Library of
Davidson College

POLITICS IN PLACE

POLITICS IN PLACE

Social power relations in an
Australian country town

IAN GRAY

School of Humanities and Social Sciences
Charles Sturt University – Riverina

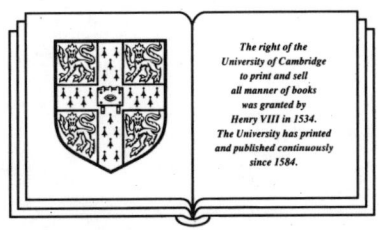

CAMBRIDGE UNIVERSITY PRESS

CAMBRIDGE
NEW YORK   PORT CHESTER   MELBOURNE   SYDNEY

Published by the Press Syndicate of the University of Cambridge
The Pitt Building, Trumpington Street, Cambridge CB2 1RP, UK
40 West 20th Street, New York, NY 10011-4211, USA
10 Stamford Road, Oakleigh, Victoria 3166, Australia

© Cambridge University Press 1991
First published 1991

Printed in Hong Kong by Colorcraft

National Library of Australia cataloguing in publication data
Gray, Ian, 1951– .
Politics in place: social power relations in an
Australian country town.
Bibliography.
Includes index.
ISBN 0 521 40426 6.
1. Elite (Social sciences) — New South Wales — Cowra
— Case studies. 2. Political sociology — Case studies.
3. Cowra (N.S.W.) — Politics and government. I. Title.
320.99445

Library of Congress cataloguing in publication data
Gray, Ian, 1951–
Politics in place: social power relations in an Australian
country town/Ian Gray.
Includes bibliographical references and index.
ISBN 0-521-40426-6
1. Cowra (N.S.W.) — Politics and government. 2. Community power —
Australia — Cowra (N.S.W.) 3. Community power — Case studies.
I. Title.
JS8273.C67G73 1991
320.8′5′099445 — dc20

A catalogue record for this book is available from the British Library

ISBN 0 521 40426 6 hardback

To Noelene Kay

Contents

List of figures, maps		*page* ix
1	Introduction: the origins of a study	1
	Origins and methods of research	2
	The argument and structure of the book	6
2	Power: concepts and applications	9
	A theoretical analysis	9
	Structural resources	12
	Interests	13
	Resistance	15
	Arenas, issues and outcomes	15
	Some Australian studies	17
	Conclusion	21
3	A history of Cowra	24
	European settlement and establishment	24
	Development and dispersal	28
	The social consequences of dispersal	31
	The rise of commerce and services	32
	Centralisation and resistance	36
4	Elitism and local government	43
	Perspectives on local government	43
	Participation and local politics	48
	Elites and reputations	53
	Conclusion: structure and interests	58
5	Spatial politics	62
	The allocation problem	63
	Progress associations	64
	Social areas	68
	The policy apparatus	71
	Some allocation issues	75
	The non-issue of air pollution	79
	Urban and rural	83
	Conclusion: councillors and ideologies	85

6	The politics of development	88
	The issue of the Tourist and Development Corporation	88
	Regulation and development	93
	The Local Environmental Plan	95
	The decline of the railway	104
	Conclusion: councillors, officers and ideologies	107
7	Gender, race and human services	110
	Women, interests and human services	111
	Women on Council	113
	Human services in Cowra Shire	115
	The councillor perspective	119
	The Aboriginal non-issue	120
	Conclusion	125
8	The making of local politics	127
	Perspectives on councillor–officer relations	127
	A joint–elite in Cowra?	129
	Institutional explanations for councillor–officer friction	132
	Councillors and officers making local politics	135
	Town and country: deference in politics	139
	Ratepayer defence	143
	Status politics	146
	Conclusion: coalitions and interests	147
9	Ideologies and resources	149
	Rhetoric	149
	Rural ideology	151
	Subjugation of bureaucrats	153
	Political neutrality	156
	Localism	161
	Status	172
	Resources and non-resources	177
10	Conclusion: the machinery of power	182
Epilogue		190
Acknowledgements		193
Appendix		195
Bibliography		197
Index		210

Figures, maps

Figure 1	Growth of village/rural and town populations in Cowra Shire 1911 to 1986	*page* 35
Figure 2	Households with annual incomes less than $9 001 (deviations from Shire percentage)	70
Figure 3	Households with annual incomes greater than $32 000 (deviations from Shire percentage)	70
Figure 4	Perceptions of availability/quality of playgrounds	72
Map 1	Cowra Shire	25
Map 2	Cowra township	66

1
Introduction: the origins of a study

This is a study of local politics in the rural Shire of Cowra, New South Wales. Cowra Shire, in 1986, had a population of about 12 000, some two-thirds of whom lived in the town of Cowra. The Shire's economy is largely agricultural, with the town servicing the needs of its own people and those of its rural hinterland.

The study explains the maintenance of Cowra's local political power structure with analysis of social processes and associated ideologies. The problem it tackles lies in the persistence of a hierarchical social relationship, one between interested groups of people who were, and some who were not, able to consistently gain access to a political system. It reveals why, in Cowra Shire, in 1986, some people could more easily than others make local politics work for them. In order to do so, it describes the dynamics of local political activity. To develop explanation for the nature of that activity, it refers to the historical social structures within which choices of political action have been made.

In building explanation, my work applies and seeks to develop social theory which may be used to cast light on political relations in other situations. In this, and being a study of a particular place and time, it resembles many community studies. By regarding spatial and historical contexts, however, it moves away from the discrete community assumption of some earlier studies toward a concept of community in which institutions are interrelated and locality-based without being locality constrained.[1] Community studies can transcend locality, as indicated by their contribution to theoretically informed analyses of class and power in Australian society (Austin, 1982, 1984).

Recognition that social relations are constructed over space, and that localities differ socially, has helped to reawaken some of the interest in community studies which waned during the 1970s. Community studies, however, should not repeat old errors. There is no justification for attributing simple social causation to a spatial entity, as implied by the now long-discredited notion of a rural-urban continuum. This does not mean that spatial factors have no place in a causal model of social relations, nor does it mean that differences and relationships between urban and rural societies are not worthy of research. It does suggest that attention to such generalities as urban and rural may be more productive with complementary focus on the particularity of place, and social construction within and of place. The research to be reported here considers such social constructions. It draws heavily on the methods of community study, in order to observe the effects of ideology on the interpretations of individuals, to observe the meanings which individuals attached to their social situation and events around them, and to observe the way those meanings enabled some groups in local politics while disabling others.

Origins and methods of research

No community study can claim to be free from the background and idiosyncracies of its writer, and the personal events which occur before and during fieldwork.[2] This study originated with research which started in July, 1985. No field other than community studies attracted my serious attention. The project was to be a rural community study because, although I had been raised in Sydney, my parents, their siblings and most of their nieces and nephews had grown up in the country, some in towns and some on farms. I thereby had had plenty of contact with country people. I spent much of my school holidays, and some time since, staying with country relatives. This time had not, however, given me what I felt to be a satisfying understanding of the country and its people. I saw the research project as an opportunity to learn about life in the country sociologically: a means that none of my family and relatives had had an opportunity to apply.

My theoretical perspective was developed and reinforced by fieldwork experience. I found encouraging potential in the community study method and the emerging critical approach in rural sociology. Critical analysis seemed timely as late 1985 brought another of Australia's intermittent rural economic crises, this time with added vitality from developing farmer militancy, and the casual speculation on my part that when the rural economy falls down, the politically as well as economically weakest people will hit the ground hardest.

I chose Cowra because it is of medium size, its economy is based on agriculture, and it is reasonably close to the Australian National University in Canberra where I was a graduate student. It was passing through a local political crisis which, from reports in the local newspaper, was a big one. I correctly anticipated that this would make talking to people about local affairs easy. Before deciding on Cowra I looked at Commonwealth Census data, read some newspapers from other towns, and made a one day tour around most of them.

Cowra had an industrial working class. It had acquired some large secondary industries which other towns might have envied, but it had almost lost its railway industry. I hypothesised that these factors, and the

Introduction: the origins of a study

forthcoming celebration of the centenary of the railway to Cowra, would have created local public discussion. Noting the presence of an Aboriginal settlement, I also hypothesised that Aboriginal welfare would be a problem, and seeing that a Neighbourhood Centre was struggling to establish itself, I thought it too might contribute to local political activity. These very early hypotheses had much bearing on the research.

While I knew that many people in the district were involved in a fracas in the Shire Council over planning, that the district was facing the decline of its railway and that some people were trying to establish a Neighbourhood Centre, I did not know either how or where these matters would be determined. My brief, as I explained it to Cowra people on arrival, and for a few months thereafter, was to study local organisations and the way the 'community' solved its problems. After realising that Cowra Shire Council was the arena around and through which local affairs moved, my explanation changed to: 'I'm here to study local government'. To many people I was there to write a book about the town. The messages that returned to me suggested that this was how the grapevine transmitted my purpose. People often asked me how the book was going.

Cowra Shire Council was my first point of contact. I started attending its meetings in October, 1985, before I moved to Cowra in November. My reception was warm: senior Council staff welcomed me and assured me that all meetings were open and I need make no special arrangements to attend. One councillor suggested that I should not miss the committee meetings, because most of the important discussion occurred there. I missed only two meetings, including committees, during the next twelve months and attended some meetings during the following year. By mid-1986 councillors and staff were quite accustomed to my presence, helped no doubt by my practice of drinking with them, sometimes after meetings, but more often at casual encounters in pubs and at social functions. I was as much a part of council meetings as the press representatives, but I was less threatening because I did not repeat councillors' words in a newspaper. Council meetings were a rich source of data, unaffected by my presence. The seriousness of debate eliminated the possibility that some was performed or modified for my benefit. After a particularly torrid meeting, a Council officer once said jokingly to me, in the presence of another, 'Of course, we are only doing this for your benefit'. The other replied: 'Like hell we are', in a tone of annoyance.

At the first meeting I introduced myself to several councillors, as well as the editor of the local newspaper who offered me office space. A senior Council officer also offered support, but not wishing to be sponsored, I thanked them and said no more. I was received warmly from the beginning. I attributed this successful entree to my willingness to learn rather than instruct, as visiting 'experts' are often seen to do. I enjoyed the benefits of equal status with the locally powerful, although my background of parentage in farming and country-dwelling families may have been more valuable than the often-questioned status of an intellectual in a farming environment.

I was sufficiently different to make becoming a complete insider impossible. My origins in Canberra and my supposed intellectual status made me an outsider; the link with Canberra being particularly important at a time when farmers and their organisations were attacking the Commonwealth Government. I did not accentuate my Canberra base. Being seen as a potential ear in Canberra was no doubt useful as a conversation stimulant, but it could also have been inhibiting, as people were unsure of what was wisely revealed. I did what I could to dispel this interpretation of my presence, and I believe that as people came to know me and saw some of what I was doing, the idea was dropped. My 'outsiderness' was productive because, as Richards (1981) noted, being an outsider leaves one open to teaching; intimacy may be accompanied by 'the imprisonment of tight role expectations' (Stephenson and Greer, 1981: 127) and failure to recognise relevant patterns and meanings (Burgess, 1984).

I participated in the Railway Centenary Committee, and offered my labour to a Sydney-based railway museum organisation which kept its locomotives and rolling stock in the otherwise virtually unused Cowra Locomotive Depot. I worked in the Neighbourhood Centre as a volunteer, answering the telephone and doing odd jobs. I was invited to, and did, join a discussion group which undertook unexamined university extension courses. I also joined the local historical society. I almost joined the Apex Club, but when the focus of research moved onto the Shire Council, I had to forsake the Apex Club to avoid clashes of meeting times. I nevertheless maintained some contact with Apexians. I also drank in the pubs and attended social functions. I entertained people in my flat and was entertained in others' homes.

My biggest participatory role was in the Neighbourhood Centre, through which I undertook surveys with the local Home and Community Care (HACC) Committee.[3] I became identified with the Centre through that project, with assistance from radio and television interviews during pre-survey publicity. For some people, this associated me with the welfare lobby, but it did not occur until ten months into the fieldwork period. I was also identified with the Railway Centenary organising committee after I appeared in a photograph of the committee in a book published at the time of the celebrations, which occurred a few days before I returned to Canberra.

I was accepted at the Neighbourhood Centre as an academic whose skills had something to offer the district. I was accepted by the railway people for my willingness and interest rather than for skills. A few of the local railway employees were active members of the museum. They were welcoming and forthcoming, but I think for some I merely confirmed the uselessness of intellectuals. My friends at the discussion group did not show the same scepticism. My contact with the Farmers' Association

Introduction: the origins of a study

through this group enabled another survey.[4] I lived in what could loosely be described as a lower middle or working class area, known as Taragala (map 2).

I had no formal sponsors, in the sense of support coming from an individual or organisation in some official capacity (Dempsey, 1986b). Informal sponsorship was also virtually absent. The exceptions were three people who suggested others whom I might interview. I consciously avoided sponsorship for fear of identification with some group or organisation which might close the door to others. Nor did I encounter significant gatekeepers. Beyond these introductions, I am not aware of any individuals whose help was essential for access to sources, other than the senior officers who made Council records available.

If, however, one takes an exchange perspective in order to illuminate reciprocal responsibilities (Gray, 1980), and acknowledges those responsibilities, relations between myself and my informants become more complex and ethically demanding. All informants were told as much about my work as formulation of the project would allow. They knew that there would be a final product, and for some, access to that product would complete a tacit exchange. For others, notably but not only the railway employees, the prospect of communication of their plight to higher authorities was potentially and implicitly a possible reward. Such an agreement was most clear among those who helped with the HACC surveys, an agreement fulfilled by successful use of the survey report in bids for government funding. I maintained throughout the project an awareness of my responsibilities to local people, and at a more instrumental level, an awareness of the potential value of local feedback on my work.

Reciprocity was present throughout, as people took me into their confidence, offered information which I could reasonably infer they would not want me to reproduce, or expressed opinions which they may not want to see attributed to them. Only once did an informant ask that something not be repeated, and that was a very frank comment on the informant's feelings at a stressful moment. There has been no censorship exercised in the compilation of this work, except by myself in the selection of evidence so as to eliminate any risk of personal embarrassment among informants. Real names of public figures, the councillors and senior Council officers, are used, and statements made by them in their public roles are quoted, but identitities of other informants are disguised by generalisation, usually in terms of occupation.

The data presented in this study are products of a process of development at a theoretical level during and after fieldwork.[5] Two factors in particular moved me to sharpen the research into a study of power processes. One was observation of the depth of the political crisis I had detected before entree, a crisis apparently precipitated by the Council making a very unpopular decision on the basis of ostensibly bureaucratic requirements. Moreover, while that crisis attracted much attention and appeared to be embarrassing prominent people, other matters were either not raised or not responded to. The other factor was the way ideas like those of the traditional wholistic community seemed to be widely adhered to and used to make sense of the social environment in one context, while in others what appeared to be real divisions were readily acknowledged.

Perhaps the most profound impression made upon me during fieldwork was the passion with which people pursued goals which had obviously unintended consequences. The most charitable people could advocate oppression when what they saw as a common good appeared to be threatened. Others earnestly believed that their interests must be pursued, to the possible detriment of others, for some avowedly common ideal. And others who could have pursued their own interests did not, either because they failed to recognise them, they did not believe pursuit to be a proper course of action, or because they were caught unwittingly in a double bind. On occasions thinking sociologically about a respected acquaintance was horrifying, and on other occasions it was very sad. Detaching individual from social structure was one of the more trying duties of data analysis, just as it is one of the most trying tasks for social theory.

The argument and structure of the book

The community power literature, most of which has been produced in the United States, has suffered from an individualistic and static approach. Some recent developments in social theory suggest a better strategy for the study of local power relations. Concepts are developed in chapter 2 which enable the exploration of structures and processes, rather than identities of apparently powerful individuals; this chapter also reviews some Australian studies which directly or indirectly tackle problems of power. Those studies suggest tentative applications of the concepts developed earlier in the chapter, and thereby direct attention to some of the dimensions of Australian local power structures.

The study of social process is a study of history which commenced long before the fieldwork for this project. To understand the events observed in fieldwork, it is necessary to establish their historical context. Chapter 3 relates a history of Cowra Shire since white settlement. It provides background to ideas and structures by suggesting antecedents to the meanings which local people attach to people and events.

Chapter 4 introduces the local political structure, as it focuses attention on local government. It offers description of the institution of local government, its place in local politics and participation in it, and briefly discusses the local political structure in terms of the reputations of political actors. This discussion offers a base for what follows rather than definition of a power structure. It draws attention to the weakness of earlier methods as it explores the ideologies associated with reputations for power.

Introduction: the origins of a study 7

As argued in chapter 2, explanation of power relations demands study of power processes. Chapter 5 is the first of four which do so, as it looks at the processes in which local government resources were distributed. The politics of distribution are found to have been constrained by both the administrative apparatus and the beliefs of local government members about the institution and their roles in it. This constraint raises the question of the content of local politics, for it suggests that political relations may have been structured by a process of agenda setting. Some groups who had legitimate political interests may have been unable to pursue them by raising issues.

The problem of issue raising is considered again in chapter 6, this time in relation to issues and non-issues surrounding economic development. The chapter demonstrates that while the interests of some groups were not heard in local politics, others, notably farmers, were able to create a political crisis when they felt that their interests were threatened. The political profile of business and farm people provides a striking contrast with that of railway workers. Chapter 6 repeats a theme which first appears in chapter 5: that of friction between council officers and councillors over the issues which constitute visible politics.

More non-issues are explored in chapter 7. It examines the place of human services, with consideration of the interests of women and Aborigines, in relation to the local political agenda. This examination deepens the contrast between the strong position of business and farm interests and the weakness of others. Unlike the issues discussed in earlier chapters, the non-issues of human services were not associated with conflict between councillors and officers. The agenda setting process has again been found to have determined political relations.

The importance of agenda setting raises the problem of explanation for political action: what determined the interests which gained expression by creation of issues? Chapter 8 offers background to this question with discussion of institutional factors. It looks back over some of the issues discussed in earlier chapters as well as new material. The later part of the chapter focuses on the legitimacy of conflicts, as they were perceived by councillors, to help illuminate the interests which gained expression.

Chapter 9 turns to the electors, whose general interest the councillors sought to pursue in the processes which created specialised politics, keeping some interests off the political agenda. Local politics are found to have reflected ideologies which pervade rural society and have a particular focus on local government. Beliefs which political actors interpreted from their electors and responded to in the political arena had structured the political agenda.

Without necessary conscious intention on the part of political actors, the parameters of local politics were defined in such a way that some interests were given prolific expression while others were ignored. The concluding chapter draws attention to the machinery of power: the resources constructed, maintained and used to the advantage of some people rather than others. The study attributes cause to beliefs used as ideological resources, but recognises that beliefs have been constructed in the context of local property relations, relations between town and country, and the institutional history of local government.

Notes

1 Being concerned about the conceptual problem of community, and the observation that community studies assume institutions to be both locality-based and interrelated, Stacey (1969) proposed a concept of 'local social system' to replace 'community', as it obviated these problems, and suggested a less constrained agenda for locality research.
2 Community studies confront problems of objectivity and presentation of evidence associated with the participant observation method. These problems have been put most succinctly by Bell (1969: 418) in terms of participant observation data offering illustrations rather than proof, and the possibility of 'retrospective selection' of data. Recognition of these problems has brought forth calls for 'natural histories' of research, so that readers might fully appreciate the writer's perspective (Bell, 1969; Gray, 1980; and Wild, 1981).
3 These surveys were reported in Gray (1987a, 1988a). Questionnaire data were collected on local facilities, social support networks, incomes, health and housing from two sources. One was a random sample of 870 adults in Cowra Shire and some adjacent areas; the other consisted of randomly selected representatives of each Aboriginal family in Cowra (59 respondents). Both studies were aimed at considering the implications of government policy changes away from institutional care of aged and handicapped people toward home care, and found that such changes would disadvantage many people, including those who already suffered from low incomes, inadequate housing and other problems, and those who lacked personal support networks. The study of Aboriginal people revealed further difficulties, especially with health and housing.
4 This survey, as reported in Gray (1988b), collected data from sixteen farming couples on their family backgrounds, their attachment to farming in terms of beliefs and values, and their plans and desires for their children. It found some support for a proposition that farm couples who retain strongly rural, rather than business, values, feel they should pass their farm on to their son(s).
5 Other than observation, data sources used for the study include Commonwealth and earlier censuses and the local newspaper (the *Cowra Guardian*). I read every issue of the *Guardian* between 1947 and 1987, and many earlier issues of the *Guardian* and its predecessors. I was fortunate to be granted access to Council documents, including minutes of meetings. Thirty-five interviews with locally knowledgeable people were conducted. The interviewees fell into three overlapping groups: long-term residents, councillors and local organisation leaders.

The interviews, of between one and four hours duration, were minimally structured by a small number of standard questions designed to stimulate discussion as well as elicit answers. Questions about the importance and role of the Shire Council, the local status system and relations between town and country were asked of most respondents, but many of the conversations had specialised components about, for example, councillors' sources of information and organisations' dealings with the Council. Questions about the identities of influential people were put to twenty of the interviewees. I became quite friendly with many of the interviewees and spoke to them often. The interviews themselves provided revelations, but were a minor source of data overall. Spontaneous conversations, often started with an explanation of my work, were just as fruitful.

2
Power: concepts and applications

Social theory provides useful tools for analysis of local political relations. Development of theoretical tools has often been stimulated by empirical application. Discussion has emanated from 'community power' research, a field which has been virtually synonymous with a persistent, unresolved and 'rather silly' (Bell and Newby, 1971: 218) empirical debate carried on within the United States. One side (pluralists) sought to show that United States cities were governed by many; the other side (elitists) has sought to show that they were governed by few. The protagonists shared an important characteristic: neither has been as concerned to explain how the observed power structures came about, as it has been to justify its assumptions. Fortunately the debate is now largely irrelevant. The lack of explanatory force on both sides indicates that there is nothing to gain from attempting to rejuvenate it in Australia. There is, however, value in the theoretical debate which grew around the conceptual deficiencies of the two sides.

A theoretical analysis

The notion of power implies relationships among individuals and groups in which the behaviour of some has an impact on others over space and time. Explanation of those relationships seeks to answer the why and how questions. That is, why do some individuals or groups affect others, and how does it come about that they are able to, and choose to, act in a way that has such effect? Power, however, implies more than behavioural cause and effect in social relations. If one assumes that the powerful act rationally in pursuit of their own objective interests, and that not everybody's interests are the same, power may benefit the powerful at the expense of the powerless. This implies that the powerful may be identified as those who benefit from political relations. The keystone of this approach to power, which is essentially that used by Lukes (1974), is that the actions of the powerful are seen to affect the powerless to the relative detriment of the latter.

Analysis of power will be framed around a slightly modified version of the conceptual scheme of Lukes (1974), using it as a heuristic device as it was used by Fasenfest (1986), Gaventa (1980), and Bryson and Wearing (1985). Lukes observed that pluralist studies of power had taken a narrow 'one-dimensional view', by analysing only observable conflict. It was, he claimed while citing the 'neo-elitist' work of Bachrach and Baratz (1970), possible to take a wider 'two-dimensional view' of power by considering the possibility that power may be exercised and identified when no overt conflict is apparent. This 'two-dimensional view' brings non-decision making and agenda setting as well as decision making into focus, but it retains an assumption that conflict must be present, either overt or covert, for power to be available and exercised. It also introduces the role of ideology with the possibility that a powerful group could control the political agenda by developing and reinforcing social values through which some kinds of conflict are accepted and others rejected.

The 'three-dimensional view' offers sight of a greater role for ideology. The concept of 'mobilisation of bias', used by Lukes among many others, having originated in Schattschneider (1960), introduces the possibility that a powerful group could influence or even determine the values of another, thereby eliminating the possibility of conflict, both covert and overt, in a power relationship. The essential feature of the 'three-dimensional view' is that it takes analysis of power relations beyond the identities and actions of individuals into the social construction of ideology. It offers the prospect of more thorough sociological explanations of power than the pluralist 'one-dimensional' and neo-elitist 'two-dimensional' views.

That Lukes has not identified three dimensions of power relations deserves recognition. The term 'dimensions' is inappropriate, because the essential features of power as observed in the two- and three-dimensional 'views' are not independent, as dimensions inherently are. The third merely extends the second beyond the use of ideology in order to set the agenda of politics through non-decision making, to setting the agenda by distracting subordinates from perception of their own interests.

Lukes' three perspectives make potentially visible three modes of action which may be available to actors in power relations. The first mode involves overt conflict; the second consists of direct action to set an agenda or agendas without overt conflict; and in the third, agendas are set indirectly by fostering values and beliefs which disguise the real interests of subordinates. The first mode is observable as fighting over rewards, which can occur when plural interests participate in political action. The second mode of action, and its relation the third, are empirically more complex, but have been clarified conceptually by Saunders (1979). He suggested a three stage non-decision making filter, based on Bachrach and Baratz (1970). In the first stage, interests may be formulated into expressed problems, or not formulated under a mobilisation of bias, suggesting action in the third mode. In the second stage of Saunders' filter issues may be articulated, or not articulated due to anticipated reactions, suggesting the second mode. Anticipated reactions are also related to ideology, and may be an aspect of mobilisation of bias. In the final stage issues may be resolved, or not resolved after negative decision making: action in the second mode. The second and third modes may be empirically entwined as well as theoretically connected. Teasing them out relies upon the essential characteristic of the third: use of it consists of development and application of the values of weak people by powerful people. Ideology of the superordinate has a role in the second mode, but in the third, focus moves to the ideologies of the subordinate.

The concept of mobilisation of bias introduces the possibility that a powerful group could influence or even determine the values of another, thereby eliminating the possibility of conflict, both overt and covert in a power relationship. Mobilisation of bias moves the focus of power research further into the realm of the process of social construction of knowledge, ideas and values, rather than leaving it at analysis of their role in power relations. The concept of power in the third mode is close to the Gramscian concept of hegemony, variants of which have been used, for example, by Connell (1977) among many others.[1]

Research which takes the 'three-dimensional view' to seek the causal factors in power relations inevitably confronts a problem of conceptualisation of the mobilisation of bias at the level of individual action when action may be unconscious or unintended (Debnam, 1975).[2] The problem posed is one of separation of individual action and structural property, and teasing out the roles of each in power relations. The lack of conceptual tools to bridge agency and structure is illustrated in the work of elitists who, in seeking causal models, acknowledged structure but analysed individuals. The poverty of the elitist approach is best illustrated when one considers that the significance of an elite need not lie in the identities and characteristics of individuals whose significance may fade in the light of ideas which are widely shared, 'that seem to come from the society as a whole, and seem to represent a consensus' (Connell and Irving, 1985: 349). This suggests passage beyond the finding of Saunders (1979: 324), that business and local politicians acted in a partnership in which plans and ideas moved 'like osmosis'. They may not have been conscious of their own level of organisation. Moreover, the elite may be created by forces over which its members have little control (Lukes, 1986; Stone, 1980).

There is no ready solution to the problem of identification of structural determinants in the behaviour of individuals.[3] The search for cause inevitably leads back to the individual. There is nothing to gain from substituting a purely structural explanation for an individualistic one when we need to account for both structure and agency. Means to separate power from individuals are still required. If power can be exercised without conscious intention of agents, the focus of analysis moves away from intentions and actions to enablement of actions.

Structural resources

As Polsby (1979) required, locating the source of power demands more than location of those who benefit from social relations. It is necessary to identify some feature of their social position which enables them to exercise power. A concept of structural resources offers a means of such identification. Resources can include financial capacity, size of organisation membership and community dependence on it, status of individuals in the eyes of the community, and ideology (Bachrach and Baratz, 1970).

The analytical role of resources was set out by Lukes, when he stated that showing some individual or group gaining over another is not sufficient to show that the individual or group has power. Demonstration of power requires indication that an individual or group possesses resources which are causally associated with benefit (Lukes, 1986). While retaining some preoccupation with individuals, this point shows a path away from individualism by looking at the structural properties held, and used, by individuals. Attention to resources should move the primary focus of the analysis of power relations away from the wishes of actors toward a structural analysis (Barbalet, 1987). As Giddens cautioned, power and resources are not identical, and resources should not, as suggested by Layder (1985), become the sole object of study, for resources are media of power (Giddens, 1979). The study of power becomes the study of resources as the availability of the media of power relations, and the ways in which the availability, use and reproduction of resources structure social relations. This leaves a key role for the study of action, for power presupposes the making of decisions by actors, without observation of which, the products of power and its reproduction could not be observed.

Resources can have both material and ideal elements; ownership of property and beliefs about property-related institutions being contrasting but related examples. The concept of resources can be applied to each of the three modes. In the first, if resources are balanced and actors choose to deploy them, power relations may also be balanced, as indicated by the outcomes of issues. If resources are not balanced, one group may dominate and an elitist structure develop. In the second mode, those who possess the resources which enable them to do so can choose to set the political agenda. Appropriate resources may include beliefs about agendas. Such resources can extend into organisation rules (Giddens, 1979). Rules should not be overlooked as resources when they bring about a bias in a political apparatus which favours some people over others, especially when, as Saunders (1979) points out, the powerful may be able to interpret rules with the acceptance of, but contrary to the interests of, the weak. This type of action overlaps with the third mode, as resources for action in the third mode are located among ideologies, especially those of subordinate actors. Complexity is encountered when the concept of resources is applied to the mobilisation of bias; that is, when it is recognised that resources may be created in social interaction, in the construction, maintenance and change of knowledge in which all parties involved in the power relationship participate. When taking the 'three-dimensional view' one might be tempted to conceptualise the resource bestowed by the beliefs and values of the weak as legitimacy. A regime may, however, be illegitimate and still powerful when its subjects are apathetic. While legitimacy is an ideological resource, ideological resources can take other forms. The third mode consists of the construction and reconstruction of ideology, and moreover, deployment of ideas by a powerful group in all ways which develop its relationships with subordinates.

Interests

Interests may be the driving force of actor choice, and hence may demand explanation in analysis of power relations. They become, however, highly problematic when the 'one-dimensional view' is abandoned. Unlike resources, the interests of actors in power relations can never be indisputably specified. They can, however, be subjected to analysis in order to build an understanding of power relations.

Interests are the unfettered engine of power in the first mode. The pluralist approach assumes that interests expressed in political arenas are the only interests which actors possess, because they are the only interests which are empirically detectable (Dunleavy, 1980). Under this assumption, observable interests can explain action, but not power relations. The 'two-dimensional view' reveals a mechanism in which expressions of some interests, although recognised by their adherents, are prohibited from political arenas by powerful actors. When looking for the third mode the assumption that interests are recognisable by their adherents is cast aside. This is illustrated by, for example, Therborn's (1980) 'sense of representation', which suggests that the ruled may accept unquestioningly that the rulers represent their interests when in objective fact they do not.

Power analysis from the 'three-dimensional view' depends on the possibility that actors' perceived interests are not identical with their real interests. Empirical recognition of real interests, therefore, may be a process of imputation which can suffer imposition of values by the observer. This rules out rational objective analysis of power relations from the 'three-dimensional view'. It also rules out refutation. This problem pervades the 'two-dimensional view' as well, where identification of the powerful also depends on observation of conflict of interest that can only be inferred (Merelman, 1968).

There have been several heroic attempts to circumvent this problem, including those of Benton (1981), Betts (1986), Dunleavy (1976) and Falkemark (1982). However, as Knights and Willmott (1982) suggested, the imposition of values will remain as an intractable problem in identification of the effects of interests from the 'three-dimensional view'. There are two complementary courses of action which may obviate the problem. One is to boldly state one's own values and pragmatically apply a *verstehen* approach. The other involves becoming more precise about the place of interests in the analysis of power relations.

The pragmatic approach has found favour in empirical studies. For example, Crenson (1971) felt he could assume that it would be in anybody's interests not to be poisoned by air pollution. Gaventa (1980) took a similar approach, drawing on Frey's (1971) assertion that one could expect non-issues where no action is taken to ameliorate inequality in distribution of some commonly, avowedly valued good. Bell et al. (1976) and Newby et al. (1978) adopted the same position. Saunders (1979) tied this method to the allocative activity of local government in terms of interests in distribution of benefits, such as community facilities and environmental amenity, and allocation of costs, such as rate payments and location of nuisances. These encounters with the problem of interests suggest that what appears problematic in theory may not be so in empirical application.

The second approach to the problem of interests suggests that it is worth questioning what one would want to know about interests and what that knowledge might enable research to achieve. Interests may lead to starting points for research, rather than being starting points themselves. Adherence of actors to interests is contingent upon social conditions, objectives chosen on the basis of interests may be incompatible, and interests of an actor as a member of one group may be incompatible with his/her interests as a member of another (Hindess, 1982). Interests, perceived or real, are themselves subject to explanation.

The focus of research can usefully be moved onto the ways and means of objective selection and away from attempts to identify real interests and explain why they are ignored (Hindess, 1982). The importance of studying the process of interest perception is illustrated by Fasenfest (1986), who found a situation in which the interests pursued by local government were objectively perceived by the people of the city, but were pursued in a direction which imposed substantial costs. The problem posed lies not so much in perception of interests, but in the appreciation of benefits and costs when costs may be discounted by the powerful. This serves as a reminder that even the powerful might inaccurately assess the costs and benefits of pursuit of their interests, or they may not recognise their interests at all. It also draws attention to the possibility of the double-bind, or an encounter with conflicting interests.

Resistance

The concept of resistance illuminates the possibility that subordinates may identify interests which are not their real interests, and act upon them without effect on the structure of power relations. The resources of one-time superiors might in some circumstances be threatened and demolished by subordinates, but not with resistance. Knights and Willmott (1982, 1985) used a concept of individual identity seeking to explain how resistance to the power of rulers fails to change power relations because actors, in seeking self-identity, ignore or deny the interdependence of power relations. They merely find a new identity which can be accommodated within existing power relations.

Overthrow of a structured system of dominance demands the use of resources which are only available outside the system (Barbalet, 1985), rather than resistance within. It is axiomatic that in a structure of domination, the resources of rule are always in the hands of the rulers, for a power relationship can only work one way at a time. Consideration of the concept of resistance raises questions about conditions in which real threats to regimes do arise. Therborn (1980: 106) suggested that demolition occurs when the 'disorganization of legitimacy' extends to the 'apparatuses of rule'. Therborn refers not to the denial of the ideas of the rulers, but rather to the efficacy of those ideas in the machinery of government. I interpret this as an observation that opposition to ideas may occur without effect, but if those ideas are no longer seen to provide workable organised government, senses of representation, acquiescence and apathy are no longer resources of the rulers.

Analysis of power relations may be focused on resistance, as suggested in the writing of Foucault (1983). This provides an escape from a total determinism implied by emphasis on structural resources. But it is meaningless without first understanding construction, maintenance and use of resources, something which the community power literature, with its lack of attention to ideological resources, has not done adequately.

Arenas, issues and outcomes

Arenas are political institutions, the rules of which may be made into resources for some at the expense of others as they are produced and reproduced in power relations. The economic and social history of a geographical-political entity, such as local government, may contribute to the construction of arenas which provide resources differentially available among actors. Choices of means of deployment of resources are limited by the institutional arena within which political relations are enacted.

The institutional arena may have been set up in part, in whole or not at all by forces within a locality; the boundaries of the locality may have been influenced by institutional change which was enacted in an arena. Arenas may be part of 'locale' (Giddens, 1979: 202), in which social structure is produced and reproduced. Arenas may have associated social conditions which give rise to their own ideological climates. In the context of this study, the ideological climate pervading local government is especially important.

The concept of issues poses several problems, the classic among them being selection of issues and non-issues for analysis. For issue selection, the problem is selection criteria (Frey, 1971; Forward, 1969); for non-issues the problem is the infinity of possibilities (Debnam, 1975; Buller and Hoggart, 1986). When the subject of power research is social process, issue selection is not such an essential problem as it is when the objective is to identify powerful individuals. Following Crenson (1971), the process of decision, or in his case, non-decision making, is critical, rather than the issue itself. Study should proceed from analysis of who benefits to analysis of causal factors, making awareness of outcomes of issues important, but not the primary focus of study (Falkemark, 1982). Following Lukes (1986), the main criterion for selection of issues becomes their ability to demonstrate the power of the powerful. As Dunleavy (1976) observed, such issues are not necessarily extraordinary in the public view. Power relations may be maintained in routine matters.

Resolution of these problems at an empirical level ultimately falls back on the same pragmatism which has obviated the difficulties posed by specification of subjective interests. Gaventa (1980) adopted such an approach, again drawing on Frey's (1971) suggestion that lack of attempts to remedy glaring inequality in something valued indicates a non-issue. The point that non-issues may become issues, made by Debnam (1975), is largely semantic, but it does indicate the need for observation over a period of time.

Outcomes of issues are the intended or unintended products of choices made by actors in relations with others. All theoretical writing on power relations implicitly or explicitly adopts a concept of outcomes. Without specification of outcomes, power relations have no meaning. An actor may be found to possess vast resources, but without analysis of issues, actions and outcomes, the nature of the actor's power relation with others will be undefined.

Dunleavy (1976) noted that outcomes of one issue may contribute to the process of resolution of the next. Outcomes may structure beliefs in such a way as to create resources, or facilitate the creation of resources for one group rather than another. This invites a dynamic analysis of issues. Participant observation promises intimate knowledge of individual actors and the social conditions in which they learn and act. In moving out of the 'one-dimensional view', the taken-for-granted aspects of outcomes are crucial, and they can only be revealed in study of the meanings of interests, issues and outcomes to actors.

Some Australian studies

Australian sociology and political science have not shown anything like the American enthusiasm for local political studies. Nor has there been as much attention focused on local government within these disciplines, as there has in Britain. The reasons for Australian inactivity may lie in erroneous but common perceptions of Australian local government as weak and uninteresting. Nevertheless, local power relations have attracted attention, and some Australian studies have indicated elements of the three modes of power.

The earliest relevant study is McIntyre and McIntyre's *Country Towns of Victoria* (1944). They studied 180 Victorian towns having populations between 250 and 10 000, and a further thirty smaller towns. This study preceded even the beginnings of the American debates. Despite not seeking evidence for either elitism or pluralism, it has, unwittingly, come down on the side of elitism. The McIntyres found the powerful to have an ideological resource akin to Therborn's (1980) concept of 'inevitability', in that local government electors believed that 'it doesn't matter who gets in, one is just as bad as another' (McIntyre and McIntyre, 1944: 116). Oxley (1978: 14), however, examined the McIntyres' findings on local organisations, and found their evidence to show that each town had a small group of leaders, 'but they did not necessarily unite to form integrated ruling cliques'. Unfortunately, without detailed information on the processes of politics in the McIntyres' towns, the significance of integration or non-integration of ruling cliques cannot be assessed. These small groups of leaders may or may not have been ideologically in tune with each other and acting contrary to the interests of others. Moreover, we know nothing about the processes which created and maintained this pattern of leadership.

The work of Oeser and Emery (1957) is, at the same time, promising and disappointing. It is promising in that it offers an insight into beliefs, as well as power structures. It is disappointing in that, as Oxley (1978: 13) felt, they offer little evidence to support their view. Again, power relations were a very small component of the study. Oeser and Emery studied one town, which had a population of 500, and found it to be elitist. They developed a view of politics as defined by a powerful group, and as the very meagre evidence suggested, possibly by the less powerful as well. This suggests an exercise of power in the second mode, in that the farmers were able to set the local political agenda, and in the third, as their ability to do so rested on the beliefs of their subordinates. Oeser and Emery (1957: 32) imply that political activity may be in the interests of the less powerful.

They found 'a widespread belief in and acceptance of the superiority of the existing political system, a belief which is strong enough to prevent any interpretation of class relations within the community in terms other than community status and personal differences, and which supports the parcelling out of their class interests to the parliamentary institutions'.

Unfortunately the discussion is conceptually imprecise and the evidence thin or non-existent. Oeser and Emery offer only one instance of expression of such belief. 'During the eleven days immediately preceding the 1948 election only one political comment was heard in the public bar of the hotel – this was immediately quashed by the hotel keeper with the statement "no politics here" ' (ibid.). It is not clear that this amounts to use by the dominant group of their resource. It was probably only intended to indicate its existence. One should be wary of reading too much into Oeser and Emery, but at least they offer some evidence for distaste for 'politics' in local affairs in a rural community, a distaste which could become an ideological resource for a powerful group.

Two more recent studies have examined ideologies which are relevant to power, as they may become resources applied in the third mode. *The Good Old Rule* (Poiner 1990) is principally a study of power in the context of gender relations. Poiner had little prospect for the study of broader community politics because her locality, a rural area centred on a town of a few hundred people in southern New South Wales, did not contain a significant local political arena, such as a shire or municipal council, in which the enactment of power relations could be observed. Poiner's work has a strong focus on ideology, particularly ideology that is distinctly rural. Ideology is central to her understanding of the local social structure and she is much concerned with the hegemony associated with rural class and gender relations. She discusses a 'rural idyll', a system of beliefs which romanticises country life, finding deep intrinsic value in those aspects of it which are uniquely rural. The rural idyll selectively downplays, ignores or reforms aspects of rural life, building an ideology which can become a medium for benefit to the propertied class.

Dempsey (1990) is a study of social stratification rather than politics in 'Smalltown', but his analysis looks closely at local ideologies. Dempsey develops a concept of localism further than Poiner, examining ways in which it becomes a cohesive force. He explores ideological factors in power structures, specifically those in which a sense of belonging is fostered, beside social closure along class and gender lines. Dempsey found an ideology which enables the exercise of power in the third mode as it hides inequality, but did not seek to explore manifestations of power in local politics.

These studies suggest power relations mediated by ideology, in which people who have property have at least potential ideological resources at their disposal. Those resources include a sense of inevitability about the domination of a few; a belief that politics belong elsewhere, inhibiting discussion and consequently political action; and localism, which raises the value of local attachment and clouds perception of objective interests. Evidence for the first two is, however, weak, and the relationship between the 'rural idyll' and the political dimension of localism is not made clear. These studies suggest at least the possibility of elitist structures, mediated by ideology, but they offer thin evidence and no analysis of the processes in which such ideologies and their associated structures are created, used and maintained in local political arenas.

Other relevant studies include Oxley (1978), Wild (1974a) and Wild (1983). They were influenced by the most frantic period of elitist-pluralist warfare in the United States. Oxley, in *Mateship in Local Organisation* (1978), is the only one of this group to come down against an elitist interpretation, finding no evidence of individual or group advancement through local politics. The pluralistic image of local government developed in Oxley's discussion of local issues enhances this interpretation, but it does leave unanswered some important questions which would be posed after taking the Lukes 'three dimensional view' of power. We cannot be certain, either that real interests were not obscured, or that a consensus was not aided by an ability of the Council to keep controversy under the carpet. Nor can we be certain that the definition of popular will was not in the hands of one group, and exercised by them at the expense of another.

In *Bradstow*, Wild (1974a) offers a very different view. He identifies a power structure in which local government was central and elitist. Wild's principal concern was with application of a Weberian model of stratification, using the familiar conceptual trinity of class, status and power. He approached power as the ability of some to exercise their will over others. The town he selected for study (in New South Wales' southern highlands, population about 5 000) had a clearly hierarchical social structure. Wild observes the exercise of power in the second and third modes on his way to identification of powerful individuals. The observations are reported in Wild's treatment of the operation of local government, which he found to be elitist in itself, and in his analysis of local political issues which all at some stage involved local government.

His *Heathcote* (Wild, 1983) is an analysis of power in some of the clothing of a 'community-as-object' study. That is, one which would treat community, in terms of social relations, as an object for study. It is not a 'community-as-object' study because community was used as a conceptual tool rather than as the object of study. It is a power study insofar as it seeks an understanding of how power relations changed. It analyses a process through which power exercised in the second mode was threatened and eventually overcome, temporarily at least, by people who had been subordinate. This time Wild is not principally concerned with identifying the powerful.

The study concentrates on one local political issue involving strong external factors which arose in a shire with a population of a little over two thousand people in rural Victoria. The issue arose when the State Government proposed to put a toxic waste dump in the shire. The Shire Council agreed to the proposal on the condition that safety precautions be taken and some financial and other concessions offered. Some local residents became concerned and formed a committee to protest. They gained substantial local and external support. Significantly, their support included some people of high reputation in the broader State and national context and some who had considerable technical expertise. The issue raged in the Melbourne as well as the local press. The Shire Council stuck to its position, but the State Government gave way, deciding not to locate the dump where it was obviously not wanted by local people.

Wild was principally concerned to account for the strength and success of the protest group. To do so he called upon concepts developed by Schmalenbach (1961): 'community' as relationships of tradition, 'communion' as relationships of emotion, and 'society' as relationships based on individualism. He uses these concepts to analyse the process through which the protest group formed when local tradition was threatened, how it was bound into a fighting force by emotions under threat from an apparently aloof and even hostile Shire Council, and how it disintegrated when the crisis had passed. This approach moved Wild far from the more static pigeon-holing of his earlier study. The concepts of 'community' and 'communion' introduced an ideological element, this time as resources of the subordinate group.

The power relation which was threatened in this issue was a product of action in the second mode of power. Issues did not arise in this community because the Shire Council contained them. It operated in a consensus mode similar to that identified by Wild (1974a), and was also dominated by a small group of councillors. Non-decision making and secrecy were normal behaviour for the Council. Through the waste dump issue, the Council followed its usual non-decision making course, and drew on the resources offered by its technical and administrative functions. It decided to 'wait and see' (1983: 128). But the Council lost the issue because it could not stop it arising, and once arisen, its pursuers found resources to match those of the Council. Peace (1985) saw this as a more important offering of the study than that made by Wild's application of the Schmalenbach concepts. I would add the perception of interests by the protesters as an important feature of, and indeed a necessary precursor to, their successful action.

Perhaps the most valuable offerings of the Oxley and Wild studies are largely coincidental by-products of the community study method, with its emphasis on participant observation. Wild's studies illustrate power processes in the second and third modes. He identifies objective resources of technical and administrative expertise, and ideological resources in terms of shared values and belief in consensus. Wild (1983) offers a reminder that resistance does not lead to change, but Oxley's legend showed that change in a power structure is possible. These studies suggest that some communities are more elitist than others in terms of 'cliqueishness', but it would seem likely that most are elitist in terms of representation in local government.

Pandey (1972) is the only Australian study set firmly within the elitist-pluralist mould. His *Power in Barretta* offers direction for rural local power studies, because, although not exploring the ideological aspects of power relations, Pandey's work within the elitist-pluralist tradition suggested, and called for, an escape route from it. The contrast between this research and that carried out by Wild (1983) is most striking, not because Wild explored power relations, but because his study focused on process rather than static structures. Pandey studied a town of about twenty thousand people in northern New South Wales. He used the familiar reputation and decision methods to identify 'leaders'. His concept of elite, identified by observation of political activity, was more like that of Wild (1974a) and Oxley (1978) than that of McIntyre and McIntyre (1944) and Wild's (1983) analysis of council-constituent relations. He carried out a social stratification analysis similar to those of Oxley (1978) and Wild (1974a).

The political system he studied was an active one in which issues arose and were resolved competitively. Pandey found that business interests formed the most active group in local politics, and, like McNab (1970), he found a general complacency toward local politics. He also acknowledged the role of values and ideology, for some groups – particularly farmers – were widely believed to have a reasonable claim to power, while those who did not adhere to the values of the farmers were isolated and ignored. Pandey makes the point that, rather than there being a real consensus, there was only a belief in the existence of such a consensus. Local political disputes were attributed to personality clash rather than to conflicts of interest. This suggests a parallel with Poiner's (1990) concept, which I interpreted above as localism. Poiner found that rural ideology provided a mystifying force which submerged conflict under the belief in a common local interest. Pandey was not able to use participant observation methods as extensively as were, for example, Wild (1974a) and Oxley (1978). Hence ideology and values remained beyond his gaze. However, Pandey's work calls loudly for the study of interests and ideology rather than the identification of individuals. He recognised that the next agenda for community power studies would include examination of how ideologies and values are created and maintained, and used in local politics.

Conclusion

Perhaps the most striking features of the Australian empirical community power literature are the parallels between its development and that of theory. Both have revealed the elitist-pluralist debate to be sterile, and both seek exploration of the second and third modes of power action.

Australian studies have indicated varying degrees of elitism, in terms of 'cliqueishness'. They have also found a common lack of representativeness in local government. At the level of overt issues, it would seem that business interests are represented and business people are usually in a good position to exert their will and, moreover, with or without conscious effort, gain from local power structures. We know little about the processes in which this may or may not occur, because the focus of study has largely been placed on individuals rather than interests and resources.

The Australian literature offers instances of a sense of inevitability (McIntyre and McIntyre, 1944) contributing to a lack of political life in which issues are unlikely to arise. It also offers instances of deliberate agenda setting by powerful individuals (Wild, 1974a), drawing on values of consensus. Taking Lukes' 'three dimensional' perspective, it suggests that acceptance of a status hierarchy (Pandey, 1972; Wild, 1974a), localism (Dempsey, 1990; Oxley, 1978; Poiner, 1990; Wild, 1974a) and a related belief in consensus and the apolitical nature of local politics (Oeser and Emery, 1957; Pandey, 1972) may be resources available to and used by the powerful. They are adhered to by the powerless as well as by the powerful, but the political outcomes which they engender favour the powerful.

Oxley (1978) and Wild (1983) together illustrated the difference between resistance and change, and showed that power relations are not necessarily immutable. Wild (1983) pointed by implication toward the value of regarding outcomes as components of a process, as each contributes to the next. The Australian literature has left the application of the concept of arena available but open, because although local government was found to be central to power processes in all those studies which focused on power, its role in any locality will always be problematic and demand definition.

The Australian literature does not offer simple solutions to the intractable problems of identification of objective interests and specification of the antecendents to ideological resources. Interests have not been problematic because the focus of study has largely been placed on individuals, and definition of power has tended to follow the pluralists rather than Lukes. At least it is encouraging that where power processes in the third mode have been identified, assumptions about the objective interests of subordinate groups do not appear to warrant criticism.

Attributed resources have not been problematic either, largely because there have been no attempts to explain their ideological content outside the well-established stratification approach to power and status used by Wild (1974a, b) and Pandey (1972). However, even resources which appear to be objective, such as technical expertise in Wild (1983), may have an ideological element. Those such as localism and belief in consensus may in their construction be largely ideological. Other than the work of Poiner, and some in the broader context of the study of rural ideology, such as Craig (1983) and Share (1985), the Australian literature merely suggests that ideology is to become an important aspect of the study of power relations, as the theoretical literature suggests.

Australian studies have shown that those who wield power may do so because they can draw on material resources associated with local capital, ideological resources of localism and status, and beliefs about local government, administration and technical expertise. There are suggestions that such resources are associated with property. Aspects of this conclusion broadly agree with British work on rural community power (Bell et al., 1976; Newby et al., 1978), which focuses on property and tradition as antecedents to power relations, but in which localism, status and belief in apolitical local government play major roles. The British social and historical context is of course different to the Australian one. But in both situations, the processes in which resources are constructed and applied should become the first objective in the search for social antecedents to rural local power relations.

Notes

1 It is worth noting, when associating the third mode with a concept of hegemony, that, as Hindess (1976) pointed out, there is nothing necessarily radical in a political sense about Lukes' perspective on power, despite his titling of the book 'A Radical View'. Domhoff (1986: 69) considered Lukes to be a pluralist. Indeed there is no logical necessity for power relations in the third dimension to produce an elitist structure. There may be a balance between competing ideologies. However, as Woodward et al. (1985) pointed out, Lukes is empirically more consistent with the elitist view. In any case Lukes (1974) may be seen to suggest a radical agenda for empirical community power research.

2 There are potential problems in the 'three-dimensional view' which may not all arise in research practice. Identification of non-decisions and non-issues may be significant problems at a theoretical level but appear semantic at an empirical level. As Polsby (1979) pointed out, non-decisions are really a type of decision and should be treated as such in political analysis. Wolfinger (1971) and Frey (1971) debated the problem of identifying and choosing non-issues, concluding that the problem of non-issues was an extension of a perennial problem of issue selection.

3 Before turning to structuralism and searching for evidence of hegemony, it is worth remembering that if hegemony is found, the task of seeking explanation for it remains. Gramson (1985) warned that hegemony can become a research objective in itself, substituting for explanation. Hegemony merely helps to describe a structure without accounting for it. Knights and Willmott (1985) implied a similar point by attracting attention to social psychological processes. They drew on a notion of interdependence among weak and powerful actors in their searches for social identity. The powerful are dependent on the weak to produce and maintain the ideology on which structure is based. These approaches seem only to deepen the agency-structure problem. Betts (1986) attempted to blaze a trail around the dilemma. She used Giddens' structuration approach in attempting to build a model of power in which the tension between agency and structure is absent. Unfortunately Betts' model depends on separation of tacit from discursive knowledge and identification of unintended consequences as structural products. She also acknowledged the impossibility of doing so. She has taken the issue no further than a useful reminder of the value of historical study of the context in which knowledge is obtained.

3

A history of Cowra

The Shire of Cowra became a political and administrative entity in 1980 upon the amalgamation of Cowra Municipality and Waugoola Shire, the latter having covered Cowra's rural hinterland. Cowra Shire lies between the uplands of the Great Dividing Range and the western plains which lead to the 'outback' of New South Wales and Central Australia (map 1). Cowra is about 300 kilometres west of Sydney. The Shire has an area of 2 801 square kilometres, a journey by road across it covering about 80 kilometres. About two-thirds of the population live in the township of Cowra, by far the largest population centre in the Shire. Only two others have populations much in excess of one hundred.

The Shire covers the area in which the Lachlan River, one of the major tributaries of the Murray-Darling system, rising near the Great Dividing Range, breaks out of mountainous terrain onto undulating countryside and plains. Over half of the Shire's land can be considered arable, and only seventeen per cent suitable for neither cultivation nor grazing. Thirty-three per cent is 'highly regarded in the statewide context' for cropping, with grain yields exceeding those of many other local government areas in the wheat belt of New South Wales (Nott, 1983: 6–9). Wyangala Dam at the eastern edge of the Shire has made water available for irrigation. Primary production includes grains, oilseeds, fruit, vegetables and livestock products, some of which are processed locally. A highway route between Sydney and Adelaide passes through Cowra, and lesser roads radiate from Cowra to centres north, west and south. The railway through Cowra is subsidiary to the main routes to the south and west from Sydney, but Cowra is a significant rail node for its servicing of a branch line to the south west and another to the north. Travelling time to Sydney by road or rail is around four to five hours.

European settlement and establishment

Cowra Shire's economic and political resources have, during the European period, changed from concentration in the possession of relatively few people through a process in which resources were spread among many

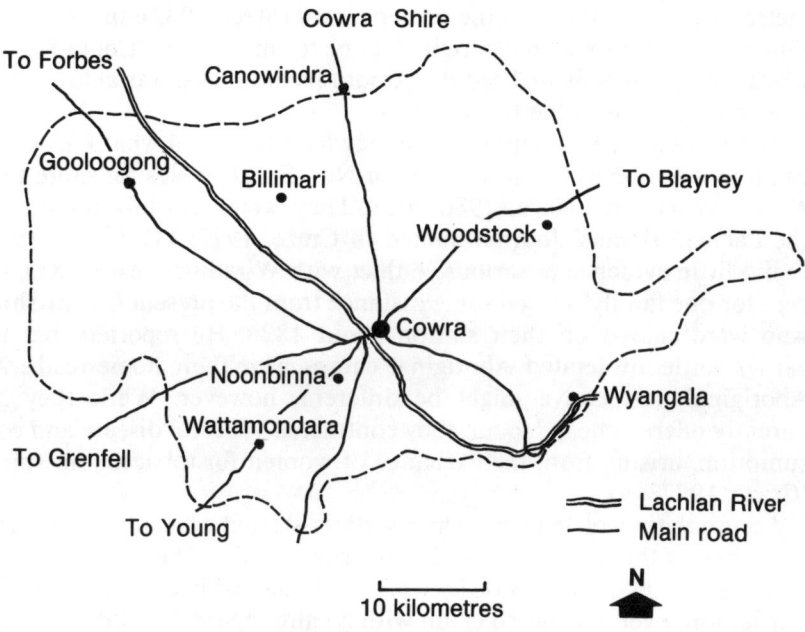

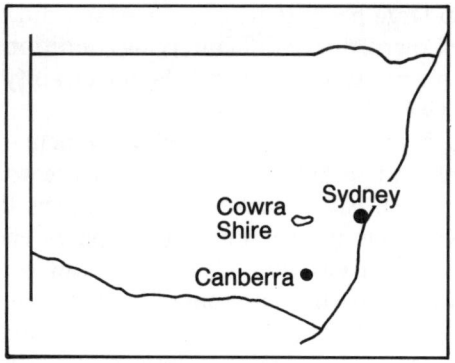

Map 1. Cowra Shire

individuals, places, enterprises and institutions. The process has continued into centralisation, as resources have again become concentrated and alienated from the people of Cowra. The early European history of the Cowra district is a story of accumulation of vast resources by a few families, a process which appears to have begun around 1830, well after the government surveyor, Evans, had reached the Lachlan River, a few kilometres north of the site of the present town (Steel, 1932), in 1815. One European settler took an Aboriginal name for his station, 'Coura Rocks', which, after someone realised that Coura meant rocks, was abbreviated, altered and given to the township.

The Wiradjuri Aboriginal people may have occupied what Europeans came to describe as the south west of New South Wales for more than 40 000 years (Gammage, 1986: xiv). They were certainly present on the Lachlan (Evans' Journal quoted in Craze, 1977: 11). Craze (1977) found little evidence of serious conflict with Wiradjuri near Cowra, except for one family, settled some distance from the present Cowra Shire, who were chased off their station about 1823. He reported that the earlier settlers tolerated Aboriginal camps near their homesteads. An Aboriginal perspective might be different, however. While they apparently offered cheap labour, they contracted venereal disease and consumption, arising from the exchange of women for tobacco and spirits (Craze, 1977: 19).

Accumulation of land by white settlers started officially in the area when one of them was granted 2 560 acres in 1827. The deed, however, was not executed until 1831, by which time he had been wrangling with officialdom over a disputed claim with an already-established neighbour (Craze, n.d.: 3). Through the 1830s, the 'squatters' and their overseers acquired blocks of 30 000 acres and larger. Overseers were paid in stock which they could graze on the owner's property. They could thereby develop large herds (Craze, n.d.). Many did not reside on their properties near Cowra, due to difficult living conditions, isolation, fear of Aboriginal and bushranger attack and the uncertainty of annual leases (Craze, n.d. and 1977).

Each property was a small settlement of its own, servicing its own people and probably others. Much of the work was performed by convicts. Grazing of cattle, horses and sheep was the main activity. Wheat was grown and milled for domestic purposes, each station having its own mill. The first activity on the site of the township-to-be was that of a pound, known to have been present in 1844 (Craze, n.d.), with the poundkeeper's residence adjacent. The first hotel appeared in 1846. The first store was also opened at around that time. In 1847 a prominent landholder wrote to the Colonial Secretary 'forwarding applications from inhabitants of Coura Rocks to purchase allotments at that place'.[1] The letter was also signed by thirty-four people, described by Craze (n.d.: 17) as 'mainly stockholders'. The development of a township was instigated by the landholders. They had to apply to Sydney to have the land made available for sale. The first sale did not take place until September, 1854, as reported in the *Bathurst Free Press* of 14 October. It was preceded by local meetings and appeals to Sydney for a surveyor.

In 1850, the village had thirty-four inhabitants, and in 1852, 120 (Craze, n.d.: 17). The census of 1856 indicates the dominance of rural activity in the 'Carcoar Police District', an area encompassing the present Cowra. The small number of people (sixteen) engaged in 'trade and commerce', and the small population of Carcoar (364 persons) and Cowra (perhaps 150) compared to the 2 943 in the district, which would have contained no larger villages and towns, suggests that economic activity was very largely rural. The returns of the first census of Cowra village, that of 1861, indicated that 'Providers of Food, Drink and Accommodation' were more numerous (eleven) than people engaged in 'Trading and Commerce' (five), and that almost half of the village's population (of 193) were either 'Scholars' (thirty-nine) or 'Domestics' (forty-eight).

During the 1850s three more hotels were built, the first policeman arrived, and a post office and court house were established. The first school was established in 1850. The owner of 'Coura Rocks', became the first Justice of the Peace. Presbyterian and Roman Catholic churches were built. O'Shaughnessy mentioned three stores in the village in 1855.[2] In the 1860s a flour mill and another hotel were opened. The hotels prospered on the traffic to and from the Lambing Flat and Grenfell gold fields to the south and west of Cowra. The village was developing as a district centre and a stopping point for travellers. Indeed, travellers to the gold fields had to stop to cross the Lachlan River, for there was no bridge. Bailliere's directory (Whitworth, 1866: 157) noted that the need for a bridge 'is much felt', and that 'the roads about Cowra are in but indifferent condition'. Communication with Sydney presented many difficulties. The *Bathurst Free Press* of 21 October, 1854 reported complaints from Cowra about delays of weeks for the weekly mail service. In the 1850s Cowra was still very much a pioneer settlement. The roles of representatives of the law, including those prominent landholders who acted as, for example, justices of the peace and magistrate, would have been very important.

There is evidence that landholders were involved in, without necessarily monopolising, village businesses. They certainly acquired village property, some of which remained with their descendants in the 1980s. The growth of Cowra during the 1860s was not especially rapid. The 1871 census counted 265 people. The distribution of occupations was similar to that recorded in 1861. By 1870 Cowra had been established, but the role of the village was small, and dominance of the landholders was profound.

Development and dispersal

A period of rapid growth, which laid the foundations of the present township, came in the next twenty years, when the concentration of activity in the hands of the landed proprietors was broken down. This is at least partly attributable to Jack Robertson, squatter, member for a rural electorate, and Secretary for Lands, who had 'pledged himself to allow men to found homes in the wilderness by undertaking to unlock an agricultural paradise to legions of small selectors' (Clark, 1978: 139). Robertson's legislation had little effect during the 1860s and early 1870s. Much of the squatters' land in New South Wales was locked by leases, and selection by settlers was retarded by loopholes in the legislation until 1875 (Buxton, 1985). Being rich agricultural land, the Cowra district was attractive to settlers, and from about 1875, it boomed.

Agriculture expanded rapidly, against the previous virtual monopoly of pastoralism. As the number of holdings grew (those exceeding one acre grew from 120 to 412 between 1875 and 1880), the area cultivated grew a little faster, from 1 949 to 7 982 acres in the same period (Sands, 1878-9: 157 and 1881-2: 38). The total area of holdings grew relatively slowly between 1877 and 1880 (from 151 312 to 160 283 acres), while the area cultivated rather more than doubled (from 3 342 to 7 982 acres). Such was the impact of wheat farming. The *Australian Handbook* (Gordon and Gotch, 1883) reported that the Cowra district had achieved the second highest grain yield in the Colony. The town prospered as farmers established themselves, and in the 1880s they were helped by good seasons, new agricultural machinery, and hungry markets.

The growing township offered business opportunities which were rapidly taken up. *Sands' Directory* of the Cowra Land District for 1884-5 listed thirteen professional people, fifty-two people in trades, sixteen hotel keepers, twenty-three storekeepers, twenty-two in other commercial activity, such as bank managers, agents, 'contractors', auctioneers and agents, and seven in government service. It had been a hectic decade, which can be summarised and compared with earlier and later decades, albeit crudely, by surveying the entries for Cowra in The *Australian Handbook* (Gordon and Gotch, 1872-1902), which shows the number of banks and 'large stores' growing from one in 1880 to nine in 1902, inns increasing from two in 1872 to eight in 1902 (having peaked at ten in 1889), and the total population (of an undefined area around Cowra) growing from 1 618 in 1872 to 11 000 in 1902.

Land legislation and wheat production were linked at an ideological level by an agrarian myth, the idea that a stout and stable yeomanry would grow consequently with the grain, which was prominent in political rhetoric among the leaders of land reform. Gammage (1987) found that the common view of historians is that the purpose of the legislation (as Robertson's pledge mentioned above suggests) was to implement the agrarian ideal. It is difficult to accept that the squatters' interests were served when the legislation was aimed at breaking their dominance, but it is unwise to assume, even with the evidence above for Cowra, that they suffered as a result of the land legislation. Gammage (1987) found that the legislation had the immediate effect of underwriting the value of land already held freehold. It contained many loopholes which allowed squatters to gain legal title to their land. Nevertheless, free selectors could obtain land. *Sands' Directory* of 1878–9 reported free selection under way in the Cowra area. O'Shaughnessy wrote: 'I rode out to the scalded plain to see if there was enough vacant land there for a selection. There was some but not enough for me' (1 December, 1878: 65).[3] In 1879 he reported selecting two blocks of 200 acres each (15 April and 21 May: 73). *Sands' Directory* of Cowra Land District for 1884–5 lists 230 farmers, 78 selectors, 23 graziers and 27 squatters. The big properties, however, declined slowly. Their owners were in the best position to take advantage of a market for wheat. They also had some excellent land. The *Cowra Guardian* (28 January, 1905: 2) noted that 'this is the centre of one of the great wheat growing districts in Australia. The largest acreage under wheat at least in New South Wales the property of one man is Brundah . . . some twenty miles south of Cowra'.

The late 1870s and the 1880s saw the rise to prominence of many local citizens who were successful in farming or business or both. The older landed families began to share prominence in local affairs with town business people. Storekeepers and professional people, as well as squatters, were prominent at meetings which led to establishment of the Cowra Race Club, the Pastoral, Agricultural and Horticultural Association (P. A. and H.), and the Progress Association in 1878. However, squatters were still considered to be of sufficient stature to be consulted before the P. A. and H. was formed (Craze, 1979: 8).

The squatters' continuing role is exemplified by George Campbell, representative in the New South Wales Parliament and an important force in the establishment of local government and the coming of the railway. The story of incorporation, as told by Ryall (1928)[4], shows Campbell's strong presence and, at the same time, his political weakness. A petition for incorporation was signed by townspeople in 1886 and presented to the authorities in Sydney. Campbell opposed the move, but succeeded only in delaying incorporation. His status ultimately remained undamaged. After the first election, in 1888, he was elected Mayor, and according to the minutes of the meeting, he was unopposed. The continued prominence of squatters is a vestige of their earlier paternalistic role. This role is illustrated by McDiarmid of Waugoola, who was instrumental in the establishment of institutions, such as the Carcoar Presbyterian Church (reported in the *Bathurst Advocate* of 13 May, 1848), and who was a patron of social life in the district. It was he who wrote to the Colonial Secretary in 1847 with the request for subdivision of the town.

Campbell was also prominent in the agitation for a railway connection to Sydney. At one stage of this movement, the thought that a neighbouring town would have the railway at Cowra's expense stirred the people of Cowra, and a public meeting to be chaired by Campbell was called to form a 'railway league'. The push had come from business and farming interests, rather than squatters (Ryan, 1986). Indeed, Ryall (*Cowra Free Press*, 15 May, 1928: 7) took a rather cynical view of the squatters' role, recollecting that the railway league received 'no generous contributions by large landed proprietors who gained immensely through the enormously enhanced value of their several properties'.

Some local people undoubtedly obtained land through selection, and some who already had much of it prospered, but the land legislation and the changes that followed it were products of an urban image of progress. Moreover, urban financial institutions and the New South Wales Government profited from land sale and investment. City merchants profited from the growth of commerce. The dispersal of economic activity from the initial total dominance of a landed aristocracy was not driven by small local interests, so much as by large remote interests who held an idealised view of rural life.

Ryall's hostile attitude to the squatters and his fervent support for closer settlement expressed both the ideals of Sydney metropolitan business, and the interests of local town business. Both the *Free Press* and the *Cowra Guardian*, which had first appeared in 1891 as the *Cowra Independent* (Martin, 1938: 10), expressed the call to unlock the land. Closer settlement rolled on, until relatively recently, pushed by the belief that it would bring growth and prosperity to the district. It was also helped by circumstances, which included the financial strain for the squatters of defending their holdings, and poor health and loss of heirs among the owning families. By the 1930s, although still passionately pursuing closer settlement, Cowra people had learned from disaster. The *Lachlan Leader*'s editorial of 1 July, 1937 called for care to be exercised with closer settlement, an 'imperative if repetition of failures of the past – some have been ghastly – is to be avoided'.

Nevertheless, demand for closer settlement was rekindled after World War II, in the name of returned soldier settlement. Government was taking an aggressive approach in resuming land by the mid 1950s, but breaking up the properties of the squatters and making them available for sale provided opportunities for others to establish large properties. By the mid-1960s closer settlement was winding down but not forgotten. Some at least still sought to pursue the ideals of putting families on the land. On 1 November, 1968, the *Guardian* reported the leader of the New South Wales opposition Labor Party as having said that his party would investigate 'closer settlement needs' as 'closer settlement had ground to a halt over the past three years'. This reaffirmed the long standing support for closer settlement by the Australian Labor Party. It could go on as long as property owners were able to accumulate large holdings, but in the Cowra district, it had finished.

The social consequences of dispersal

Selection and farming created a new social order by adding people of small property rather than taking away those of large. A passage from the *Free Press* (6 May, 1892: Supplement p. 1), entitled 'All about the Cockies', offers some useful insights. It described the 'boss cockies' or 'picaninny squatters' who held 'hundreds of acres', the 'cockatoo parrot' who had a smaller holding with a 'limited number of sheep and cattle' and the 'ground parrot' who had a still smaller holding. The '40 acre perisher', who earned daily wages from a neighbouring squatter and was dependent on a few acres of wheat for flour and a vegetable garden, sat at the bottom of the status ladder. He had one or two horses and one or two cows, but he was also 'a landed proprietor and that *rara avis* – a contented cockatoo'. This passage, while espousing the nobility of those who are unpretentious and work hard, also indicates the aspirations of all to have property, preferably a lot of it, but some is enough. Having some property opened the possibility of acquiring more, and becoming an employer rather than an employee.

As Waterson (1968: 17) observed, pastoralists were still superior in the 'Australian rural hierarchy', and '... all groups eventually came to subscribe to the ideals of the Pure Merinos and to imitate their way of life as far as their means would allow'. The 'forty acre perisher' would have had little hope of acquiring substantial means, but in some of the literature of the day, notably the *Bulletin*, he became a hero (Share, 1985: 6). He was not a hero on his own, for the battler image was drawn as the family, as depicted in the writing of Henry Lawson and Steele Rudd, and consistent with the ideal of wholesomeness in rural living expressed by the early land legislators. Women and children shared the hardship.

Perhaps the key feature of the process of dispersal of rural capital was its creation of a new class of smaller employers. A rural working class grew with settlement, and as it grew it developed a class consciousness and the means of industrial and political activity. The Labor Party campaigned in Cowra, against the views of the local press. Labor support and organisation, in 1898 at least, was weak. The *Guardian* of 19 February reported that a Labor League candidate admitted during his campaign that only the executive of the League existed locally, although he had been its president for three years. The *Guardian* of 21 July carried lists of names of people who had attended Federal Liberal Party and Labor League meetings. The Federal Liberal Party appeared to have attracted a relatively large number of prominent farming and business people. They felt they could call on an historical legitimacy. The names of prominent landholders still carried meaning, although the local representative in the New South Wales

Parliament during the early 1890s had been a storekeeper who had started business in the early 1880s. While its opponents could call on prominent names for support, Labor was in disarray.

The first farmer organisation in Cowra was formed in 1905 (*Cowra Guardian*, 20 February, 1962). The list of office bearers included names of town business people. The following quotation from a conversation I had with an elderly resident illustrates the opposing interests, and the farmers' perspective on labour and the Labor Party.

> Fred . . ., he was a farmer, had several sons. He was Labor because he didn't have to pay the men. The rest of us couldn't stand a bar of him. [Chuckle] He'd put forward his ideas at Farmers and Settlers meetings, but it was all right for him. He didn't have to scrounge to pay someone like we did because we didn't have grown up sons. He had sons working for nothing. So naturally he was for Labor.

The Labor Party's intention in supporting closer settlement was to give the small people a chance. Unfortunately small settlers often failed, and those with more property, as employers, became politically conservative. By 1914, the Farmers and Settlers had entered an association with a New South Wales employer organisation (Gammage, 1986: 113). Dispersal brought both prosperity for the propertied and hardship for those of smaller means. For Aborigines, lowest on the dominant status ladder with virtually no means at all, dispersal meant something very different: destruction of community and enforced placement in the white world. (Some of their history during this period will be related in chapter 7.)

The rise of commerce and services

Growth since the 1880s, as indicated by New South Wales and Commonwealth censuses, has been unsteady. The town's population, having more than doubled from 628 in 1881 to 1 546 in 1891, grew only to 1 811, through economic depression, in 1901. There followed another spurt of growth, to 3 271 in 1911.

By the 1900s the town had developed processing and manufacturing industries, including a dairy company, a coach factory, a brewery, a soap works, three cordial factories, two flour mills and a rabbit freezing works (*Cowra Free Press*, 29 April, 1892; *Cowra Guardian*, 24 November and 27 December, 1906 and 11 June, 1948; and Martin, 1938). In 1903 the New South Wales Government established an experimental farm (Craze, 1979). Railway branch lines were opened in 1901 and 1910 (Ryan, 1986). School facilities were expanded in 1900, again in 1907 and yet again in 1912 (Martin, 1938). In 1906 the New South Wales Government legislated to establish shire councils, in order to devolve responsiblity for road construction and maintenance. Consequently Waugoola Shire came into existence in that year. The first councillors were prominent farmers.

The Municipal Council made an agreement with a gas company for the establishment of gasworks in 1910, and in 1925 it commenced electricity reticulation. It had built its first Council Chambers in 1902 (Armstrong, 1988).

Industry had not, however, displaced agriculture. As the editor of the *Guardian* wrote on 3 January, 1907: 'It is to the district and its primary producers that the town is indebted for its growth and prosperity, and so long as that class thrives and prospers, so long will our town forge ahead'. The numbers engaged in commerce, transport, communications, manufacturing, construction and other industry together (1 278 persons) fell well short of the 1 641 engaged in agricultural and pastoral pursuits counted at the 1921 census.

The next twelve (inter-censal) years saw considerable change without upsetting the dominance of primary industry. By 1933, the number employed in commerce had grown substantially, from 313 to 497, while the number engaged in agricultural and pastoral activity fell, from 1 641 to 1 570. The 1933 census also recorded 848, or 19.4 per cent of the work force, unemployed. During World War II a munitions factory was set up in the Showground pavilion. An army camp was established on the town's outskirts, and a prisoner of war camp was erected nearby. A power alcohol distillery was added to the district's industry. The most important industrial addition was the vegetable cannery of the Edgell company; the cannery would have been largely responsible for increasing manufacturing employment, as recorded at the 1947 census, to almost double its 1933 level.

Economic activity was in the hands of many people. In 1921 the census counted 977 people who were 'employers' or were 'working on their own account', being twenty-nine per cent of the work force. The proportion had fallen to twenty-six per cent in 1933, although the number had grown to 1 143. Of those 1 143, some 463 were employers. This represents a great change from the early days of settlement, and suggests a substantial measure of local autonomy.

It is worth considering, however, some ways in which that autonomy was more superficial than it appeared. Certainly many commercial and industrial enterprises had been initiated locally. Some such as a cordial factory which commenced in the 1900s and the Edgell cannery, were local branches of firms which had started elsewhere. But when the importance of government decisions and activity and Cowra's commercial and financial reliance on Sydney are considered, a great deal of dependence can be inferred.

The coming of the railway is perhaps the strongest example of dependence, because local people had to influence the decision process in Sydney in order to obtain it. Their desire to obtain it is an indication of their appreciation of commercial links with Sydney. Waugoola Shire was established in order to achieve the aims of the State Government independent of local initiative, unlike Cowra Municipality which was established after local appeals. Later Government decisions, such as the one to build Wyangala Dam, and establish camps and industry during World War II, had a substantial impact. Cowra's commerce developed while largely dependent on city-based institutions as sources of finance. Decisions about the investment destinations of Cowra people's savings were and are made in the city. Cowra's growth is best illustrated as a product of its relationship with the city by the city-inspired land legislation that helped to set it off. The squatters were legally and commercially dependent initially, but they enjoyed a degree of independence bestowed by their economic strength and status that was not available to small proprietors.

Cowra people have seen their district's population grow very slowly. If we extract the aberrations caused by work on Wyangala Dam in the 1930s and the mid 1960s and the migrant camp in the early 1950s, the Shire's population growth would appear to have levelled off around the 1930s. It has only recently recovered to reach its 1933 level (figure 1).

The 1933 census counted 11 394 people and the 1986 census 11 569, but the town of Cowra has experienced steady growth, increasing its share of the Shire population. The decline in the rural-village share started after 1933 and, without the migrant camp and Wyangala Dam, would have continued. The 1986 census revealed slight rural growth, but this may be attributable to 'hobby farms' established near the town by people whose principal work is in the town. Accelerated town growth in the 1947–54 and 1961–66 periods was associated with rural growth under the influence of the migrant camp and Wyangala Dam, rather than closer settlement. The role of the villages as population and business centres has declined substantially. In 1911 the villages contained sixty-four per cent of the village-rural population. In 1947 they contained forty-four per cent, and in 1986 they contained about fifteen per cent of the village-rural population, or about four per cent of the total Shire population.

Through the post-war period primary production has declined from occupying thirty-four per cent of the employed work force in 1947 to twenty-four per cent in 1986. Growth has come from commerce and the service industry. In 1986 forty-nine per cent of the Shire's work force was engaged in such activity whereas twenty per cent had been so engaged in 1947. The largest components in this sector in 1986 were retail trade (fourteen per cent of the employed work force) and health and education (thirteen per cent of the employed work force). The manufacturing, construction, transport and communication sectors have retained their employment levels without substantial change.

In the immediate post-war period, Cowra people found their district's businesses to be prospering. The Edgell cannery continued production, contradicting wartime fears that the post-war decline in demand for canned food would force its closure (MacColl, 1944). On 16 December,

A history of Cowra

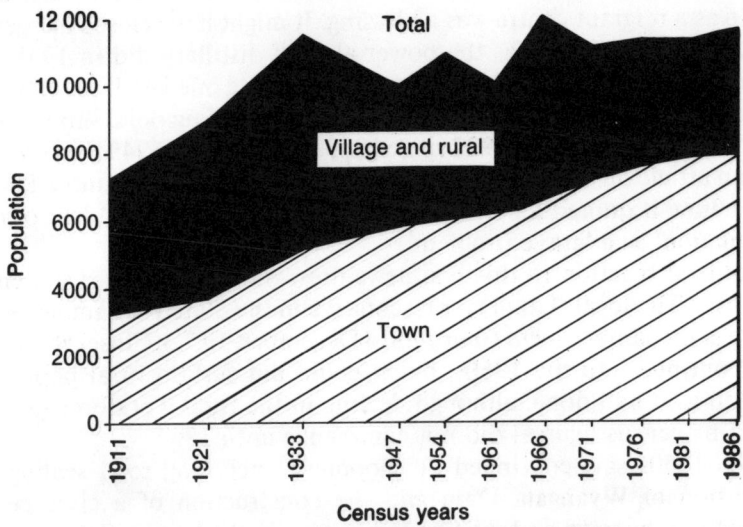

Figure 1. Growth of village/rural and town populations in Cowra Shire, 1911 to 1986

Notes
Sources are New South Wales and Commonwealth Censuses. Census figures are available for the rural and village areas only since the incorporation of Waugoola Shire in 1906.

The following aberrations have altered what may have been a steady trend of relatively slow growth in the total population since the 1921 to 1933 period:

The height of the peak in 1933 and the rapid growth in 'rural and village' between 1961 and 1966 can largely be attributed to growth in Wyangala Village due to construction and reconstruction work on the dam.

Much of the growth in 'rural and village' between 1947 and 1954, and much of the decline in the following period, were associated with the establishment and closure of a hostel for European migrants about three kilometres from the centre of the town.

'Full-blood' Aborigines were not enumerated before 1966. Their enumeration in 1966 contributed about one quarter of the indicated growth in the town's population between 1961 and 1966.

1949, the *Guardian* announced that town business was growing and had been, according to local business people, for the preceding four to five years. Work had started on conversion of the former army camp to a migrant centre. In the early 1950s the town grew rapidly, boosted by the arrival of migrants and the high natural population increase of the post-war 'baby boom'. A new power station, gasworks and motel were all local initiatives. An airline service, a new hospital, a technical college and an ambulance station were also welcomed, but were products of decisions made elsewhere.

The decision by Commonwealth authorities to use the former army camp as a migrant centre was a blessing. It might have closed altogether, as it did in 1956, and as the power alcohol distillery did in 1948. The *Guardian*, on 31 October, 1947, ran a large page one headline, 'Startling Figures for Cowra District', and revealed that Waugoola Shire's population had decreased by 1 927 since 1933. On 4 March, 1949 the *Guardian* ran an article on the 1947 census entitled the 'Passing of Country Towns'. On 7 June it quoted a parliamentarian who described the 'drift of rural population' as a 'grave problem'.

Political reaction to this bad news drew on the old closer settlement formula. The local (Labor) representative in the State Parliament sought more of the same (*Cowra Guardian*, 4 December, 1951). Closer settlement did continue into the 1960s, but it could not sustain rural population growth as it had done, although decline in the rural workforce (as indicated by census figures) did not commence until 1954.

The 1960s saw continued development, including road sealing, the extension of Wyangala Dam and the construction of a civic centre. Growth in the town and the Shire was rapid in the first half of the 1960s, but slowed after the completion of the dam (figure 1). The total population fell by 1 060 between the 1966 and 1971 censuses. At this time the metropolitan cities were growing rapidly and city planners looked to decentralisation, offering new hope for country towns. However, in September, 1970, a representative of the New South Wales Department of Decentralisation and Development visited Cowra and reminded its people that decentralisation was intended to solve the city's problems, not Cowra's (*Cowra Guardian*, 8 September, 1970).

Centralisation and resistance

A process of centralisation operating within the Cowra district, and as part of a more general process operating through Cowra's external relations, can be observed as far back as the early selection period as commercial activity focused on the town. At the broader level of city-country relations, it could be observed in 1883 (as O'Shaughnessy noted in his diary, 20 November, p. 134) that a local hotel had been bought by a Sydney firm. Centralisation has, however, been most obvious in the post-war period, as the district has focused on the town, and the Shire has become more closely tied to and dependent upon metropolitan Sydney.

The *Guardian* announced an early post-war indicator of change to come on 16 January, 1951, with a page one headline: 'Big General Store Changes Hands, Reid Smith Pty Ltd Sells to City Firm'. The store was one of the two largest in Cowra, and had always been locally owned and operated. It had been bought by Reid Smith from D.C.J. Donnelly, a prominent citizen and local parliamentary representative, around the turn of the century. The other large store, 'Squire Pepper', was sold in 1955 to an out-of-town chain. It had three premises on or adjacent to the main street at the time, having started business in the 1880s. The Cowra flour mill was also sold by its local owners to out-of-town interests at about the same time. It was soon closed.

The later 1950s found Cowra struggling to maintain sovereignty over its water and electricity services. The *Guardian* of 28 August, 1956, announced that the Cowra power station was to close, eliminating twenty-five local jobs, as Cowra was connected to the central State grid. On 4 December, 1956, the *Guardian* declared that 'Cowra will be the bunny' and that the plan would be 'a terrific blow' for the district. On 15 February, 1957 the *Guardian* feared that the 'Big electricity grab will cripple Cowra', and that 'If the plan is adopted it will mean virtual stagnation for Cowra as a business centre'. In 1958 it appeared that a similar type of administrative arrangement might divest Cowra of control of its own water reticulation. Waugoola Shire eventually became part of such an arrangement; Cowra Municipality did not, although the threat arose again in 1966 and 1974 (Armstrong, 1988). The 1958 threat caused local alarm. Cowra's mayor observed that a 'stripping process' was under way, seeing such changes as removing important responsibilities, and their associated resources, from local government (*Cowra Guardian*, 2 December, 1958). In 1959 the first motel to have been built in Cowra was sold to a 'national company' (*Cowra Guardian*, 27 October), and establishment of another was announced by out-of-town interests (*Cowra Guardian*, 31 July).

The 1960s and early 1970s may have provided a respite from publicised external intervention, for the pages of the *Guardian* were largely free from announcements like those above. The vulnerability of local commerce, however, again became apparent in 1976, when a clothing factory which had started from a local base in 1972, ceased production (*Cowra Guardian*, 18 June, 1976). 1978 brought particularly bad news when the department store formerly owned by Reid Smith was closed (*Cowra Guardian*, 7 April). This followed soon after the closure of another chain store. The Reid Smith store had a sufficiently important role in the town's commercial life for its loss to prompt deep concern about the town's capacity to provide for the district's inhabitants. This was capped by the announcement in the *Guardian* of 15 August, 1978, that the Sydney-owned Cowra Steam Laundry was about to close. In 1948 the *Guardian* (9 July) could boast that Cowra's steam laundry was the second biggest in New South Wales. Less than one month after announcing the Reid Smith closure, the *Guardian* (5 May) announced that Cowra's telephone exchange was to close. This closure was deferred, and did not eventuate until 1984 (*Cowra Guardian*, 11 June). The old Reid Smith store was sold to another chain in 1979 (*Cowra Guardian*, 3 April).

Reminders of Cowra's dependence on, and vulnerability to, external decisions have strengthened since the late 1970s. On 23 October, 1979 the *Guardian* announced that Cowra Hospital was to lose twenty-one of its one hundred beds. 1980 brought the enforced amalgamation of Cowra Municipal and Waugoola Shire Councils, and in 1982 the Central West (electricity) County Council closed its Cowra store.

In 1984 the *Guardian* was acquired by a newspaper chain. For some time its local content had declined as it enclosed a regional news section produced out-of-town and circulated across a wide area of New South Wales. By this time Woolworths had opened a large supermarket in Cowra. In 1982 the local bakery wrote to the *Guardian* (12 March) complaining that Cowra's externally owned and controlled supermarkets were not buying local bread. This practice had cost four jobs. On 16 July, 1984 the *Guardian* headed an article 'Supermarkets Threat to Small Shops'. It continued: 'Cowra's small shopkeepers believe a war is being waged against them by supermarkets and there is nothing they can do to stop it'.

Cowra had, however, been fighting back for many years. The possibility of the establishment of a local abattoir had been discussed at least as early as 1928 (*Cowra Free Press*, 22 June). In February, 1966 the Waugoola Shire President called a public meeting to discuss the matter. At a later public meeting, attended by 250 people, a decision to form a company was made (*Cowra Guardian*, 19 April). Fifty per cent of the capital was raised locally, with the remainder coming from a Sydney company. The abattoir commenced production in 1970. The Chamber of Commerce has been active since the 1950s, appealing for Cowra people to give custom to local shops. The *Guardian* editorial of 24 June, 1955 asked its readers to support local business, warning that 'invading firms' offer poor service and no refunds. Local interests were able to rescue local assets which might otherwise have fallen to outsiders. In 1981 one local bid to purchase the old Squire Pepper store failed, but a second succeeded, as did a bid for the Central West County Council store (*Cowra Guardian*, 27 July, 1981 and 22 June, 1984). Both were let. A local initiative obtained the *Guardian*, but could not prevent its eventual sale.

Cowra has received stimuli to economic growth. The more prominent include a vineyard and a Japanese Garden, both of which were established in the mid-1970s. The latter received substantial assistance from Japanese institutions that wished to symbolise and perpetuate Cowra's relationship with Japan which emanated from World War II. All Japanese military personnel that died on Australian soil during World War II are buried at Cowra, including the many who perished while attempting to escape from a prisoner-of-war camp near Cowra. This makes Cowra a special place for Japan and Japanese people, and for Australia and Australians as well. The mass escape bid, while having great significance in military history for the large number of prisoners involved, has offered Australia a contact with Japanese tradition, and an opportunity for Australians to perceive an aspect of a culture which usually seems distant and mysterious, and internationally very important. (The significance of

Japanese cultural tradition for events around the escape bid is discussed in Carr-Gregg (1978).) Cowra's Japanese Garden and its 'Cultural Centre' attract Australian and other visitors, many of whom, I suspect, find the cultural exhibits curious, and the Garden most pleasing. The tranquillity of the Garden makes it easy to forget the violent origin of this apparently very successful point of contact between Australia and Japan.

Cowra's third large secondary industry, a wool scouring plant, employing about eighty, was also established in the mid-1970s. Although local initiative had an important role in attracting this industry, it is owned and controlled elsewhere, largely in Japan, by big corporations. It was assisted by State Government financial aid to decentralising industry. Local initiatives to attract industry, and retain commerce, have been handled by Cowra's Tourist and Development Corporation, as well as by local government. It was set up in 1967 with support from the Chamber of Commerce, Waugoola Shire Council and financial help from Cowra Municipal Council. Cowra has resisted change, but, not surprisingly, has failed to deflect the national and international forces that have generated centralisation.

The number of primary production establishments in Cowra Shire has declined from 603 in 1977 to 551 in 1986 (Australian Bureau of Statistics, 1977–1986). Even government policy seeks to increase farm size rather than number (Nott, 1983). Closer settlement appears to have slipped into reverse. Its reverse momentum has two directions; the second being the rise of absentee ownership and agribusiness. Cowra people have told me of three large and valuable properties which have recently been sold to absentees. Cowra business people are aware that absentee owners, like the squatters, may do their buying elsewhere.

Agribusiness is important to Cowra. Many of Cowra's vegetable growers are contracted to supply the Edgell Company. That company started as a family business in 1906, and was very successful. In 1961 it was taken over by a company large and diverse enough to be in the 'agribusiness' class. In 1982 it was swallowed by the even larger Adelaide Steamship Company (Adsteam) which in 1983 had control of over 450 separate companies (Lawrence, 1987: 142).

Cowra farmers' contracts with Edgells may be commercially advantageous in removing an element of risk, but they also remove an element of independence. As a Cowra farmer explained, the contracts encourage overproduction, placing a burden on the soil and threatening the long-term viability of the land. This element of the farmers' independence has been given to a company which has captured ninety per cent of Australia's market for frozen vegetables (Sargent, 1985). This perspective on centralisation makes the concentration of wealth among the squatters look feeble.

The history of the power alcohol distillery offers a parallel intervention by agribusiness. Being no longer required for alcohol distillation after

World War II, the distillery was sold to a locally-managed, although not locally-owned, stock feed company. The importance to Cowra people of its local base was illustrated by the emphasis placed on its local management in an article about the company in the 1 November, 1968 issue of the *Guardian*. Cowra was the firm's headquarters. The business was acquired by a Sydney-based company in the early 1970s, and has since been taken over by a large national company with interests in flour milling, baking and other food production, as well as stock feeds. The latter company captured almost two-thirds of Sydney's market for bread with a 1986 takeover (Sargent, 1985; Lawrence, 1987). Cowra's stock feed facility is a very small component of its enterprise.

Dispersal created a large number of businesses, some but not all of which were big enough to support their proprietors. Some indication of the range of farm incomes in Cowra Shire was obtained in survey data collected in 1986 (reported in Gray, 1987a). Of the fifty-four respondents to the survey who stated that the main occupation of their household's main income earner was farming or grazing, eighteen said that their total incomes were below $10 000 in 1985–86. Four said that their incomes were above $39 999. Those whose farm does not support their families must seek work elsewhere, and although there are no relevant statistics available for Cowra Shire, it seems likely that they are doing so in large numbers.

Farm mechanisation reduced the need for labour in the 1950s, and the declining terms of trade since have made it increasingly difficult for farmers to take on employees. The number of employees in Waugoola Shire fell from 854 at the 1954 census to 599 in 1961. The traditional farm worker who lives on the farm and receives food produced on the farm as part payment for labour is now rare. Unfortunately statistics on farm labour over time for Cowra Shire are not available, but my conversations with local farmers indicated a decline. When asked if he knew of any farmers who had a live-on-farm employee in the district, a prominent member of the Cowra Farmers' Association could think of only two.

The necessity for off-farm employment, and the loss of rural employment, indicate increasing dependence on the town, turning around the traditional local rural-urban relationship. An increase in the proportion of the rural workforce employed in non-farm occupations has become evident in Cowra, having been thirty-six per cent at the 1976 census, and forty-four per cent at the 1986 census. The shift of employment to the town is best illustrated by comparing the growth of the workforces resident in town and country. While the town workforce grew by sixty-five per cent between 1947 and 1986 censuses, that of the rural area of Cowra Shire grew by six per cent. Despite growing numbers of farmers working off-farm, the town's share of employees in Cowra Shire grew from sixty-eight to seventy-seven per cent during the same period. The town's share of the Shire's employers also grew, from thirty-six to forty-six per cent.

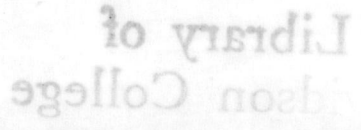

The political labour movement has organised well in Cowra but has not enjoyed success since the late 1950s. The State electorate in which Cowra is situated had a Labor representative from 1941 to 1959.

The most dramatic change in the workforce since World War II has been the growth of its female component. The proportion of Cowra Shire's workforce which is female grew from seventeen per cent in 1947 to thirty-seven per cent in 1986. While the female workforce was growing by 200 per cent in this period, the male workforce grew by five per cent. The proportion of women in the workforce working in service activity has, however, declined only slightly, from sixty-three per cent in 1947 to sixty per cent in 1986.

Despite the entry of large organisations, the role of small business has remained strong. The ratio of employees to employers and self-employed for town residents was 4.3 to 1 in 1947, and had moved only to 3.9 to 1 in 1986. For the rural area, it moved from 1.1 to 1 to 0.9 to 1. Centralisation has brought reliance on large industries, described as 'heavy reliance' by an economic consultant in 1986 (Peat, Marwick, Mitchell), but it has by no means eliminated the economic and social structures created by dispersal.

The most powerful feature of the history of Cowra Shire is the importance of political decisions made in Sydney in the middle of last century, which, more than any other factor, sent Cowra on a course toward growth and prosperity. Growth was sustained by closer settlement which continued into the 1960s, helped on two occasions by large injections of government employment on Wyangala Dam, and rescued from post-war decline by the maintenance of the cannery, the 'baby boom', and for a time at least, the migrant camp. In the 1970s it was helped by the establishment of two large manufacturing industries, one largely through local initiative.

However, one-third of Cowra's 1986 workforce was employed either by government or by one of the three large manufacturing industries. The prospects for development of locally-based large scale industry appear bleak, and government now seeks the opposite of closer settlement. The reality of this change was brought home to Cowra in a New South Wales Department of Agriculture report in 1983 (Nott, 1983), which claimed that the average farm size in Cowra Shire was too small. The Minister for Agriculture, in his Foreword to the report, said that 'over half the rural holdings in Cowra Shire are already too small for efficient utilization'.

Cowra Shire is dependent on government in two ways. It employs twenty-one per cent of the local workforce (1986 census). There are more government employees than farmers, the latter being sixteen per cent of the workforce. The only growth in government employment, however, appears to be in local government. Between 1976 and 1986 censuses, State and Federal Government employment in Cowra declined by four people. The other form of dependence, on government decision making, is more powerful. Government decisions can affect the range and quality of the district's services, and increasingly importantly where industrial viability depends on government assistance, the extent of employment it offers. Cowra depends on its ability to marshall the support of government.

Notes

1 Colonial Secretary, Register of Letters Received, July-December 1847, held in the Archives Office of New South Wales.
2,3 The Diary of Thomas O'Shaughnessy, 1835–1903, copy held by Cowra and District Historical Society.
4 J. C. Ryall was the founding proprietor of Cowra's first newspaper, the *Cowra Free Press*. In 1928 he published a series of articles in the paper in which he recalled the history of the town. Ryall was an active and vocal townsman. He was also a strong supporter of closer settlement, and was implicitly opposed to the squatters, as references to the *Free Press* will indicate.

4
Elitism and local government

Examination of the structure of local government in Cowra, with consideration of the possibility of elitism, reveals the arena of local politics. One might ask if the structure is elitist or pluralist, but that question does not lead directly to fruitful answers. It rather poses problems, providing a base for exploration of power relations. The community power and local government literature offers some background on local power structures, but, unfortunately, the fields covered have not coincided, although there is a place for them to do so. The Australian local government system was cast in a British mould, and local power studies have been largely American. British and Australian local government studies have seldom sought to analyse power relations. They have rather explored democratic and administrative aspects of local government using the tools of political science. The British have debated the conceptual and empirical problems of local government as manifestations of the role of the state in capitalist society more often than they have tackled the problems of local power relations. The various approaches to the study of local government are, however, instructive in the way that they have defined its problems for study and formulated research agendas.

Perspectives on local government

Perspectives on local government fall very roughly into three camps: Marxist and Weberian in sociology, and those which focus more narrowly on political apparatuses and processes. The Marxist approach sees a problem of inequitable distribution of power and wealth as a product of local government being an arm of the state, through which a ruling class maintains its dominance. Writers such as Cockburn (1977), Magnusson (1986), and in the Australian context, Mowbray (1984) see the problems of local government determined by class relations, finding the roles of local government to be necessary to the maintenance of the capitalist system. Those working from a Weberian perspective range from, for example, Saunders (1979, 1981, 1983), and Elliott and McCrone (1982), who reacted against the determinism of the Marxist approach but continued to see the problems of local government as having a class component, to the 'urban managerialists', including Pahl (1975) and, in Australia, Jones (1981), who, from an empirical basis, found the problems of local government to lie in relations between bureaucratic institutions and people. Those who confine their attention to the machinery of democratic processes resemble pluralists, as they look at the performance of local government against criteria of democratic ideals. Such work is exemplified by Bowman (n.d.), Painter (1973) and Johnson (1979) in Australia, and a host of British studies including Hampton (1970) and Dearlove (1973). My approach is closest to that of Saunders (1979), acknowledging the fruitfulness of a class perspective while accepting an important empirical place for people-institution relations.

Local government has been widely ignored in the study of Australian society, and not without reason. The reasons, however, increasingly appear mistaken. They include the belief that local government's functions are determined by State government, which is substantially correct; the belief that its functions are menial, which is partly correct; and the belief that it is of neither consequence nor interest to the people it 'governs', which is manifestly incorrect. The importance of local government to the people of Cowra, and its role as a link with central government, make it *the arena* of local power relations. For Cowlishaw (1988: 163), the importance and power of Brindleton's council were indicated by its ability to 'determine the terms of public debate by informal control of the newspaper, through [its] influence in organisations and informal social life, and through the deference shown to [it] by others who run the town's institutions'.

Australian local government is a product of English tradition and the dispersed pattern of settlement in Australia (Chapman and Wood, 1984). Local councils were established by colonial and later State governments to provide the infrastructure services essential to development. Colonial and State governments did not seek to create local governments which were either independent or parliamentary. The local councils of New South Wales are still products of, and subject to, State legislation, and they operate much like management committees. They lack many features of a parliamentary system, such as full time salaried elected membership and 'parliamentary privilege'. They have, however, taken on greater roles in service provision and local advocacy; they are partly funded from Federally-collected income tax revenue; and they are elected by all locally-resident adults and local property owners (although voting is not compulsory for non-resident ratepayers).

For Cowra, the relationships between local and State and Federal governments are important, despite the power which the State government wields over local government functions. Local government has been described as 'ancillary' to State government functions (Bowman, 1983: 165), and closer to the materialist mould, 'an extension of the state apparatus', with 'somewhat tenuous autonomy' (Halligan and Paris, 1984: 65). At the extreme, it functions as an agency of State government, enforcing state regulations. As Halligan and Paris (ibid.) point out, however, the relationship is not so simple, for co-operation between local and State government is necessary, and there is room for consultation and negotiation. The process of centralisation in Cowra's history has made access to central decision-making increasingly important, as local demands to make the relationship serve local interests have grown. State and Federal government rhetoric surrounding local government sometimes emphasises the value of consultation and negotiation with the local level. The Advisory Council for Inter-Government Relations (1984) included representation of local interests as well as community development, co-ordination of services and acting as local catalyst in the wider political arena, among the reasons it cited for the establishment of local government in Australia. Local government has been seen to have important roles as a local 'entrepreneur' (Bowman, 1983: 169) and as a local community leader (Jones, 1981: 16).

The responsibilities of local government, as initially laid down by New South Wales Government legislation, were narrow, and would appear menial in these times of broad ranging government activity. They did not include local advocacy (Jones, 1981: 43), but did include 'roads, rates and rubbish', which attract no glamour. They have, however, grown substantially, and have always been fundamental to local economic activity and quality of life. The traditional road maintenance role has great importance to rural dwellers who are highly dependent on transport, a significance quite different to any attributed to it by urban dwellers. Water, sewerage and public health are fundamental to town life.

State government is nudging local government into a wider variety of roles. Kilmartin, Thorns and Burke (1985) and Mowbray (1987) associated this with a political climate of increasing conservatism. The New South Wales (Labor) Minister for Local Government, in 1986, wrote of such expansion in a positive tone, emphasising local co-ordination and advocacy roles (The Hon. K. Stewart, Foreword to Colebatch and Degeling, 1986: 4). The then New South Wales opposition (National Party) spokesperson on local government was quoted in 1987, with a more aggressive posture, as saying that 'We believe in the principle of devolving more power to Local Government through legislation' (Local Government and Shires Association of New South Wales, 1987: 12). The same parliamentarian (who was to become the local representative after changes of electoral boundaries and government at the March, 1988 election) stated at a meeting, which I attended in Cowra in 1987, that all State welfare programs would be handed over to local government, if his Liberal-National Party coalition was to gain power.[1]

Cowra Shire Council is a large organisation, having a turnover in 1986 of about 7.7 million dollars (Cowra Shire Council, *1987 Estimates*). Local organisations called on it to share some of those resources. A local bush fire brigade appealed, successfully, for the donation of a truck which was surplus to the Council's requirements. A group trying to establish a neighbourhood centre sought assistance, unsuccessfully, with accommodation. The Council has an important role in the distribution of goodies from State and Federal government, as illustrated by the process of distribution of Commonwealth Bicentennial grants to local organisations. When a member of the local Bicentennial Committee put forward a proposal for a 'Bicentennial project', he said that the first step towards the project would be acquisition of the support of Council. The potential for debate over allocation of council priorities is essentially what prompted Wild (1974a: 157) to state that 'most controversies in a small town that do not start in the local government council usually finish there.' Some even saw the activity of the Council to be crucial to the economic prosperity of the town, or rather they saw its inactivity as a threat. A local businessperson wrote of the Council, in a letter to the *Guardian* (23 February, 1987):

> The few foresighted, competent councillors are drowned out by the pathetic gaggle of amateurs. Until they are replaced or inspired by the drive and entrepreneurial enthusiasm of Orange and Dubbo [large regional centres] councils this town will continue to stagnate and collapse under the weight of its own, Council driven, inertia.

The support of the Council could be crucial when local organisations sought help from State or Federal authorities, as those authorities saw the Council as a potential guarantor for the venture proposed. The committee which eventually set up the neighbourhood centre, having received State government assistance after much uncertainty and delay, felt that it had been greatly disadvantaged by the Council's unwillingness to support it. An executive member of a group involved in a proposal to have an economic plan drawn up for Cowra using State funding was pessimistic about the proposal because of an anticipated adverse reaction to a request for support from the Council. A voluntary worker who had important roles in establishing facilities for youth and the elderly found the Council's support to have been crucial in both cases from the earliest stages. 'If it doesn't support you, you are doomed to failure'. A member of the committee which set up a child care centre told me that the project 'got nowhere' until Council offered support.

It seems that State and Federal authorities saw local government as a legitimating agency for requests from local organisations. This was not a new phenomenon. In 1960 the Municipal Council found that, for the town's Old People's Welfare Committee to obtain Federal funding for an aged persons' nursing service, the Council would have to offer sponsorship (*Cowra Guardian*, 19 January: 11). To local eyes, however, the Council had become more than a channel of communication. It was the locale for civic activity. As a 'local knowledgeable' and prospective candidate for the 1987 Council election said: 'It's something that everybody who is civic minded thinks at some time that they'll have a go at. Just about everything significant needs Council support at some stage'.

While my experience with local organisations indicated that the Council was seen as a convenient place to look for support from government, it was also seen as a convenient place to express dissatisfaction with government. This could even extend to the possibility of local influence on Federal Government policy. A group of candidates, mostly business people, at the 1974 Municipal election, included in their platform a preparedness to express local needs to Canberra (*Cowra Guardian*, 17 September: 5). At a 1986 meeting of Cowra Shire Council, a letter from a nearby district council of the Livestock and Grain Producers Association (or LGPA, which has since changed its name to the Farmers' Association) was discussed. The letter expressed a desire to have the Federal Government '... make an attempt to transfer the current Welfare State into the Work Ethic State. Social Service recipients could work one day a week or one week per month for their pay ...'.

The accessibility of local government officials and elected members, and the visibility of its taxation made it a ready target for complaint. When I asked a councillor if he thought that people reacting to Council decisions were really expressing their anger at State and Federal government, he replied:

> Definitely. Because they can't get at the State government... Because there is no easy way of venting their anger they do it the easy way and take it out on local government. Say with water rates. They make a much bigger fuss about small changes in water rates than about big losses in their pensions.

As Jones (1981: 105) pointed out, rates are a very visible form of taxation compared to, for example, income and sales tax. They became a target for farmer protest during the 1985–86 rural recession (*The Land*, 1986).

There were other significant organisations in the district, but rather than the Council entering their arenas, they entered the Council's. A Ratepayers Association was the only group set up specifically to oppose the Council. But it merely reacted to Council decisions which ratepayers perceived as a threat, like a change in water rating, as referred to by the councillor quoted above. One of its 1986 leaders confessed to me that it was not a force in local politics.

Cowra has a Chamber of Commerce and a Tourist and Development Corporation, both of which participated in the Council's political arena. They both make decisions which affect the entire locality. The larger and more active Tourist and Development Corporation received Council funding, and its Board of Directors contained Council representatives. Its affairs tended to be issues for Council to debate rather than vice versa, through its partial dependence on Council support, and the Council's interest in its investment in the Corporation. The Corporation had an indirect interest in the Council, in that the latter's policies could affect district development. The Council was the arena in which those policies were determined, largely in the context of planning and building regulation decisions. The Chamber of Commerce was smaller and had not played such a prominent role in the establishment of industry. It promoted local business and initiated and entered debate on Council affairs, debate which culminated in decisions taken in Council meetings.

The Council's network cast its influence across other public authorities. It had delegates to regional water and electricity reticulation organisations and a regional library service. It had delegates to the local sport co-ordination body, the Showground Trust, a State Recreation Area Trust and local committees responsible for a retirement village and the annual local festival, as well as the aforementioned Bicentennial Committee and the Tourist and Development Corporation.

Political life in Cowra focused on the Shire Council as the arena of local power relations.[2] Its functions were seen as significant, and sometimes seen as crucial. It was relatively accessible government, which showed some possibility for accepting local influence, and even extending that influence into State and Federal arenas. While other organisations provided a specialised link with central government, no other provided a general local representation function which was looked to for support. Amid growing local perception of the detrimental effects of post-war centralisation, the resources of Cowra Shire Council had taken on greater significance.

Participation and local politics

The history of local government shows the creation of a peculiar kind of arena, established to service property and enable the growth of cities and towns, while removing the burden of infrastructure costs from the colonial governments. Property issues were written into the agenda of Australian local government from its beginning. This has not changed substantially.[3]

The class role of local government has not been changed from below. In Australia it has certainly not been presented as a seed-plot of revolution as it has in Britain (Corrigan, 1979), although one council was controlled by Communist Party members, in a colliery district (Shire of Kearsley) between 1944 and 1947 (Mowbray, 1986). The Labor Party, however, remains the only major party to actively and overtly endorse candidates for local office. The conservative parties have apparently been happy with local government. This need not be surprising, as local government can be seen 'partly as a co-operative of landowners' (Jones, 1981: 23).

A continuing dominant property service function of local government fits easily into images of it held by both local and State government. It is really not seen to 'govern' at all, at least by State authorities and its own participants. It cannot make laws. State institutions have seen it as 'mechanisms for providing infrastructure services ...' (Chapman and Wood, 1984: 11). Its participants see it 'not as a part of the governing system, but rather as a limited, functional, managerial system' (ibid: 14).

Many writers, including Bowman (n.d. and 1983), Atkins (1979), Power, Wettenhall and Halligan (1981), Chapman and Wood (1984) and Sinclair (1987), have found Australian local government elected representatives to be largely male, middle aged or older, and to be of small business, farm or professional occupation. Burdess (1984) found that there were three times as many employers and self-employed people among local government members than among the New South Wales population as a whole. The reasons for this go beyond the range of functions of local government into rules of the institution which, for example, demand substantial personal resources. Participants are required to perform a demanding task in their own time. Moreover, farmers, business people and professionals fit easily into the image of local government as property manager. The conservative ideal of local government is elitist rather than pluralist; it is seen as an organisation rather than as a political arena.

Several Australian rural community studies have found this ideal to correspond to reality. McIntyre and McIntyre (1944) interviewed 'ordinary' and 'prominent' people and found at the same time elitism in local politics and 'cynicism' and 'disillusionment' towards local government, which was seen to be unrepresentative, and ruled by a few, or even just one individual. Oeser and Emery (1957) depicted a town's political structure as thoroughly dominated by an elite of farmers. The town was similar to Cowra insofar as its economy was based on wheat production and its sphere of influence extended for about twenty miles. Unfortunately, as mentioned in Chapter Two, the evidence offered by Oeser and Emery is thin. Cowlishaw (1988) found a small town council traditionally dominated by graziers, but offered little analysis of the processes of dominance outside the context of white–black relations.

Oxley's (1978) finding of a pluralist structure was based on observation of the passage of local issues, his informants not identifying an elite, and his analysis of the resources of the local 'high-stratum' people after studying two towns in a shire in the central tablelands of New South Wales. Two-thirds of the shire's population of about 5 000 lived in the 'Two Towns', one being industrial and the other servicing the surrounding grazing district. The Shire Council was found to be sufficiently important for him to analyse power relations within it. He found councillors bowing to popular will, and the Council 'not covertly controlled by its local bureaucrats or by any self-appointed clique' (1978: 73). Oxley attributed this to a smooth-running democratic process, in contrast to the findings of McIntyre and McIntyre (1944) and Oeser and Emery (1957). Oxley's observed democratic process worked because the business of the Council was open and offered no opportunity for the advancement of individual or group interests, electors were neither apathetic nor had a sense of inevitability, councillors were budding politicians who did not want to upset their constituents, and they did not wish to risk loss of the public esteem which was the main reward of office. Oxley, however, also offers evidence from a local legend that the 'Two Towns' were not always so pluralistic. The legend told how the Shire Council, which had been dominated by wealthy graziers who neglected the industrial town, was brought to order by a militant union and Labor Party member who, after gaining a seat on the Council, raised the industrial town's interests to the fore. The grazier elite was overthrown and the Council operated pluralistically.

The graziers had been superordinate and the industrial townspeople subordinate in power relations, yet Oxley found that the industrial townspeople's interpretation merely separated the two sets of interests, rather than counterposing them. In the townspeople's interpretation of the legend, they found an identity with each other, across strata. This could be interpreted as localism, but in Oxley's work it is an indicator of egalitarianism, which denies, or rather, balances ideology associated with structural fact in terms of status. It is therefore a parallel to resistance, which seeks to alter a subjective aspect of power relations without challenging the structure on which those relations are based. Oxley's work offers two important reminders. One is that the place of local government in power structures is problematic, and the other is that power structures are not immutable, across either time or space.

Wild (1974a) offers the most extensive analysis of elitism in rural local government. He used an extensive analysis of reputations and positions as well as study of local political issues in Bradstow. He identified 'influentials' in reputational and positional surveys, and from observation of issues, found that reputed power was used, a small group revealed in reputation and position analyses consistently having its way. Wild prefaced his search for 'influentials' with an analysis of local class and status systems. He was then able to claim that 'influentials' came from the high status groups, being local employers and a group of wealthy people who had strong extra-local connections. He labelled these groups 'bosses' and 'Grange-ites' respectively.

The Municipal Council was controlled principally by a clique of 'bosses', among whom the Mayor and the Town Clerk were prominent. The tactics adopted in Council business by the Town Clerk and the Mayor in alliance offer illustrations of power processes in the second and third modes. They ruled by consensus. The Mayor maintained a relationship with the aldermen which allowed him to make decisions without their approval, determining the agenda of local politics. To demonstrate an exercise of power in the third mode by the Mayor, it would also be necessary to show that the power relation between the Mayor and the aldermen was not operating in the interests of the aldermen. Wild does not explicitly say that this was so, being more concerned to establish the nature of the Council's decision-making as background to his discussion of issues, but it would seem likely that the aldermen would have been better off not to have virtually assumed the Mayor to be infallible. Cowlishaw (1988) offers a brief description of similar agenda-setting arrangements between a shire president and a shire clerk.

Elitism extended beyond Bradstow's Council membership. The ways in which the 'Grange-ites' were able to exercise dominance in local political issues also offers an example of power in the third mode. Wild used the concept of dominance to imply that the Grange-ites exerted their influence without a direct role in local politics. Their view of what Bradstow should be prevailed when it appeared that their interests may have been threatened. The Grange-ites' and bosses' interests were at times opposed, usually related to matters of town development, such as the establishment of an army depot which the bosses wanted for the sake of business, but the Grange-ites did not want, for fear of spoiling their residential amenity. The Grange-ites won consistently, largely because their ideals were shared by the Mayor and the Town Clerk. In the case of the army depot, all the aldermen wanted it, but they sought a compromise which would not spoil 'Grange'. The Grange-ites' ideals prevailed because they defined the type of environment everybody wanted.

In *Heathcote*, Wild (1983) associates a council's elitism with its nature as little more than an administrative arm of the State Government, and its desire to find a safe course through the minefield of potential conflict between State and local interests. Wild also found the Councillors to be an elite when compared to the socio-economic characteristics of their constituents. In doing so, he applies a broader meaning to elitism than the more specialised concept he used in his earlier study, *Bradstow*. In his analysis of the relations among councillors, he uses the elitist-pluralist concept of a small clique, as identified by reputations.

The obvious outcome of the issue analysed in Wild (1983) was victory to previously powerless people, but there is little evidence that this amounted to more than resistance, for it appears that little change arose in an elitist power structure. The only effect on the council was replacement of one councillor by a member of the protest committee. This would seem unlikely to be sufficient to alter power relations in the locality over a longer term. We are not to know, because the study examined only one issue.

Pandey (1972) also suggests an elitist power structure, this time in a much larger rural town. He found that there was much overlap between a group of social and economic 'influentials', and political leadership was difficult to objectively define (1972:171). Behind-the-scenes influences were obscure, but potentially important to issue resolution. Comparison of the findings of his decision and reputation analyses revealed a forty per cent overlap among the names listed (206). However, Pandey found the reputation method identified people who were thought by informants, from apparent association with a high status group, to exercise power, when the decision analysis revealed that they had not done so. Pandey concluded that the methods he had used provided an incomplete picture of the power structure. Overall, he tentatively concluded that he had found a structure which tended more towards elitism than pluralism. Pandey had opened a door to further study, because, as he acknowledged, the local political system may or may not give effective expression to all interests. The elite may not consciously act in concert to further its own ends, but it may not always allow others to further their interests either. Pandey was constrained by what he had observed.

The recent history of local government membership in Cowra Shire shows signs of elitist membership, in that farmers, business people, professionals and men have been prominent. People of other occupations and women have, however, appeared. From 1947 to 1986, forty-two of the fifty-four persons who served on Cowra Municipal and Cowra Shire Councils were in farm, business, management or professional occupations. The remainder was distributed among trades (five), railway employment (two), bandmaster, council employment, clerical, 'home duties' and retail employment (one each). Local business proprietorship was the most prominent occupation, claiming twenty-one of those who served. Waugoola Shire's councillors were all farmers and male. The first and only women (two) in local government in Cowra were elected to the Municipal Council in 1971. One served two terms and the other served four; the latter including five consecutive annual terms as Mayor. Cowra Shire Council, at the beginning of 1986, had five councillors (including one woman) in local business, five farmers (two had retired and one also had town business interests), one tradesman and one teacher. Their ages ranged from early forties to late sixties. The presence of a small number of councillors who are not male, farmers, professionals and business people suggests that the councils have not been entirely elitist, in the manner that elitism was identified by Wild (1983) in terms of occupation and gender.

The possibility of an elite might loom, as observed by Saunders (1979: 227) if it were found that the turnover of councillors was particularly slow, indicating a climate in which conservative ideas would have time to spread among potentially radical newcomers and allow opportunities for alliances to develop. Cowlishaw (1988: 152) found Brindleton's elite to be stable, with one member having served for thirty years while others had held their seats for several terms. The fifty-four people who served on Cowra Municipal and Shire Councils between 1947 and 1986 occupied 134 terms of office (excluding by-elections). Waugoola Shire had particularly strong continuity. Twenty-three councillors occupied its ninety-nine terms of office, compared to forty-three occupying the ninety-nine terms of office (excluding by-elections in both councils) of the Municipal Council between 1947 and 1977.

While the turnover was slow, there have usually been plenty of candidates for electors to choose from, at least on the Municipal and Cowra Shire Councils since 1947. Only in 1968 did Cowra Municipal Council have the same number of nominations as seats. For Waugoola, this occurred in 1968 and 1977. One hundred and nineteen people nominated for the ninety-nine seats contested in Waugoola's general elections, while 160 nominated for the same number of seats on the Municipal Council. Cowra Shire elections have attracted large fields: thirty-two nominations for twelve seats in 1980, twenty nominations in 1983, and eighteen for eleven seats in 1987. This suggests that the process of co-optation by incumbents of acceptable nominees made possible by a popular lack of enthusiasm for nomination (as described by Sinclair, 1987) has not dominated Cowra local government.

Seats were, however, difficult to wrest from incumbents, particularly in Waugoola, as Painter (1973) found them to be in other councils. Only eight sitting members were defeated in Waugoola's elections from 1947, and five of the fifteen newly elected councillors of the period had sat previously. During this time fifteen sitting Cowra Aldermen were defeated. Cowra Shire saw eight councillors lose their seats in its three elections, none of whom fell in 1987.

Once elected to local government in Cowra, one's seat is reasonably secure, but I would not have expected so during fieldwork. I heard people speak of a necessity for a clean-up in the Council, expressing similar feelings to those revealed by McIntyre and McIntyre (1944). While I did not take a poll, I was left with no doubt that local affairs had inflamed sometimes passionate dissatisfaction around the electorate. Expressions of dissatisfaction and even anger came as readily from, for example, wealthy landowners as from employees, and from women as readily as men. Throughout fieldwork I detected a desire for a fresh start, reminiscent of the despondency reported by McIntyre and McIntyre (1944) but with evidence of determination rather than fatalism. But after the 1987 election it seemed that much of the electorate secretly wanted to maintain an elite.

Elites and reputations

Pursuit of the objectives of traditional elitist-pluralist enquiry would require three further steps: reputation, position and issue analyses. The traditional search for evidence of an elite, the reputation survey, makes a minor, but useful, contribution to this study, as it did for Saunders (1979). Reputation surveys seek perceptions of power relations. Like many other such projects, mine used the question: 'Who do you feel are the influential people around Cowra?' If that invoked a query, I added: 'Who would people feel could help them to get a local project going?' Individual influence also came up in conversation about local politics; some people volunteered an opinion about the location of influence without being asked.

The data analysed consist of the statements of twenty people whom I believed to have a good knowledge of local affairs. Three of them volunteered opinions before I would have asked them. Of the twenty, seven were farmers, four had town businesses, four were skilled or semi-skilled workers and the remaining five were professionals. Six were councillors, and five were women. All had lived in Cowra for fifteen years or longer. I did not ask respondents to think of any particular number of influentials. I did encourage them to think of as many as they could. I probed where necessary, especially among those who had volunteered opinions. This often caused difficulty. None could think of more than six influentials, two said emphatically that there was only one, and most could think of only two or three. One respondent said that there were none and was embarrassed by the question. On all but four occasions the question was asked in a pre-arranged interview situation.

A glance at the results would, in a traditional analysis, indicate an elitist structure, although as Wild (1974a: 151) pointed out, this alone means little. Nineteen names were mentioned. One name was mentioned by fourteen of the twenty respondents, another by nine and another by five. Among the remaining sixteen only three were mentioned more than once (one three times and the others twice). Among the twenty knowledgeables, just a few names came consistently to mind. Five of the six who were mentioned more than once were either Shire Councillors or Council staff. The other was a prominent local business person who took no apparent interest in local affairs in 1986, and from my reading of the *Guardian* and other conversations with local knowledgeables, had not overtly done so in the past.

If this study were in the traditional elitist-pluralist mould, it might now search for these reputed influentials around important positions. The above descriptions indicated that there was an association between having a reputation for influence and proximity to the Shire Council. The town's most important local organisations, including the Tourist and Development Corporation, the Chamber of Commerce and the Services Club were represented among the reputed influentials, by senior members or recent office bearers who were also councillors. There is however, one confounding factor. The locally politically very active LGPA was not so closely represented, with none of its then or recent executive mentioned, and indeed no such people on the Council.

The opinions expressed offered evidence of the way individuals interpret the power structure of their locality. The thinking behind their attributions of power was often more revealing than the identities of the individuals named. As foreshadowed above, there is at least as much value in qualitative analysis of responses to the reputation survey as there is in the accounting exercise carried out above. The notion of reputation is problematic, and worthy of specification. One might propose a two-way connection between reputations and influence. Individuals are perceived by others to be influential at the same time as perceptions (reputations) reinforce the legitimacy, or illegitimacy, of influence. That is, reputations sustain power as well as indicating perceptions of it.

Bailey (1971: 22) offered a starting point for analysis:

> A self is a set of reputations, and these reputations spring from belonging to a community. The reputations arise from the interactions in which a man engages and from the messages which these interactions signal about him. These signals, in their turn, are triggers which set off in the mind values and beliefs, which are linked to one another, not simply as aggregates but in patterns of inclusion and exclusion.

In these terms, analysis of reputations could start by looking for 'signals', 'values' and 'beliefs' which indicate evidence considered and ideologies applied to judgement of reputations. Conversation surrounding responses to the reputation questions contained passages which can be interpreted as such phenomena.

The analysis indicates three types of response, two of which show reaction to signals from one locale of interaction, and the other from another. The first locale of interaction drawn upon by respondents was the local political arena: the affairs of the Shire Council. The second was what could be called the status system. As Birch (1959) and Anton (1963) noted, reputation for power may be mistaken for status. Analysis will draw on conversations which developed from the reputation questions, and other conversations in which the names of reputed influentials arose.

Eight respondents to the reputations questions made their judgement by thinking about recent local political issues and the people who were prominent in the processes of resolution. This was quite direct in three cases, where the respondents thought back over their own experience, their reading of the *Guardian* about local affairs, and what they had heard through gossip networks, to conclude that certain people had their way. The tendency to use participation in issues as criteria for nominating influentials led me to add doubt to an already dubious method for revealing the power structure, in particular its ability to reveal 'concealed influentials', as Wild (1974a) believed that he had found by putting his influence questions to those individuals most often nominated. My attempt to do so merely added to the scores of the other popular nominees. The knowledge I had gained from attending Council meetings and conversations at other meetings and social functions appeared to be more thorough at times than that of some respondents. Those outside the

Council could, however, be well informed on some matters, particularly any with which they had been involved. By the later part of my fieldwork, people were thinking of me as knowledgeable, and asking me questions about local politics which I would earlier have thought myself more likely to ask them. The five respondents who did not draw upon knowledge and experience of issues were stating more general expectations. They thought about recent issues, casting a darker shadow across the reputation method as used by elitists, and suggesting that it may be more useful as an indicator of issues perceived to be important than as an indicator of power structures.

The other signals from the political arena were sometimes given a more structural interpretation which did not focus primarily on issues and individuals, and did not draw on personal experience. Seven respondents mentioned a senior Council officer, but indicated 'The Council' and the officer's relationship to it as the source of influence, rather than the person. Consider the contrast between the following statements. A leader of a group which had recently sought help from Council said: 'I'm led to believe that he runs the council. [The Shire President] agreed with [our proposal]. [The officer] knocked it on the head and there was no further discussion about it'.

The decision was attributed to the officer as an officer. In the following statement, made during a conversation which led to the subject of local political influence, an adverse decision was attributed to the Council first, and to an officer's influence over it later in the conversation. It is significant that a spontaneous discussion of the issue brought names to mind, rather than my question seeking names.

> [The water rates issue] is another case of the Council upsetting its constituents. They decreased the amount of water allowed free and increased the excess rate. People are getting exorbitant bills. The least that the Council should do is explain . . . What can you do? [Officers] really run the show. The Councillors are irrelevant.

The difference is subtle, but it does indicate that the Council was also seen in a generalised manner as a source of power, and the Shire Clerk in particular was thought powerful because of his position in its administration. Two respondents mentioned the Clerk after my prompting, and spoke with certainty of his power exercised through the Council, but may not have thought to nominate him as an individual. Only people who followed Council affairs closely would have been in a position to observe struggles between officers and the Shire President at the individual level, as the previous informant quoted believed he had done. Signals travel by devious paths to reach those who attribute reputations. The 'What can you do?' question indicates a sense of inevitability to which officers' reputations would have contributed, and which would have accrued as a resource to them if shared by other relevant actors.

Three of those who nominated local business people not on Council were drawing on a similar perception. Their impression was that town businesses ran the Council, and they nominated people they knew to be prominent in business. One added that they were influential because they were 'achievers'. All three of these respondents were farmers.

Those who nominated some councillors were drawing on another source of signals, emanating from the status structure. Some were blessed with enormous prestige and esteem, the signals indicating to recipients the most valued personal characteristics. For some, prestige came from family background, and they were esteemed for the extent and generosity of work in local organisations. Some were not seen to have sought status, and were not condescending. In the words of a respondent who replied to the question without hesitation, nominating such a personality: 'He is from a long standing family and he is not pushy. We need good solid citizens like him. He is a thorough gentleman, my favourite person, the most solid citizen. He isn't socially minded; you know, up there with the Joneses, name dropping.' Another respondent spoke of a popular impression of the same person: 'He is the only [influential]. He is respected and always will be. People take notice of what he says.'

Two respondents spoke of another councillor in similar terms. Three had difficulty nominating one such councillor, because he had recently suffered a defeat and loss of what they had seen as total support, but felt that they had to nominate him. Two attributed influence, or popularly perceived influence, to some families. A respondent, of professional occupation, said: 'If someone said what do we do about something, everyone would say speak to someone [of a family name], but really there are lots of people who work away quietly.' A tradesman respondent did not give one family name legitimacy, saying 'The [family], they run this town. They tolerate you, that's all'.

Seven of the nine who mentioned a Council officer added a note of illegitimacy to their assessment of his influence. This ranged from the inevitability stated above to a simple 'He is powerful but he shouldn't be'. He is the illegitimate wielder of the Council's generalised power. His position is one of authority rather than leadership (Oxley, 1978). His lack of legitimacy had several components. Most obviously, as a bureaucrat, his power did not derive from the democratic process which bestowed a formal legitimacy upon the councillors. Nor did he possess the valued attributes of longevity of residence and the esteem associated with being a successful battler with the insecurities of business and farm careers.

His name, along with those of two councillors from prominent families, would have been comfortable for people to mention in a climate of egalitarianism in which thought of leadership is uncomfortable. The senior officer's position as a bureaucrat was seen as inherently unegalitarian, in its separation from the traditionally equalising forces of the physical and business environments, and its formal and impersonal bureaucratic authority (as noted by Dempsey, 1990: 56).

The two councillors from prominent families were held in such esteem, and another was so obviously active in local affairs, that influence for them was, for all respondents except perhaps the one who saw inequality implicit in a family's position, quite acceptable. The willingness to mention those four, the reluctance of one person to name any and two to name more than one, and the tendency to think of 'behind-the-scenes' people initially in generalised terms suggests that respondents were either not wishing to look for 'behind-the-scenes' manipulators, or knew of none. It was easy for respondents to infer during the reputation survey that I was looking for an elite. Only four respondents spoke of anything that could be interpreted as 'behind-the-scenes' activity by a group of influential people. None of those four was disparaging about such activity; two were quite positive about it, one suggesting that the influential business people deserved more influence, and the other saying that there was a group of women active in local affairs who deserved more prominence and recognition.

Only the respondent who attributed great power to one family, having given his opinion spontaneously before I could ask the usual question, gave any impression of an elite operating the local political system. He was the furthest of all respondents from the family in prestige terms, and in the same conversation referred to an 'establishment' in the town. I heard others of similar status position also use the abstract term 'establishment', without attaching individual names to it, and in the same conversation speak of a member of a prominent family as a personal friend. 'Establishment' was used to describe unspecified prominent local business proprietors. This suggests that a generalised and powerful group was thought to exist but without, for some people at least, upsetting particularistic egalitarian ideals. The reputation survey indicated that some knowledgeable people felt that they could see a small group, prominent in local government and most of the district's important organisations, being the only influentials. It has offered some preliminary indicators of ideological factors entering power relations, in the form of legitimacy and status, which, while not eliminating the possibility of pluralism, offer some evidence that the ground may have been difficult for it.

Conclusion: structure and interests

The reputation survey, by suggesting the identities of people thought to be influential, has also focused attention on the Shire Council as the local political arena, by showing how knowledgeables thought of some of the people close to it as influential, and drew on issues resolved in it to make their judgement. The Council was also seen in a generalised manner as a source of power, usually represented by the Clerk who pursued its interests. So too was the unnamed group of people which some survey respondents described as an 'establishment'. This thinking is structural, in that it is constructing an abstract entity which is beyond its individual members. Those entities were attributed interests of their own. They were symbolised for the Council by the person of the Shire Clerk, and for the 'establishment' by families, people who were assumed to pursue particular identifiable interests. It is similarly possible to expect other councillors to have pursued interests that they 'represented'. The model of elitism used by Wild (1983) is based on this approach, for it assumes that there is an interest for employed people, farmers, women and other such identifiable groups to each represent and pursue in local government. It implicitly proposes that people of different backgrounds, according to gender or occupation (or loosely, class), bring different motivations for action to the Council. The existence of such structural interests, which might be represented, creates the possibility of pluralism.

In these terms an elitist council, of the type identified by Wild (1983), would be one in which a narrow range of interests was represented, rather than one merely controlled by a small group. In Cowra, councillors appeared not to represent only the interests of middle class males, thereby suggesting elimination of the elite-as-clique model despite the results of the reputation and position surveys. The presence of a Labor Party member and former candidate for election to State Parliament (one of two Labor Party members on Council in 1986) suggests a possible counter force, just as the presence of a woman on the Council may have helped women to gain the greater prominence and recognition that one respondent sought for them. She described her role to me as representing women. There is, however, no logical or empirical necessity for councillors to pursue sectional interests.

All town and rural dwellers had interests in local government services. Everybody in the Shire had an interest in public health. Everybody in the town had an interest in water, sewerage and drainage, and everybody in the rural area had a keen interest in road construction and maintenance. All had an interest in the Council's financial management. The Council had a public pie which had to be sliced and shared among many people, all of whom elected representatives who could collectively decide where the knife was to cut. This political role was perhaps most obvious in the planning function, in which the Council was responsible for allocation of the Shire's spatial resources. The slice which some people received could not also be received by others, implying potentially conflicting interests. The local advocate and entrepreneur roles discussed above added another dimension to the Council's pie, bringing the prospect of goodies from elsewhere, including State and Federal governments, for which local interests could compete. Bowman's (1983: 179) observation that there was little in local politics to attract attention until people saw their interests threatened would need qualification before application to Cowra in 1986, because many people had felt their interests to be threatened. There would, therefore, appear to have been a recipe for a pluralist polity, in which many interests were actively represented.

Local government, however, has been interpreted traditionally not to operate as a pluralist polity, but has rather been seen as a managerial institution: a kind of *people's corporation* placed in the trust of an elite. This popular interpretation rests on ideology rather than objective assessment of interests which might be expressed in a local political arena. The narrow range of local government responsibilities should not necessarily produce an elitist structure, when everybody has objective interests to pursue, facilitated in the pluralist ideal by the apparatus of democracy. The roles of councils have not prescribed the range of interests seen to be relevant to them. Rather, their image, or subjective interpretations of their role, and, more importantly, interpretations of the role of councillors, have produced an elitist pattern of representation, in association with the difficulties for wage earners and others of finding the personal resources to participate in local government. The judgements made by respondents to the reputation survey indicate positive value placed on leadership by business, which accords with the status system, and negative value placed on the prominent position of bureaucratic authority. Elitist leadership by business rested easily with the popular view of local democracy being a managerial institution.

Notes

1 He did not make clear how the programs would be financed, but given the National Party's distaste for taxation, welfare and 'big government', local government might be seen as a place to which costs as well as powers may be devolved, into oblivion. Rural local government has not shown enthusiasm for such activity (Secretariat to the Joint Officers' Committee of the Local Government Ministers' Conference, 1980). It is quite possible for the State Government to overcome reluctance by simply legislating welfare into the role of local government, as the National Party spokesperson implied that it would, although it had not done so by the end of 1990. Devolution in this situation would mean imposition. Some writers, such as Sharpe (1979) and in Australia, Robin (1986), have seen devolution as a process of decentralisation in which genuine power is distributed. This would seem an inappropriate interpretation in circumstances when all that is devolved is unwanted responsibility. In New South Wales there has been some devolution of planning powers since a change to legislation in 1978. As evidence to be presented in chapter 6 will imply, this devolution is in large part illusory. Those writers who have seen decentralisation have, however, highlighted the prospects for expansion of the roles of local government, which can only widen its position as a political arena.

2 As this information was collected in a fieldwork situation in which I came to know each organisation through contact with people associated with it, as well as through newspapers and observation, there is a possibility, implied by the work of Granovetter (1972), that I only came to know some of the relevant organisations by following the pathways provided by connected individuals. I do not believe that this risk is significant because I learned something about each of a large number, perhaps hundreds, of locally relevant organisations, and the acquaintance networks I established in Cowra cut across class, gender, political and other barriers where network bridges might be weak.

Elitism and local government

3 Cowra Shire Council has retained the property service function without significant deviation from it. In 1986 it regulated, serviced and planned the Shire, and undertook some entrepreneurial activity. These activities were supervised by its three executive staff: the Health Surveyor, the Shire Engineer and the Shire Clerk. Under a policy decision made in 1983, the Shire Clerk became the 'Council's Chief Administrative Servant and undisputed head of Council's staff' (Cowra Shire Council Policy Register, entry A.2.02). Each of the executive staff was responsible for a department with specific responsibilities. The Health Surveyor was responsible for much of the regulatory activity, which included building inspections, licences, health and nuisance inspections, litter, and dog and stock impounding. He was also responsible for services which cover immunisation programs and maintenance of buildings including the women's rest and baby health centres. The Shire Engineer had largely service responsibilities, which corresponded most closely to the traditional local government role. They included road construction and maintenance, water supply, sewerage and drainage, street cleaning, parks, the aerodrome and the swimming pool. He also had town planning, and the entrepreneurial activities associated with a gravel crusher and a caravan park. The Shire Clerk was responsible for administrative and financial matters, including annual estimates and the rate collection system, and had the entrepreneurial activity of gas supply. A 1986 organisation chart also lists co-ordination with the State local government department and 'policy advice' among the Clerk's functions.

5
Spatial politics

Power can only accrue to those who have sufficient resources to turn their concerns into issues, unless their concerns correspond to what is determined in the political arena to be appropriate matters for its attention. In that situation, under pluralist assumptions, competing interests are balanced. The 'people's corporation' image of local government, however, suggests contrarily that everybody's concerns are the council's concerns; there is, therefore, no need for pluralism and no need for political action. Yet from time to time people do act. They may, however, be deflected from pursuit of their interests in the second stage, or ignored in the third stage of Saunders' three-stage non-decision making filter (1979).

This does not require conscious direction from one or a few individuals, as Wild (1974a) found to occur in Bradstow. Wild observed that Bradstow's Town Clerk had three obviously intentional tactics for agenda setting: simply leaving potentially threatening or controversial matters off Council agendas, putting matters before the Council in such a way that the aldermen interpreted his wishes as the most desirable course of action, and keeping matters which might embarrass the Council off the agenda to protect his own legitimacy. Wild offered an example of a town planning decision, made as the Clerk wished after he had misrepresented a planning proposal as something which the aldermen would not desire. His knowledge of their values enabled him to use those values as a resource, in order to ensure that the aldermen would make the decision he wanted. In this activity the Town Clerk worked in concert with the Mayor, but such conspiracy is not necessary for identification of power relations enacted through agenda setting.

Cowra's 'people's corporation' has organisational interests which lie in the efficient administration of its functions, and the traditional functions of local government, to which it has adhered, serve interests associated with property. Strict adherence to property services functions, however, does not alone rule out pluralism. People with property interests may compete for services, in an albeit confined pluralist-looking polity. The problem for subordinate groups is, as Saunders (1979: 62) put it, 'negotiating the rules of access as operated by local authority 'gatekeepers''.

Rules of access may be available to the powerful as ideological resources, especially when they are tied to the organisational objectives of local government by the 'people's corporation' image.

The analysis of issues and non-issues in this and following chapters is framed around a typology of policies developed by Peterson (1981) and used by Dye (1986). Different kinds of policy issues provide different windows on power relations (Yates, 1978). The study of policy development, however, should not be equated with power analysis, for in policy development study the outcome analysed is the policy, not a power relationship. The typology, based on its specification by Dye (1986: 37), describes four types of policy:

- *allocational*, being the distribution of costs and benefits of traditional property service functions;
- *developmental*, being aimed at or otherwise associated with local economic development;
- *redistributional*, which redistributes wealth from rich to poor; and
- *organisational*, which determines membership of boards and committees.

Direct application of the typology in Australia is made fuzzy by the regulatory functions passed from State to local government, such as administration of health and building regulations and the Dog Act, which do not fit neatly into any of the four policy types. However, the issues to be discussed do, with minimal wedging, fit into one or more of the first three types. Issues will be placed in the typology according to the ways in which they were interpreted, and hence the substance of the debate, or 'non-debate', surrounding them. For this reason, organisational policy will not be discussed separately, as decisions about representation of the Council on other bodies were intimately connected to the functions of those bodies, and each could be related to one of the other policy types.

The allocation problem

Allocational policy determines how the services which local government has decided to deliver are allocated, and how the costs of those services are to be apportioned. Even routine services may be delivered differentially across the social and spatial dimensions of a locality. The problem which it brings forth is one of equity in service delivery.

Allocation is seen in the 'people's corporation' image as a process of bureaucratic decision making, in which elected members play their part by exercising rational decision criteria as senior members in a partnership with professional bureaucrats, striving for equity. If elected members rationally determine which services are to be offered and the rules for their allocation, they might quite happily leave the rest to bureaucrats (Rich, 1982: 7). This image, however, rests uneasily with the previous chapter's depiction of Cowra Shire Council, around which appeared a plurality of competitors for allocation of Council largesse.

If allocation is found to be inequitable, a problem of explanation arises. It is usually seen to be a matter of ascertaining whether allocation is determined by class factors (that is, do the rich use access to local government to obtain more than the poor?), or by decisions made under bureaucratic rules. In the United States, despite obvious differences in the standard of services between rich and poor areas of cities, much research (such as Vedlitz and Dyer, 1984) on the allocation problem favours the bureaucratic decision rule explanations over those which hang on the operation of class bias (Rich, 1982: 2). In parallel with the British urban managerialism approach, this discounts an appreciation of class effects on agenda-setting processes.

The allocation problem concerns institutional responses to public needs, responses dependent on institutional perception of need, or failing such perception, public expression of discontent. Rich malcontents may be more likely than poor ones to express their wants. The poor would be more likely to opt for 'loyalty', putting their faith in elected members, or 'neglect', such as not voting; they may not have the resources to depart for greener pastures, and 'exit' (Lyons and Lowery, 1986). Participation by the rich in matters of urban allocation may be aided by their social interaction with other people of high status, and the prospects of their needs being articulated are consequently greater (Giles and Dantico, 1982).

Allocation is sometimes explained by the 'squeaky wheel' model of local politics. This suggests that the noisiest people 'get the oil' because they make the wheel squeak loudly. Bowman (1983) saw the 'squeaky wheel' process as a product of the difficulty of policy formation in Australian local government, where policy has been pre-determined from above. In apportioning responsibility to central government, this view ignores the role of the local arena, and distracts attention from two important factors: the cumulation of responses forming de facto policy through precedent, and people not being equally capable of turning the wheel to make it squeak.

Progress associations

Some history of Cowra will show that people have been able to raise allocation issues, under the banners of progress associations. McIntyre and McIntyre (1944: 117) found that a progress association 'assumes some degree of leadership, and carries out some of the activities demanded from the council, although it has no official status'. Oeser and Emery (1957) found a progress association, but an inactive one, the lack of action being attributed to poor leadership. These studies were carried out at a time of rapid growth in Cowra and great activity among its progress associations. They appeared in new and growing urban areas, also noted by

Painter (1973), but like many such movements, faded after making satisfying gains (Pahl, 1975).

The residents of Mulyan, Taragala and West Cowra owe a great deal to progress associations, particularly the small bands of energetic citizens who took initiatives to establish amenities in their areas during the 1950s and 60s (map 2). The standard of urban services in Cowra during World War II was reported by an outsider, from the Social Studies Department of Sydney University, to be very poor. Streets and footpaths were found to be in bad condition, and 'only half-hearted and sporadic attempts have been made to plant trees along the sidewalks'. The problem was implicitly attributed to the Municipal Council's business-like approach: 'although Council has shown initiative in extending electricity and water supply, it has shown little interest in town improvement of a less revenue-producing nature' (MacColl, 1944: 35). The *Cowra Guardian* of 19 August, 1952 (p. 1) quoted an alderman as complaining that 'Cowra's streets and footpaths are in a deplorable condition' with 'potholes in every street . . . We are losing our civic pride'.

The progress associations were established in both urban and rural areas to participate in their respective local government arenas. When the announcement of a Taragala Progress Association was made in 1932, its president was quoted in the *Cowra Guardian* (26 November, p. 1) to have said: ' ". . . they should have had an organisation of this character in existence years ago, as the Council has had its own way far too long". He hoped they would be able to wake that body up, and that it would be found that they were a power for good in the life of the community'.

The organisations appear to have been most active in the early post-war period. West Cowra's Association was particularly active in 1947, doing such things as cleaning the recreation ground and asking the Council to move the saleyards, having raised money from dances and street stalls.[1] In 1951 it purchased land for a park and in 1955 it agitated, at length successfully, for connection to the town sewerage system. The *Cowra Guardian* of 4 November reported that Mulyan's Association had asked the Council, successfully, for a 'silent cop' (traffic dome) and a drinking fountain. In 1950 it led one of many protests, continuing into the 1970s, to Council about drainage problems. The *Guardian* of 1 April, 1952 stated that Mulyan Progress Association was building 'almost a civic centre' (p. 1), which contained a hall, park, tennis courts and a playground. In 1960 it announced that it had obtained land on which to build a bowling green.

Taragala Progress Association was revived in 1948. Fifty attended its first meeting. It built a cricket pitch in its first year, and gave the Mayor the honour of bowling the first ball. The following year it tussled with the West Cowra and Mulyan Associations for Council's priority. The *Guardian* of 8 February, 1949 reported that Taragala Progress Association 'wants to know why parks in West Cowra and Mulyan are being provided

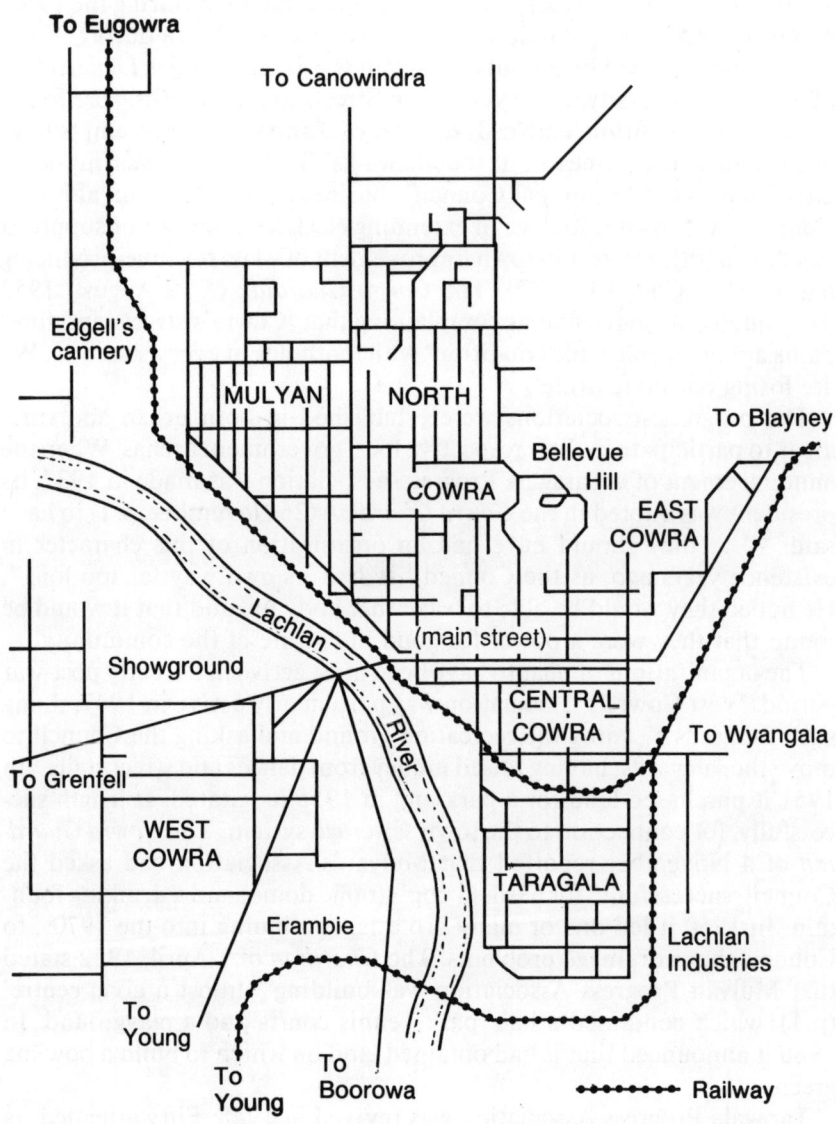

Source: Cowra Tourist and Development Corporation

Map 2. Cowra township (not to scale)

with playground equipment, while equipment promised for the Taragala park has apparently been forgotten' (p. 9). It continued agitation through the 1950s.[2]

There have also been progress associations in East Cowra, a small, older part of town adjacent to the Blayney road (map 2), and in the villages. The village associations were also active in the 1950s, lobbying Waugoola Shire. Woodstock's Association was reported in the *Guardian* to have been resuscitated in 1950. The small village of Noonbinna had formed one the previous year. Other villages also had associations (map 1).

During this period, both councils appear to have been pluralistic, inasmuch as these groups actively pursued what they perceived to be the interests of their areas in the local political arenas. An alderman from the early 1950s recollected that the Council operations had been like a tug-of-war between, on one side the Mayor, my informant and their allies, and on the other, the representatives of the progress associations, whom he described as 'Labor'. Prominent members of the Labor Party were actively involved in the town's progress associations, but not all their leadership was associated with that organisation. A long time local Labor Party member pointed out to me that at least one of the leaders was of more conservative persuasion. The associations did, however, represent the interests of people in the poorer parts of town.

The image of Labor progress associations versus conservative Mayor and allies may have been fostered by two personalities: Leo Lynch, a prominent and vigorous Labor Party and Mulyan Progress Association member, and Mark Whitby, the formidable and conservative Mayor. Whitby and Lynch sparred many times.[3] With Whitby in the Mayoral robes, Lynch and his allies remained in opposition. The parliamentary metaphor is not unreasonable, but it is justified more by the strength of Whitby than cohesion among his occasional opponents. Lynch certainly had support, as indicated by the result of the Mayoral election of 1960, which Whitby won by five votes to Lynch's four (*Cowra Guardian*, 13 December), but to suppose that Lynch was the leader of a co-ordinated group intent on unseating the forces of conservatism would be stretching the evidence beyond recognition. The point is that this actively political climate was conducive to participation. If regarded only from Lukes' 'one-dimensional' perspective, the 'people's corporation' resembled a pluralist political arena.

The progress associations put up candidates at municipal elections. In 1947 the West Cowra Association put up two candidates. Neither was elected, but they received the second and fifth highest votes from West Cowra (*Cowra Guardian*, 9 December). Its secretary was elected to the Council in 1956. In that year the voters of Woodstock elected one of their people to Waugoola Council. The *Guardian* (4 December, p. 11) reported that it 'was evident that the township of Woodstock had organised local people to vote solidly for a townsman'. However, such localism did not always win the day. In 1965 Taragala's support was not sufficient to secure re-election for its long time champion and Progress Association leader.

In 1951 the Municipal Council decided, with Mayor Whitby's support, to investigate the possibility of dividing the town into wards. The alderman who proposed the investigation believed that wards 'would give such areas as Taragala and West Cowra more representation on the Council' (*Cowra Guardian*, 23 January, p. 3). Whitby observed that six of the nine aldermen lived in the same part of town. Waugoola Shire was divided into ridings (not coincident with progress associations although some villages and rural areas had them). If one accepts Wild's (1974a:144) partial attribution of pluralism in 'Marston' council to the existence of wards, then, had Cowra divided into wards as suggested in 1951, it may have continued to display its superficial pluralism into 1986.

Social areas

Allocation obtains a spatial dimension where spatial population elements have differential access to local services. This is most likely in urban situations where distinct social areas exist along class lines. A journey across the township of Cowra would reveal a spatial dimension to social heterogeneity, and a trip through the countryside and villages would also reveal signs of wealth and poverty. The town, village, rural distinction was obviously clear cut, except for the few hobby farms on the town's outskirts, whose residents were to all intents townspeople. Natural features and the railway gave the town its physical divisions: the Lachlan River separates West Cowra from the rest of town; the railway to Eugowra separates Taragala from Central Cowra; Bellevue Hill separates North from Central Cowra, and the northern slopes of Bellevue Hill and the road to Canowindra separate North Cowra from Mulyan (map 2).

Mulyan and Taragala contain much public housing. West Cowra still has a spacious, almost pioneering atmosphere. It has new and older housing, most of it post-War, set among paddocks. It also contains the golf course, showground and rugby field. Central Cowra is the oldest area, through which the main street passes. The houses are larger up the slopes of Bellevue Hill, north of the main street. North Cowra proceeds from the top of Bellevue Hill, with a number of grand old houses nearer the main street, along a ridge, the upper parts containing large, newer houses to the north. Down the slope to the west the houses are smaller, and in the vicinity of Redfern Street (the Canowindra road), which I have defined as the boundary, North Cowra looks like Mulyan. Fortunately these apparent social boundaries correspond closely to 1986 Commonwealth Census Collection District boundaries, simplifying a social area analysis.[4]

Illustrated in figure 2 is the distribution of low socio-economic status attributes among areas, showing that Mulyan and Taragala have percentages of households with low incomes which deviate furthest, and highest, from the Shire percentage. In contrast, 1986 census data show North Cowra and the rural area to have been below the Shire proportion for low income households, and other low socio-economic status indicators including employment as labourers, unemployment and lack of motor vehicles. They also show Mulyan and Taragala to have been well above the Shire's incidence of each of these indicators. The villages were well above the Shire figures for all such indicators except labouring occupations, for which demand in rural areas had declined in the post-war period. West Cowra did not deviate far, except on unemployment. Its unemployment may have been associated with the relatively large proportion of Aboriginal people in West Cowra's population, some fourteen per cent, due to the presence of the Erambie Aboriginal settlement in the collection district. A relatively high frequency of low incomes and lack of motor cars in Central Cowra may have been associated with the relatively aged population in the older parts of town. Analysis of high socio-economic indicators shows the complementary pattern. This is illustrated by the distribution of high income households, shown in figure 3.

The rural area and particularly North Cowra had relatively low proportions of low income households and high proportions of high income households. North Cowra was close to the Shire proportion of labour force in high status occupations and households in large dwellings. The rural area skewed the distribution of these attributes, due to the frequency of small, non-employing farms and large farm houses. Mulyan and Taragala show the most consistently low indicators of socio-economic status. The villages had very few high income households, but they did have some people of high status occupation, and are close to the Shire figure for large dwellings. These indicators reflect the presence of some farmers in their populations. Broadly, Mulyan and Taragala were the poorer parts of town, with the villages also showing signs of problems. North Cowra and the rural areas were relatively wealthy while West and Central Cowra are harder to classify, the former having neither a concentration of low incomes nor a concentration of high status occupations, and the latter having a relatively large proportion of low incomes but low unemployment and a low proportion of labouring occupations, all of which may have been related to the advancing age of its population.

Dwelling purchase/ownership reflects the distribution of public and other rental housing rather more than socio-economic status. The frequency of home purchase/ownership did not fall as dramatically as some of the other variables in the poorer areas. The lowest proportion, that of Mulyan which contained much public housing, is sixty-five per cent. Seventy per cent of Cowra Shire's households owned or were buying their dwellings. They paid rates, and had an interest in property.

Cowra's social areas are not as obvious as those of company towns, such

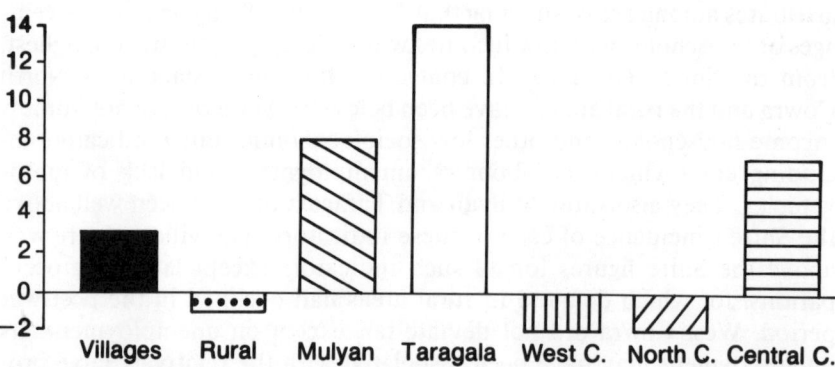

Figure 2. Deviations of area percentages from Shire percentage of households with annual incomes less than $9 001 (Shire = 19 per cent)

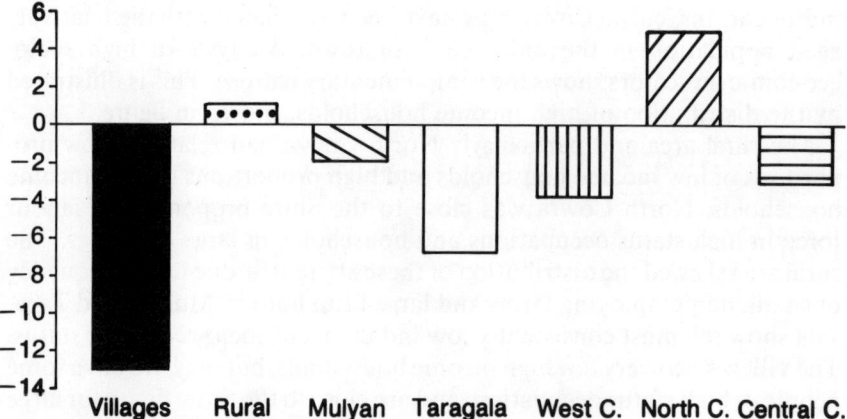

Figure 3. Deviations of area percentages from Shire percentage of households with annual incomes greater than $32 000 (Shire = 15 per cent)

as Whyalla (analysed by Campbell and Kriegler, 1981), where settlement grew around an organisation and its hierarchy. As one might expect of a town established on a hillside, the wealthy live nearer the top, but there was no formal exclusion; at least, that is, during the late 1980s among white people. The situation of Cowra's Aboriginal people has been different, and will be discussed in chapter 7.

The socio-economic differentials were more visible to the casual observer than differences in service provision. A quick glance would have suggested that all streets were sealed and in good condition; there were parks for recreation, footpaths for walking, and water and sewerage were available. There were no areas of manifest deprivation. Residents, nevertheless, perceived service provision differently around the social areas. This was indicated by a 'Community Needs Survey' which I

Spatial politics

co-ordinated while working with a local committee, as reported in Gray (1987a). The data were collected from 509 randomly selected adults who responded to questions about the availability and quality of facilities which were of interest to the committee. The responses form a scale from one (when the facility was perceived to be unavailable in the area) to four (when the respondent felt the facility to be good). Numbers of respondents ranged from thirty-two in West Cowra to 129 in North Cowra, and were approximately proportional to the population of each area.

The results are illustrated in figure 4, which shows that the mean score given on perceptions of availability/quality of playgrounds was highest, and deviated some way from the Shire mean, in North Cowra. When other facilities, including sports fields, parks and meeting rooms are considered, the only consistent feature is the positive response from North Cowra. Many rural dwellers felt themselves to be beyond easy reach of these town services. Mulyan and Taragala were below the mean, except for Taragala on meeting rooms and Mulyan on sports fields. Central Cowra shows small deviations on all items, in contrast to West Cowra, which on the three for which it is below the mean perception, is the lowest. When all the services covered by the survey are considered (including shops and schools, as reported in Gray, 1987a), the consistent above mean response from North Cowra and below mean response from West Cowra (except on sports fields) are striking. This suggests that while North Cowra residents had little interest in attacking the status quo, West Cowra residents would have had a collective interest in political participation, and they would hypothetically have been more likely to perceive a greater stimulus for action.

They did take action in the local political arena during 1986, under the auspices of the West Cowra Progress Association, the only such organisation active in the town at the time. Contact with the Council was not organised, other than spontaneously on particular issues, in the other areas, except in the village of Gooloogong which also had an active progress association, and in farmers acting through the LGPA. Otherwise individuals contacted the Council as individuals. There was no other avenue, unless the Ratepayers' Association was available. This lack of activity suggests a problem, for it indicates that people were not pursuing their interests, as one might expect them to do. An explanation for this quiescence lies in the policy apparatus of the Council. Analysis of the apparatus provides some background to issues and non-issues, including an attempt by West Cowra people to 'make the wheel squeak'.

The policy apparatus

Unfortunately for West Cowra, the Shire Council's policy apparatus allowed an efficient decision making process at the same time as it

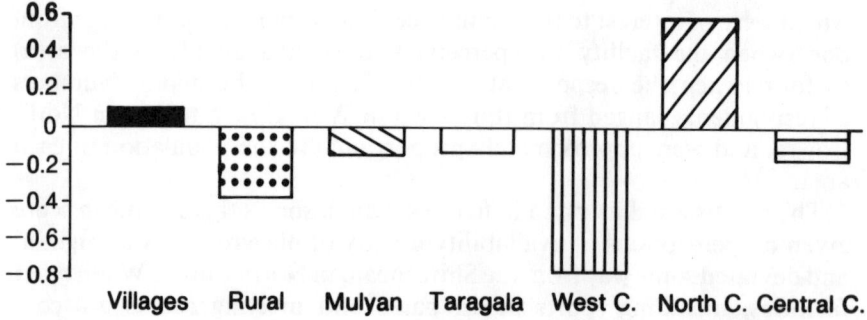

Figure 4. Deviations of area mean scores from Shire mean score on perceptions of availability/quality of playgrounds (Shire mean = 2.43)

minimised interference from 'squeaky wheels'. It was intended to allocate resources according to rational criteria based on assessment of need, making the sound assumption that the noisiest wheel is not necessarily the neediest. Progress associations may still have attempted to further the interests of their areas, but they would have done so without the legitimacy offered by a pluralistic-looking arena. The resources available to the 1950s progress associations were no longer available because the policy making process had been formalised, and the ideological climate was not conducive to pluralism.

The Council maintained a Policy Register, which it updated after discussion of recommendations made by its Policy and Resources Committee. This document laid down the order of priority for projects among the Council's service activities. It was the instrument of allocational policy. It covered seemingly everything that the Council did, from development regulations through priority order for road sealing to the closing time at the Civic Centre bar. Items such as the first and third were reviewed when necessary; works matters such as the second were determined for three-year periods, except where longer term priorities could be fixed, such as occurred with priorities for the sealing of urban lanes which covered a nine year period. This meant that policy development became largely a process of updating, and was therefore seen to be routine. Of the Council's three committees (the others being Finance and Works), Policy and Resources met least frequently: prior to each second rather than each monthly Council meeting. Its meetings were often relatively short due to brevity of discussion and they attracted less attention from the press, two of its meetings being the only occasions on which no reporter from the *Guardian* was present at Council or committee meetings which I attended. The April 1986 meeting lasted just twenty-five minutes. On two occasions I found out at the last minute that the committee meeting had been cancelled due to lack of business. I found no evidence of spatial interest groups seeking to affect the policy making process at the Policy and Resources Committee stage.

Senior Council staff saw the policy machinery as smoothing the budgetary (and hence allocational) process at the same time as it facilitated the application of decision rules with due regard to precedent. The Register was instituted after the 1980 amalgamation. Previously each department of the two Councils put up budget estimates which were like shopping lists for the councillors and aldermen to peck at. A former Waugoola councillor told me that that the Council effectively had three works committees (to handle the engineering function), because each riding decided on and pushed for its own priorities. He said it was administratively very inefficient. A plethora of 'squeaky wheels' within the organisation would not have been in keeping with good management of the 'people's corporation'. The formalised process eliminated this.

Some councillors expressed mixed feelings about the formalised policy process, because it had taken away some of their room to push for initiatives, but those who expressed such feeling to me also acknowledged its value in the rational decision-making process. Bruce Golsby, known by his fellow councillors to be a strong supporter, valued the smooth running apparatus which the system provided. (The Councillors, Shire President, Clerk and Engineer are introduced in the Appendix.) Ab Oliver also valued the system. After his re-election to the Shire Presidency in 1984 he was quoted by the *Guardian* (26 November) to have said that the Policy and Resources Committee was very important. As a councillor explained to me: 'if someone approaches you and asks when such and such a bridge is going to be replaced, you can show him its priority in the policy register'. The councillor added that Policy and Resources Committee offered an opportunity for members to take an overall view, rather than just listen to the 'squeaky wheels'.

Other councillors were not so happy with it, because they found all cases to be treated on their merits anyway, making policy irrelevant, or because it detracted from the councillors' ability to initiate policy. 'They reflect on what is served up to them.' This backhanded implication was as close as any came to a suggestion that the 'squeaky wheel' system had merit. Changes to the policy register were initiated by officers, who applied efficiency criteria. For example, when formulating the list of priorities for lane sealing, the Engineer gave priority to those lanes which were most expensive to maintain. It was up to the councillors to anticipate any inequities which might have arisen. In the event of a councillor perceiving an inequity, he or she would have had to show cause why the 'people's corporation's' efficiency should be compromised, not always an easy matter for one who placed value on efficiency, a value which all councillors espoused. Here also lay a seed of conflict between officers and councillors.

There was from time to time an undercurrent of debate at meetings about the role, and hence necessity of the Policy and Resources Committee because it was seen to be unnecessary duplication of the other two committees, while it was giving councillors and officers the same management task. The former problem surfaced, as occurred at the Council meeting of 24 March, 1986, when Bruce Golsby pointed to a recommendation from the Works Committee about road priorities, saying that priority review was a matter for Policy and Resources. His attempt to have the matter referred to that Committee failed.

Nobody suggested that the policy process was inefficient, nor that its efficiency was anything but highly desirable. A councillor who found the policy process to be irrelevant added the caveat that it did eliminate the risk of self-interest. It was the view that local government makes case-by-case decisions as a bureaucrat might, rather than policy, which made the Policy and Resources Committee appear superfluous. In this view local government is no more than management through rational decision-making, which does not require policy development. These ideas had determined the 'rules of access'. Issue-making was an encounter with an organisation rather than entry into a pluralist arena.

People from anywhere other than North Cowra who wished to request services or make complaints were unlikely to find a direct avenue to the Council via a local representative. All nine urban-dwelling councillors and all three senior Council staff in 1986 except one (Cyril Treasure, Shire President, living in Taragala) lived in North Cowra. Only one councillor consistently raised problems in his own area. The burden of allocation of Council services fell heavily on the policy apparatus. The survey results presented above suggest that services had not been distributed evenly in the perceptions of residents, but at the same time the system appeared to work fairly well, in that there were no glaring deficiencies which the Council had not considered.

Two questions remain, however. Was the uneven distribution identified a product of unwillingness or inability to raise issues? Or was it a product of issues raised being quashed on bureaucratic decision rule grounds? The answer to both questions is yes. Any suggestion that the relative satisfaction expressed in North Cowra and the rural area was a product of councillor self-interest could not be sustained. Decision rules rendered effective expression of interests by dissatisfied residents difficult. Some examples of issues, or non-issues, will show how the bureaucratic apparatus discouraged the pursuit of allocation issues among those who lacked the appropriate resources.

Some allocation issues

There are three ways in which complaints and requests could be voiced to the Council. People could approach the Council by writing, usually in the person of the Shire Clerk who placed the matter before the Council, or by asking a councillor to raise a matter in 'general business' at the end of a Council meeting. A third, more direct approach was available when the Council or its Works Committee convened a meeting in a village, during which it received requests. The Council conducted full meetings in villages in 1985 and 1986, but discontinued the practice after meeting at Wyangala in October, 1986, in favour of having only Works Committee meetings in villages.

All matters were indeed considered on their merits, but not before reference was made to the Policy Register if it had an appropriate entry. For example, the West Cowra Progress Association wrote to the Shire Clerk asking for attention to drainage problems. The Clerk placed the matter before the Works Committee (meeting 16 September, 1986) without a recommendation from Engineer Jim Finnimore because the letter had been received too late for his consideration. At the meeting Ab Oliver asked if the requested work was in the list of priorities. The Engineer replied that it was not, because it would have been prohibitively expensive. The Committee decided to meet Association members at West Cowra after the next Works Committee meeting. They did so, but made no recommendation for action to the October Council meeting.

That was the end of a short saga of frustration for West Cowra Progress Association, for they had first sought to raise the question of their drainage problem at the August Council meeting. They had asked a councillor to raise it for them, but the councillor had failed to do so, perhaps because the meeting had been particularly heated and demanding over other matters. They saw the councillors as avenues for access to senior officers. They wrote to the Shire Clerk.

Matters raised in general business were usually minor problems of maintenance or regulation which implied no difficulty for Council management. Councillor Tim West drew the Council's attention to problems in Taragala Park, and raised some difficulties in relations between village dwellers and the Health Surveyor. Barbara Bennett appealed for a pedestrian crossing in Mulyan. Jack Mallon raised drainage and other problems in Woodstock. Col Newton sought improved signposting in a village. Most councillors raised minor matters on behalf of people beyond the areas of their own residence at some time. To that extent the rules of access were easy. Individual councillors were accessible, but, as West Cowra's problem with drainage illustrates, the rules of access could be complicated when the stakes were higher.

The Works Committee meetings held in villages also worked well. People raised minor issues for the Council's attention, sought help in settling local disputes and in one case obtained a promise of a small subsidy for construction of a bus shelter. These meetings were very casual affairs, unlike the first village full Council meeting I attended, at Woodstock, and to a lesser extent the Wyangala meeting twelve months later. At the former, the three Woodstock people who spoke when time was made available for them at the end of the meeting did so nervously and tentatively. Their diffidence may have been increased in the more formal atmosphere of a full Council meeting, and the presence of such well known and locally important people as the councillors. This means of contacting the Council demanded confidence in what could be seen as an intimidating atmosphere. A councillor told me that at the early village meetings, 'they looked at us as if we came from Mars'.

The policy development process appears from this evidence to have worked well. I did not, however, see major issues raised in it. There were certainly no attempts made to obtain additional or improved facilities for areas such as the earlier progress associations made, as one might anticipate given the differential perception of facilities recorded in the survey described above. Without the pluralistic arena there was no mechanism likely to produce expressions of such interests. There was very little room for major initiatives from councillors. The factor which enabled all this is the ideological climate of the Council, in which all its participants sought to make it a smooth and efficient organisation, in contrast to the 'parliamentary' style of old. In this climate councillors were attracted by questions of efficiency. Allocation became a matter of choosing an efficient solution, while still wishing for a fair solution, but nevertheless aiming at organisational rather than interest group goals. Interest groups therefore remained 'off-stage'. They had no reason to act when they saw the 'people's corporation' attending to its efficiency and so looking after everyone. Or when they did appeal, their cries may not have been heard above the clamour for efficiency. This was best illustrated by the debate which surrounded the upgrading of the water supply to West Cowra.

Getting water into West Cowra had long been a bigger problem than letting it out. In 1967 the *Guardian* (15 December) reported that West Cowra Progress Association had said that the water supply problem had deteriorated over three years to a point at which people could not flush their toilets. The problem stemmed from the height and distance of parts of West Cowra in relation to the main water works on Bellevue Hill. A reservoir and additional reticulation were provided to West Cowra in 1971. In 1980 the Municipal Council started investigations into further improvements. In 1982 more cries were heard through the *Guardian*, which, on 8 February ran a page one headline 'West Cowra out of Water Again – Residents Angry'. In August 1982 the Council convened a public meeting which decided to proceed with an augmentation scheme.

The later stages of the scheme in West Cowra were carried out in 1986, necessitating some final decisions by the Council about the design of the reticulation system. This decision making process turned attention away from the needs of West Cowra and focused it on the technical problems associated with finding an efficient solution. This is not to say that West Cowra's needs were forgotten, but rather that the primary problem to be resolved became one of which possible solution was most efficient, rather than which would best solve the problem for West Cowra, as it might if equity had been the issue. The difference is that in the latter circumstance, the Council might have been persuaded to solve West Cowra's problem and then face the problem of finding an efficient solution. Instead, the matter became one of finding an efficient system in the course of debate over the likelihood of each of several proposals solving the problem. It became embroiled in a struggle between some councillors and the Shire Engineer in which the interests of West Cowra were not ignored, but did fade into the background. The councillors saw their job as maintaining efficiency.

The first debate occurred in a Works Committee meeting on 18 March. Jim Finnimore, Shire Engineer, had recommended that the Council install new pipes to take water to West Cowra across the Lachlan River bridge (then under construction), while consultants drew up plans for West Cowra's new reticulation system. Tim West challenged the size of the pipes, believing them to be inadequate. He was supported by Shire President Cyril Treasure and Councillor Harold Upston, who both felt that the pipes should be as big as possible. Others were sceptical. Ab Oliver did not see it as the councillors' role to determine the size of pipes, preferring to leave such technicalities to more qualified people. Stephen Bell pointed out that the Shire Engineer believed that his recommendation would meet demand, and that the cost of bigger pipes would have to be justified. But Tim West and his allies won the day: the recommendation was altered as they sought, before being put to a full Council meeting.

This debate was an overture to a long drama. Jim Finnimore was frequently called upon to justify the recommendations of the Council's consultants. At the March Council meeting Harold Upston said that some cost figures 'shoot holes' in the consultants' recommendation. Tim West said he believed that there was a fault in the design of the bridge which was to carry the new pipes. Both sides believed that their plan would put enough water into West Cowra.

The next round occurred at a special meeting of Council, called to discuss increases in water rates and the West Cowra scheme. People had received what they felt were unreasonable water rate bills. The billing was in line with policy laid down earlier to pay for augmentation, including extensive alterations to the treatment plant which were almost complete. Complainants called a public meeting at which the Ratepayers Association was revived and some Council staff denounced. The special Council meeting was held in a tense atmosphere, with six visitors, an unusually large number, in the public gallery.

The Shire Engineer reported to the meeting that the Council's consultants had offered two options, and Tim West and Cyril Treasure had designed another. His view of the West/Treasure plan was that it may not guarantee sufficient water for West Cowra, and that he could not sanction it without a technical analysis. Cyril Treasure spoke against sending the proposal to the consultants. This was one of several occasions on which I heard councillors state as a matter of principle that Council should avoid consultants in general, believing them to be expensive and unreliable, and above all, unnecessary. Jim Finnimore was left exasperated, saying that he felt he no longer knew the ground rules, but the Council decided to heed his advice and seek an analysis of the West/Treasure plan by consultants.

The matter came up again in the May Works Committee meeting. The consultants reported that the West/Treasure plan would work but without guarantee that the highest houses in West Cowra would get adequate water supply. The Council was then faced with a decision to construct an additional reservoir to guarantee supply, if the councillors accepted the consultants' doubts. Tim West and Harold Upston did not accept the consultants' doubts, leading to more friction with the Engineer. The Committee decided to put all options to the next full Council meeting.

At that meeting councillors considered a modified West/Treasure plan, which was adopted. Bruce Golsby and Councillor George Noble spoke against the plan, because of the possibility of it not meeting West Cowra's needs, a point which Jim Finnimore repeated. The five West Cowra residents in the gallery left somewhat disappointed that the Shire Engineer's recommendation had not been adopted. So, no doubt, was the Shire Engineer, because his task of finding an efficient plan to meet Council's objectives had been usurped, as the Council's agenda had become technical rather than political.

Questions about the extent of the problem in West Cowra were raised, but it was the technical aspects of the problem that were debated. There was no evidence that West Cowra people had lobbied, or if they had, whomever they lobbied failed to steer the debate towards objectives and away from means. A struggle between councillors and officers leaves little room for others, unless they, like the councillors, can muster technical arguments. Unlike the protest group in Wild's Heathcote (1983), West Cowra Progress Association did not, or could not, raise such resources. This suggests that the technical bias in the agenda of local politics had obscured the interests of the subordinate, no matter how strong the desire of the powerful to look after them.

Agenda setting can be no more deliberate than the products of an earnest interpretation of councillor responsibility. No councillor sought to do anything other than seek the best solution for West Cowra in terms

Spatial politics 79

of efficiency and fairness. All participants in the issue acknowledged that something should be done for West Cowra, and to that extent West Cowra had negotiated the 'rules of access' and established an issue. Another controversy, over air pollution, will indicate that so much is not always achieved by area interests.

The non-issue of air pollution[5]

A protracted 'non-issue', in which some residents of Taragala sought to rid themselves of an air pollution problem, offers a good example of interests pursued but eventually almost forgotten. Taragala residents were bearing costs associated with a new factory (Lachlan Industries), costs which to them were manifest as falling land values and physical discomfort. They felt that these costs were unreasonable, and so expressed their interests by protesting.[6] The problem became apparent soon after the Lachlan Industries wool scouring plant commenced operation in 1975. Wool scouring removes grease and dirt from wool in order to eliminate unnecessary weight before shipment. It produces an obnoxious waste. The factory's disposal system allowed it to settle in open ponds in order to break down. Evil-smelling gases were to be contained by a crust on top of the ponds, but it did not form as planned.

The first complaints were voiced in 1975, when eleven residents raised their concern with the then Health Surveyor. He responded, as quoted in the *Guardian* of 30 September (p. 1), by saying that there was 'no way of dealing with it at the moment', and that it 'could get worse before it gets better'. He added that he was not certain of the source of the smell. The following month Taragala residents obtained eighty-five signatures on a petition which was presented to the Municipal Council and a Senator who happened to visit Cowra. The Senator passed it on to the State Minister for Health. In December Taragala residents formed an 'Anti-Pollution Committee', which wrote to the Town Clerk, calling on the Council to seek an injunction forcing the company to stop the smell. The State Government was doing no more than the Council, having replied that, unlike the Taragala people, it saw the Municipal Council working to rectify the problem. The Council advised the complainants in January, 1976 that it had established a special committee to handle the matter and discuss it with the company and appropriate State agencies. Such discussions occurred in February, 1976, and the company agreed to cover the pond with a kind of plastic sheet.

Unfortunately this measure did not solve the problem (*Cowra Guardian*, 28 February, 1978). By early 1978 it had become obvious to the complainants that minor changes to the disposal system would not prevent the odours. Meanwhile the Council had responded to renewed complaints by offering a form to be completed by Taragala residents so that the problem could be documented. It seemed that the councillors were uncertain of the extent of the problem. Very few people submitted forms. The form read:

> Information Regarding Smell Alleged to Come from
> Lachlan Industries, Cowra
>
> Please fill in this sheet as accurately as possible. DO NOT EXAGERATE [sic] *OR* record the time that the smell lingers in the house afterward. These dates and accurate times are needed to try and track down any particular process of action causing the smell to arise.
>
> Return the completed sheet to Health Surveyor's Office, preferably each Monday.

The sheet had spaces for recording dates, times and comments. This approach may have been the only course available to the Health Surveyor when he was called upon to advise the Council on the extent of the problem. One of my informants believed that the Health Surveyor was quite sympathetic, despite saying 'put up with it'. The Health Surveyor could do nothing about it because so few people filled in the forms. In more than three months only three forms had been returned (Health Surveyor's report to Council, 28 March, 1978). He went to Taragala, but only at times when the smell was not bad. He raised the matter at the Council, but his hands were tied without documentary evidence. My informant said that 'it was worrying the life out of him'. He was sufficiently concerned to go to Taragala to ask the residents. But again he found little to offer as evidence.

The Council did, however, write to the company, advising it of the complaints and asking it to review its treatment methods. The company replied that it would modify the treatment. Correspondence continued through 1978, with the Works Committee meeting the company in May. Again the company said it would work on the problem. The Council wrote again in October and Lachlan Industries replied in December.

The modifications did not stop the odours, although the Council had expressed pleasure with developments (*Cowra Guardian*, 22 May 1979). Complaints were again made in early 1981. The company described its efforts in an article in the *Guardian* (29 May). The Council defended it. The following extract from a letter from one of the complainants, published in the *Guardian* of 27 February (p. 2), shows how the debate was warming up.

> It never fails to amaze me why Council aldermen should state that Lachlan Industries has gone to great extremes and spent $2000 to rid us of this smell when there would be at least 200 homes in the vicinity which have depreciated by that amount each over the past three years.
>
> Ninety-nine per cent of these homes belong to the working people

who have worked all their lives to purchase their own homes. (Not many Silvertails this end of town.) . . .

A letter from another complainant, published in the *Guardian* of 2 March (p. 2), said: '. . . We have been let down badly by the Council in that they (1) gave us an assurance at the time of the proposal to build the plant that there would be no pollution problems and (2) they are either not interested in complaints from the residents of Taragala or they have no power over the company . . .'

The Council had conducted a public meeting when the factory was in the planning stages. Taragala people were not only calling on it for help, they were blaming it for their problem. They did so with reason, for Council had approved the siting of the factory. On 9 March (p. 5) the *Guardian* reported on a survey it had conducted among Taragala residents:

> The response by residents was overwhelming with 100 per cent of the people surveyed on a random basis, complaining of an unpleasant odour from the plant which is situated very close to the residential area of Taragala . . .
>
> In describing the odour a variety of comments were received ranging from 'like a sewer', 'the treatment works', 'decaying sheep carcasses', 'the foulest smell you could ever imagine' and so on the list continued.
>
> Some real estate agents commented that the values of homes in Taragala had suffered as a result of the smell which is quickly being associated with the area . . .
>
> However, many of the people felt that the plant was very worthwhile in many facets of its operation. These aspects included the bringing of industry to the town and increased employment for local people.
>
> Even so, they felt that something should, and could be done about the stench . . .

The leading complainants began to aim more energy at the State Government, but had not yet given up on the Council. The Council's decision to refer the matter back to Works Committee at its March meeting would not have encouraged them. At that meeting Tim West defended the complainants, suggesting that strong action against the company was warranted. He said that the smell was so bad that 'one day the odour had made it impossible for athletes to train at River Park because the smell took their breath away', and that 'the company was on shaky ground'. One alderman was quoted in reply: 'Lachlan Industries have carried out every request Council has made to eliminate the odour'. Another alderman was quoted to have said that 'he didn't find the smell particularly offensive' (*Cowra Guardian*, 23 March, 1981, p. 1). The last statement prompted a letter to the *Guardian* pointing out that the councillor who said it lived four miles away. A letter published (on 24 April) after the April Council meeting expressed disgust that the Council had again referred the matter back to Works Committee. The State National Country Party leader entered the debate, quoted in the *Guardian* (27 July, p. 1) as saying that 'Lachlan Industries was an extremely important industry to Cowra and District and had co-operated totally with authorities to eliminate any environmental problems'. Yet the problems persisted.

The threat of loss of jobs was prominent in the minds of the councillors and others, although one of my informants believed that the company had made no such threats. The inferred threat moved sixty-eight employees of the company (from a workforce of about eighty) to write to the *Guardian* (21 August, 1981) asking the complainants to desist. By this time there were only two remaining active, other support having melted away. Employment by the company was not a reason for many Taragala people failing to support the complainants. A resident estimated that about ten employees had lived in Taragala at the time. Among those who signed the letter only three were Taragala dwellers. It seems that Taragala had learned to live with the pollution.

The Council continued to correspond with Lachlan Industries. It also sought assistance from the State Pollution Control Commission, asking it to recommend a solution. After receiving the recommendation, the Council sought confirmation from Lachlan Industries that it had taken the recommended measures. Nevertheless, the problem continued. Complaints to the State authorities continued into 1983 and 1984 from the solitary person who was willing to carry on the fight. By the end of 1985, the problem had all but disappeared. One resident told me in 1986 that an occasional whiff could still be detected, but ten years after the plant commenced operation, the problem had been pretty well solved. There was still local conjecture in 1986 about the effectiveness of the measures taken, suggesting that over the ten year period the problem would have solved itself anyway. It seems likely that eventually the Council's efforts had some effects, but they certainly did not have the prompt and positive effects that Taragala residents sought.

The complainants had lacked the resources to enforce quick, decisive action. Without such action, as Parenti (1970) pointed out, protest groups are unlikely to succeed. Time was a resource of the Council. Moreover, the value placed by councillors on the presence of the industry in Cowra put the onus on the complainants to convince the councillors that Taragala was bearing an undue cost, not outweighed by the general economic good which they saw the town obtaining at a time in its history when it appeared to be confronting economic decline. The Council's 'rules of access', demanded precise and documented evidence. When confronted with such a response to their complaints, the complainants could do little as they watched their support wane.

The company played a minor role. As Blowers (1983) noted in a study of an air pollution issue, companies are strongest politically when they are weakest economically, or in this case, the locality is seen to be weak. The company had no need to act while the Council was effectively defending it by not finding sufficient reason to attack it decisively. It obtained the benefit of the doubt. In 1986 two councillors who had been involved in the matter told me that the smell really was not bad enough to warrant the fuss. The councillors had to be convinced and the complainants failed to convince them, other than Tim West, that they should speak out against the company. Air pollution in Taragala, although it was raised in the Council, shows the characteristics of a non-issue from the perspective of Taragala people, in that debate was dominated by questions about the existence of a problem, rather than action which would immediately and certainly stop the pollution. To that extent, Taragala people were unable to 'make the wheel squeak'. This 'non-issue' offers a good illustration of how a spatial interest group could have its interests submerged beneath what those who benefited saw as an interest common to the whole district.

Urban and rural

Discussion of spatial politics has so far focused on matters internal to the town. An urban-rural dimension had been added when the Municipal and Shire Councils were amalgamated in 1980, although the affairs of the two councils had been intertwined through common interest in town facilities, such as the saleyards, and at times in more personal ways in the presence of Mark Whitby's son being Waugoola's Shire Clerk (he retired in 1985 as Cowra Shire's Deputy Clerk after 48 years in Cowra local government) and Ab Oliver's brother being Waugoola's President. The amalgamation eliminated the relationship by combining the budgets, organisations and electorates of each.[7] It did so amid vociferous protest from Waugoola, protest which arose from fears that rural interests would be forsaken. Urban-rural relations were on the agenda from the inauguration of Cowra Shire. This provides a contrast with the relationship between the interests of Taragala people and the local political agenda as described above.

Waugoola Shire and Cowra Municipal Councils had long lived at close quarters, but when it appeared that enforced amalgamation was imminent, Waugoola screamed. It had heard murmurs about amalgamation long before 1980. The Boundaries Commission, a State agency established to examine possible amalgamation of local government areas, raised the prospect in 1974. A *Guardian* editorial (2 July) reported that the Town Clerk saw advantages in amalgamation, but Waugoola was opposed. The matter hovered about during the late 1970s as new councils were created elsewhere in rural New South Wales, with Waugoola standing firm in its attitude. When the State Government announced amalgamation in 1980, Waugoola attacked. The *Guardian* page one headline of

2 July, 1980 read 'Council Disgusted over Government Methods'. Two days later it reported that the Shire President, Cyril Treasure, was 'totally opposed', demanding a riding system (a division of the shire into voting areas or 'ridings') to ensure representation for rural interests. Rural dwellers also feared that they may not receive value for their rates, seeing town services as a potential sponge. This was expressed in a letter about the water augmentation scheme from a rural ratepayer published in the *Guardian* on 14 December, 1984 (p. 2): '... I became worried that it will be rural ratepayers paying for the convenience of town residents having water running out of their taps whenever needed, a situation I hope doesn't arise, and that the people using the water pay the majority of the cost of such water.' The amalgamation proceeded without the establishment of ridings. Nevertheless, such overt friction had placed rural-urban relations on the agenda of the new Council.

Both the representation and rating issues were raised during 1986. The representation matter arose after a councillor (Harold Upston) resigned. This raised the possibility of reducing the number of councillors from twelve (an unwieldy number because the Shire President's casting vote could give him two votes). At a Council meeting (25 August) an urban-resident councillor suggested that application be made to the State Local Government Minister to have the number reduced to nine, but after argument from rural councillors that such a change might eliminate rural representation, application was made to have an eleven-seat council. The application was approved with effect from the 1987 election.

The rating issue emerged at annual estimates time, when a relative increase in rural rates was proposed to bring rural, urban resident and business rating into line with an arrangement made at amalgamation. The arrangement was that the relative revenue contributions from the three sources should be maintained, with adjustments for those facilities which had been and would continue to be used by rural people, but paid for by town people. The drought of the early 1980s intervened and the adjustment had been deferred. Indeed the rural contribution had been allowed to decline relatively. The 1987 budget process raised the prospect of moving back to the post-amalgamation arrangement.

The Shire Clerk drew the attention of councillors to the arrangement when presenting the 1987 Budget Strategy, referring to an entry in the Policy Register. He added that under this policy rural rate revenue in 1987 'would increase from 49% to 50%' (Shire Clerk's Report to Finance Committee, 15 September). On 6 October the *Guardian* reported on page one that: 'This year ratepayers living in residential areas can expect to pay one per cent less than they did last year for their rates while rural rates will increase by one per cent and commercial rates will remain the same.'

The farmers reacted. The President of the Livestock and Grain Producers' [Farmers'] Association wrote to the Shire Clerk, stating that the Cowra Branch of the Association was 'concerned at Council's decision to raise rural rates for 1987, when rural industry's capacity to pay is at the lowest level for many years'. Some pert questions about Council's operations and efficiency followed. The farmers had assumed that an increase in the rural share of rates implied an increase in the rural rate. This was an understandable interpretation of the Clerk's proposal, as he had indicated it in his report to the September Finance Committee with the words 'I had proposed that the increase in rural rate in 1987 could be avoided through [action under] Section 118, [meaning a change in hobby farm rating], but that was rejected by [an earlier Council] resolution . . .'.

The strength of the Council's reserves allowed the Clerk to budget for a decrease in general rate revenue, so avoiding raising the rural rate by lowering the residential rate in order to raise the rural share. That is how he presented the estimates to the 17 November meeting of the Finance Committee. Regardless of any effect of the farmers' letter on the Clerk's decision, it was reflected in his presentation of the estimates to the Council. His emphasis appeared in the statement that: 'The General Rate Revenue is DECREASED by 2% with the decrease being entirely on residential properties where rates will fall by 5.5% but with NO RURAL RATE INCREASE . . .'. The farmers had been heard. The Council decided to offer to meet with them, and it discussed the terms of its reply to the questions in their letter. The reply told the farmers that they had not understood the way the rate burden was shared, but they got their zero rate increase.

The amalgamation virtually guaranteed that rural interests would be represented in the arena. Even if no farmers were elected, it is unlikely that access to the Council would have become as difficult as it was for Taragala. Separation of rural and urban interests was readily perceived on both sides, unlike spatial interests within the town.

The amalgamation alone cannot simply explain the farmers' ready and effective access to the arena, when in terms of senior staff the Municipal Council virtually took over Waugoola and rural area resident representatives have been a minority on the Council. Of the twelve Cowra Shire Councillors in 1986, two were farmers, two had active farm interests and another two were retired farmers. But the Council did not divide into opposing rural and urban forces along those lines. No councillor jumped to defend the farmers' position on the rates issue; they did not need to. Farmers were more powerful than their numbers on the Council. Their ability to maintain effective expression in the arena is what demands explanation. That explanation partly lies in the ideology of councillors and the climate in which deference to rural interests is legitimated. Rural people assumed a right of access, which they were accorded.

Conclusion: councillors and ideologies

The ideologies of local government councillors are, as argued by Dearlove (1973), just as important to local politics and policy making as those of parliamentarians in their arenas. Ideology has a very important role in determining what is and is not legitimate for the agenda of local government. In the issues and non-issues discussed above the councillors applied their values and beliefs, showing particular value placed on organisation management.

The policy apparatus was aimed at efficiency of management while hoping for equitable allocation of resources. That hope rested on the assumption that needs could and would be communicated by those in need, an assumption which appears dubious in the light of the 'Needs Survey' results, the history of Taragala's air pollution problem, and the clouding effect which management and technical concerns could have. The assumption appears to have stronger foundation in the rural context, where concerns could be expressed with confidence that they would be heard and responded to, if not acted upon.

While the value placed on organisational efficiency rested happily with a 'people's corporation' image of local government, it inhibited or even cancelled the prospects for pluralism. The 'peoples corporation' image projected a model of consensus, but that consensus was more constraining for some than others. The councillors strove for efficiency, but so did the senior officers. Both made for the same objective, and collided along the way. The collisions distracted attention from some of those interests which were expressed, and left little prospect for latent interests to be recognised. Unless, that is, they were illuminated by the values of councillors or officers, as the interests of Lachlan Industries were, or were accepted as valid matters for the agenda, as were rural protests.

Notes

1 Progress Association affairs were reported in the *Cowra Guardian*. On 9 December the *Guardian* reported that the Mayor had attended a West Cowra Progress Association meeting, and had said that the Council appreciated its efforts: 'had it not been for this association we'd have had very little correspondence to put on the table at a number of our council meetings' (p. 8).
2 In 1949 Taragala Progress Association sought a new bridge over the Eugowra railway. It lobbied for park improvements again in 1953. In 1954 it announced that it was to build a hall and tennis courts at its own expense. Council agreed to let the Association use Council land. It again agitated for park improvements in 1960. It reported a good year in 1959: 'Completed projects were lighting improvements to the tennis courts, installation of sewered toilets to replace the existing buildings, modern facilities for the kitchen and repair to the kitchen ceiling ...' (*Cowra Guardian*, 19 February, p. 3).
3 For example, when Whitby did not want a pensioner rate rebate scheme applied to mortgaged properties, Lynch objected (*Cowra Guardian*, 5 April, 1960). When Lynch claimed that the cost of a lunch for a State Government minister should be debited to the Mayoral allowance, Whitby described the suggestion as 'despicable' (*Cowra Guardian*, 15 February, 1957, p. 2).

Battles between these two aldermen largely dominated the Municipal arena from Lynch's election in 1953 until his death in 1962. Whitby was first elected in 1925. He served for 40 years, including 27 as Mayor, his last year as Mayor being 1963 (Armstrong,

1988). He had a substantial impact on Cowra's local government. A 1986 (non-Labor) councillor told me that he felt that the Council was still climbing out of the detrimental effects of Whitby's conservatism, attributing to it the town's lack of services, as identified by MacColl (1944), as disputed by the progress associations, and as seen by this councillor as a problem still to be overcome. He was thinking in terms of parks and recreation facilities. Whitby held tight to the traditional ideological reins of local government: fiscal and political conservatism. At his retirement, a fellow alderman was quoted in the *Guardian* (13 December, 1963, p. 1) as saying that 'Cowra Council was one of the best financed councils in the State and this was due to Alderman Whitby's conservative approach'. He made no secret of his conservatism. At the inauguration of electric lighting in a part of the main street in 1932, Whitby said: 'It has been said that Cowra is a conservative town – well maybe it is, and it is better that it should be that way than the opposite, and I have no objection in saying that your town should be second to none in the State' (*Cowra Guardian*, 2 November, p. 1). When asked to comment on a debate in the Central West (regional electricity) County Council about a proposal to give an employee time off work to enable him to attend a meeting of a council on which he was an alderman, Whitby said, as quoted in the *Cowra Guardian* (7 May, 1953, p. 1):

> 'We all suffer a loss through attending council meetings at times. But when we enter local government we are prepared to give our time and lose a certain amount of income. . . . Everyone should realise that they are expected to give their time and portion of their income in the interests of local government . . . I definitely oppose this motion. I think it is dangerous to local government.'

4   The village category includes the villages of Gooloogong and Woodstock which were large enough to form Census Collection Districts. The others ranged in population from a handful which was hard to discern from the rural population to something over one hundred. Gooloogong and Woodstock constituted perhaps two-thirds of the total village population. I formed the impression that they were the wealthiest villages. The boundaries in the town were all clear cut, except for the North Cowra-Mulyan division, which followed the topography rather than the Census map. The Collection Districts which I have included in North Cowra covered some of the poorer parts of Mulyan, but as North Cowra was by far the largest area (1 274 households compared to 972 in the rural area, 504 in Central Cowra, 408 in Taragala, 381 in Mulyan, 282 in West Cowra and 167 in the villages), it did not significantly alter the result.

5   With apologies to Crenson (1971).

6   Taragala's problem was not the first pollution matter to raise controversy in Cowra. The Municipal Council confronted opposition when it gave permission for a shearing shed to be built in West Cowra in 1954 (*Cowra Guardian*, 19 January). Aldermen Col Newton and Leo Lynch protested in vain. West Cowra Progress Association attracted 100 people to a protest meeting (*Cowra Guardian*, 29 January), all to no avail. Three years later the Municipal Council allowed a mushroom farm to be operated in Mulyan, again followed by unsuccessful protest from Leo Lynch among others.

7   Cowra's amalgamation formed one of seventeen new country councils under the New South Wales Local Government Areas Amalgamation Act of 1980. Nineteen new councils had been created by amalgamation between 1975 and 1980 (Law Book Company, 1985).

6
The politics of development

The numerical dominance of farming and business people on Cowra Shire Council and its predecessors, and the looming possibility of economic decline in the district might lead one to expect that matters relating to economic development would have accounted for much of the energy expended in Cowra's local political arena. One might also expect, given the 'people's corporation' image, that the Council would take the form of an elitist club, whose members were united in the struggle for growth and development against the tide of urban capital accumulation. The latter expectation, however, is not justified. Controversy did arise over development matters, injecting a superficial note of pluralism into the arena.

In development politics, as in spatial politics, benefits can only be realised by those who are able to raise issues and pursue them to a satisfying outcome. Issues arose over the Shire Council's role in development matters, and they were raised by people putting forth both business and other, opposing, interests. Development politics offer further evidence of resources being available to farmers to create issues and achieve desired outcomes. The issues which were created clouded the interests of the non-farm sector, and not all the development-related issues which town employers and employees could be expected to pursue found their way to the surface.

The issue of the Tourist and Development Corporation

Political relations between the Shire Council and the Tourist and Development Corporation had what could loosely be described as a class dimension, arising because the Council used rate revenue to help fund the Corporation, which was established to assist business. Non-business ratepayers questioned the probability of their own interests being served by furthering those of business. Problems with development organisations had a long history. Cowra and Waugoola Councils were both involved with the Lachlan Valley Regional Development Committee after World War II. This Committee of neighbouring councils appears to have had a difficult history. In 1949 the *Guardian* reported (16 September) that Waugoola was hesitating to take part in the Committee's revival after a two-year lapse and Cowra had decided not to join. In 1952 Cowra was again reluctant but a public meeting resolved to join, contrary to the wishes of Mayor Whitby (*Cowra Guardian*, 22 April). Waugoola withdrew from the Committee in 1953 (*Cowra Guardian*, 17 March). A report on re-constitution of the Committee, and Cowra's membership, appeared in the *Guardian* of 15 April, 1958. Reluctance to participate in the Committee appears to have been caused by a desire to avoid a cost burden to ratepayers.

The Cowra Tourist and Development Corporation emanated from a trust formed in 1967 with financial support from Cowra Municipal Council. This support had been recurring, and was therefore open to debate each year at Council's estimates time. Increases in that support had created controversy. In 1970 and 1971 the Council's contribution was increased despite objections from some councillors. On the latter occasion the Mayor had to use his casting vote to secure the increase (*Cowra Guardian*, 25 September, and 19 October, respectively). On the former occasion the *Guardian* quoted Col Newton objecting to the increase because of the cost to ratepayers. By 1975 the Japanese Garden project had brought the Council and the Corporation closer together, as the Corporation had leased the Garden land from the Council. In that year, a letter explaining that no Council money was being spent on the Garden was published on page one of the *Guardian* (14 February). In 1976 the *Guardian* reported that the Ratepayers' Association was concerned that the demand for water for the Garden would deplete the supply available to town residents.

Ratepayers' concern was again expressed in 1986 when the Corporation's five-year lease on the Japanese Garden site became due for renewal. The Council split into two camps, one which wanted to increase the Corporation's independence while not losing Council's support, and another which wanted greater control by the Council. This dispute was complicated by the presence on the Council of five Corporation Board members, three of whom were appointed by the Council to represent it (Barbara Bennett, Ab Oliver and Stephen Bell) and the others being Board members before election to the Council (Don Kibbler and Harold Upston). The voting rights of the two latter councillors were in continuing dispute, after the Shire Clerk had recommended, in 1985, that they not be allowed to vote on matters relating to the Corporation, for fear that the Corporation may be able some day to gain a majority of seats on the Council, and effectively take it over. Legal advice that they could not be prevented from voting had been obtained, but an informal agreement had been reached that they not vote when a conflict of interest might be construed. That agreement was still subject to dispute, exacerbating the tension between Corporation supporters and others on the Council.

The controversy over the lease of the Japanese Garden site started with a Finance Committee recommendation in March 1986 that certain clauses of the lease be altered and some added upon renewal. The changes would have greatly increased the Council's influence over the Corporation by stipulating that surplus revenue generated by trading at the Garden be used for purposes other than administration and maintenance of the Garden, only with Council consent. Further, the proposed lease added clauses which would have obliged the Corporation to obtain consent from the Council before raising loans or advancing funds to other projects.

This was unacceptable to the Corporation. Ab Oliver presented the Corporation's case at the Council, moving that it agree to the Corporation by-passing it, and dealing directly with the New South Wales Lands Department, which had ultimate responsibility for the land as a recreation reserve. He pointed out that, although the Corporation had had financial trouble early in the Garden project, the situation had stabilised and the Corporation had obtained substantial support from Sydney and Japan. He acknowledged that the Council may be liable for losses, but believed that the Corporation's reserves eliminated the risk. He felt that dealing directly with the Lands Department would overcome past friction and may obviate accusations that the Garden was a burden on ratepayers. Ab Oliver also praised Don Kibbler for his work on the Garden project as Corporation Director, pointing out that his efforts had been a powerful force in the establishment of the Garden.

Cyril Treasure asked: 'What is wrong with the recommendation?' Ab replied that the problem lay in the consent requirement. Cyril expressed uncertainty that the Lands Department would be an easier landlord. Col Newton was the first to speak against the motion, saying that the intention of the new clauses was to ensure that the Council was aware of the affairs of the Corporation. Don Kibbler discounted this concern, saying that he believed that public doubts arose through fear that the Gardens may become a drain on rate revenue, but he assured Council that the New South Wales Government would help in an emergency. Bruce Golsby said that as the Council supported the Corporation financially it should retain control. Neville Pengilly expressed disagreement with that point, believing that the Council should not interfere. Stephen Bell went further, questioning those who would want the Council to have a hand in running a proven successful venture. Tim West repeated the doubts expressed by Bruce Golsby, saying that he was uneasy about the Garden accounts. Ultimately the motion to allow the Corporation to deal directly with the Lands Department was carried. So ended the first round of debate.

The Lands Department responded with a plan to establish a Trust from which the Corporation would lease the Garden site. The plan provided for the Shire President to be a member of the Trust, retaining Council involvement but eliminating the prospect of control which some councillors sought. The same scepticism about the destination of ratepayers' money

The politics of development

was raised. Bruce Golsby repeated his view, saying that the Council was 'saddled with a monster'. Col Newton did likewise, saying that the Council would only be going along to pick up the tab while the Corporation milked the profits. He called for public nominations to the Trust. But the Corporation side won the day.

Unfortunately for the Corporation, negotiations with the Lands Department revealed that a lease from the Trust, which would be appointed by that Department, would also require consultation with the lessor on financial matters. The issue was discussed at the June Council meeting, after the Shire Clerk had recommended a modified version of the original proposal, which he believed satisfied some Corporation demands. The Corporation asked that the matter be discussed 'in committee'. This request raised debate. That it should do so is not surprising, given that the councillors who sought to increase Council control of Corporation affairs did so because they wanted assurances that ratepayers' money was used in ratepayers' interests, and having related matters discussed 'in committee' was not compatible with their goal of opening Corporation affairs to ratepayer scrutiny. Nevertheless, the council resolved to close the meeting to the press and the public. Col Newton was particularly concerned, saying 'I have done everything to divorce myself from this'.

The final lease agreement closely resembled the Finance Committee's original recommendation, with an additional clause providing for arbitration of disputes between the Council and the Corporation by the Lands Department. The Corporation had won the local battles but lost the war, because, like the Finance Committee, the State Government sought safeguards. While Corporation representatives could raise the necessary numbers on the Council to have the Council release its control, the Corporation could not find a more accommodating landlord.

The persistence of this issue indicates resources in the possession of people who saw themselves as ratepayers in confrontation with business. Businesses, however, also paid rates. The councillors who had businesses might have seen themselves in a double bind. One (Bruce Golsby) chose to oppose the business interest. But it was a financial rather than political double bind. Business people could feel that they were expressing a general local interest whichever side they supported. The Corporation representatives could see a general benefit from tourist development which they did not want hampered by political debate that may convey an undesirable impression to supporters of the Garden project. This view was especially apparent in the debate over 'in committee' discussion. Ab Oliver summed up the Corporation view, as quoted in the *Cowra Guardian* (25 June): '... matters should be discussed in committee when publicity of the proceedings would be prejudicial to the *public interest*, by reason of the confidential nature of the business to be transacted' [my emphasis]. The Corporation's opponents in this matter saw a different public interest: that of protecting the ratepayers' investment.

The desire of some councillors to see the Corporation's affairs open to scrutiny was expressed over several matters. When the Corporation submitted plans to the Health Surveyor for approval of a building in the Japanese Garden, the Health Surveyor felt that he could not approve them without Council consideration. This followed the normal procedure: any development or building application which did not unambiguously meet the regulations laid down by the State Government, and which the officer concerned therefore did not feel could be approved, was to be referred to the Works Committee. The ambiguity lay in the purpose of the building. The Corporation proposed a building which could have served as both exhibition space and a flat. The regulations required different standards of fire protection, a flat requiring the higher standard. The Health Surveyor recommended it be classified as such, but the Corporation members on Works Committee (Ab Oliver and Harold Upston) disagreed. The recommendation went to the Council in favour of the lower standard, amid disagreement from Tim West and Cyril Treasure. Again the Corporation had the numbers.

At Council, Col Newton raised a query about the matter, with support from Bruce Golsby. The point of contention was the possibility that the Corporation would be seen to be receiving favoured treatment. Col Newton sought clarification of the change made by the Works Committee to the Health Surveyor's recommendation. Cyril Treasure supported this request, expressing concern that the matter might be seen as irregular because of the change made by the Works Committee. The full Council accepted the Works Committee recommendation, but again the 'opponents' of the Corporation had raised a contentious issue.

They did so again when the Corporation sought the Council's blessing for its application for Government assistance with restoration of an old mill building as a tourist attraction; and on this occasion a personal dimension which had earlier been obscure became clearer, while still remaining largely below the surface of Council debate. The Corporation proposed to seek a grant to purchase the mill from Don Kibbler's wife. The Shire Clerk recommended to the Council's February, 1986 meeting that it not support the project, on the grounds that the stated purchase price was excessive and that the project was not viable. Col Newton spoke for the recommendation. He believed that the project was not viable and that if the Council became involved, it would be 'propping up the Tourist and Development Corporation'. Harold Upston indicated his opposite perspective, replying that support for the Corporation was irrelevant, and that support for the 'local community' was the issue. Despite some support, from Bruce Golsby, the supporters of the Clerk's recommendation did not have the numbers. Ultimately, technical and other problems stopped the project before the mill was purchased.

Don Kibbler took no part in this debate, but his presence as Corporation Director had some significance for Council-Corporation relations. While Ab Oliver praised Don's skills and perseverance, he could not alter a popular perception of him as a 'tall poppy', an outstandingly successful local businessman. To the Corporation members, Don was almost a hero, but he had achieved success without the credentials associated with traditional leadership in rural communities. This did not overtly accrue as a resource to his opponents in Council debate, because they did not steer debate onto a personal level. Its significance lies in the legitimacy that it added to the issue.

Regulation and development

Conflict surrounding the Tourist and Development Corporation was only one feature of the politics of development in the local arena, and when compared to issues which were raised about the Council's more direct role in development, it was perhaps a minor issue. As one might expect, the Council had assisted development, but some councillors sought to have it do more, or at least refrain from what they felt to be the placing of obstacles before development. This precipitated conflict similar to that between councillors and officers over the technical matters related to water reticulation.

The Council helped business during 1986 by its annual donation to the Tourist and Development Corporation, by helping the Cowra Golf Club establish an industrial subdivision, by helping the Corporation fund an economic survey of the district, and by subsidising the water supply of the three large manufacturing industries. Business interests clearly benefited from these activities and policies. Yet councillors saw opportunities to question the actions of the Council, and even accuse it of hindering development. These opportunities arose largely from the Council's regulatory role.

The most dramatic of such issues offered a parallel to the Japanese Garden building matter. Two issues arose over the imposition of fire regulations, as alterations to shops in the main street were planned. As with the building at the Japanese Garden, the Health Surveyor confronted irregular matters which he deemed to require consideration by the Council. To that extent it was the Health Surveyor who raised the issues, but some councillors saw them not just as a technical problem, but as a case of regulations hindering development. The alleged ability of the Council to do so became an issue.

In the first case, the Health Surveyor was confronted with a sensitive problem. The owner of a building containing three shops had applied to make alterations to just one of them. The alterations would have to be made in compliance with fire regulations. That much was easy. The matter was, however, made difficult by all three shops in their pre-alteration state failing to comply with then current fire regulations. Council policy provided for enforcement of regulations when old buildings were modified. The Health Surveyor observed that all three shops had a common roof, so making one comply and not the others made little sense, but alterations to all three would be a substantial imposition. He decided to recommend that the owner be required to draw up plans to upgrade all three shops, but only require alteration to achieve compliance on the one to be altered. Harold Upston, Tim West and Stephen Bell expressed reservations about the recommendation, but it was accepted at the Works Committee. Harold was particularly concerned that the call for plans would hold up work, and that imposition of regulations on old buildings would open a 'Pandora's box' of further requirements that would be difficult to meet.

That issue was easy, however, when compared with another which the Health Surveyor raised at the same Works Committee meeting. Another shop owner in the main street wanted to make alterations in an old building which was shared with other shops. This owner had already started to make alterations. Making the situation still more sensitive, the shop allegedly had an illegally installed ceiling, and another shop owner in the building had made alterations, allegedly without approval. The alterations necessary to bring the shop into line with a strict interpretation of the regulations appeared to the Health Surveyor to be unreasonable demands, so again he compromised. He recommended to the Works Committee that sufficient conditions be applied to ensure what he judged to be a reasonable degree of fire protection. Adherence to those conditions would, nevertheless, have been expensive.

Harold Upston emphasised his view that even the compromise would be an unreasonable demand. As Stephen Bell explained, the problem lay in imposition of regulations on one shop owner while letting the others off the hook. The meeting discussed a move to make the other shops in the building comply with the conditions to be imposed on the one which planned alterations. Both Tim West and Harold Upston opposed such a move, but it was accepted and passed to the Council for consideration.

Discussion at the July Council meeting further revealed the concerns of councillors over the matter. To Don Kibbler, the problem was one of deciding how far the Council could go in applying regulations before it would start to hinder development. Jack Mallon and Neville Pengilly also expressed concern about effects on the business. Harold Upston turned his attention to what he felt was unfair treatment of this shop owner, in the light of the changes that had already been made. He had, at the Works Committee meeting, threatened to resign if the Health Surveyor's recommendation was accepted at Council. It was accepted, and Harold resigned, amid a flurry of statements which indicated his belief that Council officers were engaged in a vendetta against business. (His resignation precipitated the by-election mentioned in chapter 5.) The vote on this occasion was close. With Ab Oliver absent, Cyril Treasure's casting vote carried the motion to accept the recommendation after Col Newton,

Tim West, Bruce Golsby, Barbara Bennett and George Noble had voted for it, probably having accepted the point made by Tim and Bruce that neglect of the regulations could leave Council responsible, and the ratepayers liable to great cost of damages. The matter later got bogged down in the necessity to obtain co-operation among the shop owners and ultimately the Council had to take stronger action, but not before Cyril Treasure, as Shire President, had sent a circular to all businesses explaining the Council's action.

Planning matters, more than any other form of regulation, obtained response from those who expressed the business interest. This willingness may have been influenced by success in the major planning issue to be discussed below. Some discussion of minor issues, which arose in the wake of that major issue, will provide an overture to the latter.

The Shire Clerk's report to the August Policy and Resources Committee recommended that the wording of the requirement that developers meet the full cost of street sealing be altered for the sake of clarity. Don Kibbler objected on the grounds that developers might be discouraged. He moved accordingly but his motion lapsed for want of a seconder. The recommendation proceeded safely through Council. The October Council meeting considered a Works Committee recommendation that a 'parking code' be adopted in the form of a plan which would require developers to provide a specified standard of parking space around buildings. Don Kibbler and Jack Mallon spoke against the recommendation; Jack Mallon on the grounds that having a plan could potentially remove discretionary powers from Council, and Don Kibbler on the grounds that merely having policies can discourage developers: 'people see policies and go somewhere else'. The council accepted the recommendation.

These regulation and planning issues gave little joy to those who pursued the business interest in that their wishes were not met, but their potential to raise issues had at least reminded the Council officers that they could seek compromise and so avoid unnecessary damage to business interests. There was no indication that the Council served the whims of business, but the issues did show that business interests were effectively raised for debate, and account was taken of them.

The Local Environmental Plan

The formulation of a planning document for Cowra Shire brought about a major wrangle, in which farmers raised their voices and were heard so clearly that although partly inconclusive, their performance in local politics could give them much satisfaction. This issue occupied in total far more of the time and energy of councillors, Council staff and active citizens than any other. It was the only issue in which a large number of people outside the Council participated. The local representative in State Parliament was quoted (in the *Forbes Advocate* of 23 May, 1985, p. 1) to believe that 'the controversy over the plan for Cowra was the greatest to grip that area since World War II'.

The issue brought about a 'disorganization of legitimacy' (Therborn, 1980:106). Legitimacy was not lost, but the apparatus of the 'people's corporation' was aggressively threatened, and under such threat the old pillars of local government began to crack. The 'people's corporation' temporarily lost its image as a guardian of all interests. It had pursued a policy which was, most charitably, popularly seen to be aligned with an interest of its own and, most deprecatingly, seen as an alien interest which it could not defend. Hence it wilted before what it saw as popular demand. This does not mean, however, that it turned pluralist, for not all interests surfaced in the debate. The Local Environmental Plan (LEP) issue demonstrated more than any other the ability of farmers to raise issues which are large enough to cloud all others.

By clouding other interests it resembled the West Cowra water supply issue in two ways: in that other interests were catered for but not as a product of pluralistic bargaining in the political arena, and in that it became a field of conflict between Council officers and councillors. It established popular rationale and informal precedents for, and hence helped to legitimate, opposition by business. The LEP contributed more to the legitimacy of action aimed at the influence of Council officers than any other issue.

The issue followed implementation of the New South Wales Environmental Planning and Assessment Act (1979), which gave local government power to initiate and develop planning policy, and at the same time, required that councils adopt a process of public consultation (Toon, 1984). A formal procedure was laid down. It included preparation of an environmental study, the exhibition of that study, an invitation for public submissions on the study, preparation of a draft plan with due regard to be given to public submissions on the study and consultations with other government agencies, public exhibition of the draft plan with an invitation for submissions, public hearings if and as requested by a person or persons making a submission, and preparation of a final plan to be forwarded to the Minister for his consideration and ultimate gazettal (Nott, 1982). For Cowra, the process ran aground after the draft plan exhibition stage.

The Act sought a broad approach to planning in which social, economic and environmental factors are considered and plans are subject to a wide range of technical and popular critical input (New South Wales Department of Environment and Planning, 1981). A government statement on the Act concluded: 'For it to fulfil its potential, those responsible for its administration must accept the challenge, and the community must take advantage of the opportunities provided for its involvement' (ibid: 38). The last sentence begs that venerable question: what is the community? It will become evident that in Cowra 'the community' as it operated for this issue consisted largely of farmers. There is much evidence which shows that higher status groups tend to be the participators (Buller and Hoggart, 1986), or that response tends to come from an articulate minority (Newby et al, 1978) so that participation can put power into the hands of 'a gaggle of small groups of committed activists', thereby reinforcing the power of the middle class which is best able to organise (Sandercock, 1978: 125). So it happened in Cowra, but commitment from some people swept many others along, to the extent that a farmer could, not altogether unreasonably, say to me in 1986: 'The whole community stood up and said no!'

The notion of public participation presents a problem to those who wish to retain the 'people's corporation' image. Councillors may believe that they have been elected to make decisions in the interests of the whole community. The proposition that formulation of a plan should be done in consultation with the public denies that belief. If the community which councillors serve is a singular interest, there is no need for the pluralistic planning process which the new Act sought; and if the councillors were trusted by the electors to look after everybody's interests, then why would there be need for further input into decision making? The Act asked councillors to step down from their 'representative' role as it introduced an element of participatory government, which, in Cowra at least, was quite foreign, and as Painter (1973) found elsewhere, was not wanted. Veteran councillors, who had in their careers considered many demands made on the Council and had often decided who to favour, could have found it tempting to look upon participators as just more 'squeaky wheels', especially as one group led the squeaking. Circumstances arose in the course of the participatory planning process in which such a view made sense to councillors, while others, like the farmer quoted above, looked upon their own participation as action resembling revolution.

The issue had a long gestation, prior to its explosion into a political crisis in 1985. At the time of the amalgamation, the Municipality was making its development decisions under an Interim Development Order, but Waugoola had avoided planning and planners. The *Guardian* of 19 September, 1969 (p. 1) reported that Waugoola Council had rejected a request by the State Planning Authority for its representative to address the Council. Cyril Treasure, as Shire President, was quoted: 'Council is not ready for such a move at this stage'. Another councillor was reported to have said: 'Council has enough control now without adding to their worries', but the Shire Engineer appears to have been more positive: he 'could not see why Council did not want the officer to address Council'. The State Planning Authority drew up an Interim Development Order and forwarded it to Waugoola for its consideration in 1974, but the Council told the Authority in 1976 that it did not wish to proceed, and hence no planning instrument was available to it at the time of the amalgamation (Armstrong, 1988).

Waugoola Council was directed by the Minister in 1980 to prepare a Draft Local Environmental Plan. After amalgamation consultants prepared an environmental study (Jackson, Teece, Chesterman, Willis and Partners, 1982) for the new Shire of Cowra. It was made available to the public, and after receipt of only seven submissions, the consultants produced a draft plan. Jim Finnimore later expressed regret (in his Shire Engineer's report to Council of 26 March, 1984) that there had been so little public input at the study stage.

The draft plan touched one particularly sensitive nerve. It included a provision that subdivisions in rural areas be no smaller than forty hectares, in order to preserve commercial viability in the agricultural industry, which was expected to be lost if many small 'hobby' farms developed in place of larger units. During the process of consultation with government authorities, however, this figure was increased to 400 hectares, about twice the average size of existing farms in Cowra Shire. The change was promoted by the Department of Agriculture, which, as mentioned in chapter 3, sought to encourage farm consolidation. The Department of Environment and Planning agreed, but Cowra Shire Council did not. Negotiation brought the minimum rural subdivision down to 200 hectares, close to the Shire average. The draft plan included provision for the Council to permit smaller subdivision if it believed that it was intended for a reasonable purpose, such as a dwelling to be occupied by someone connected with the farm or for a viable small-scale agricultural undertaking. It was not so draconian as to altogether prohibit small subdivision, but it did impose the necessity of obtaining the Council's consent.

The necessity for the Council's consent became the point of contention, being another situation like the Tourist and Development Corporation Garden lease, in which objections were raised against the Council having such power, despite the apparent alternative being a weakening of local power in favour of authorities in Sydney. The draft LEP would, as a planning instrument, transfer power to approve development from Sydney authorities to Cowra Shire Council, but business and farming people chose to oppose the plan, perceiving the power it would vest in the Council to be a threat to rights to alienate their land.

Opposition became apparent soon after the Council decided in October, 1984 to exhibit the draft plan. Council decided to convene three public meetings early in 1985 as means, additional to the submission process, for obtaining public input. The decision to exhibit the draft plan was contentious. Some councillors had reservations about it, feeling that the public would interpret the draft plan as Council's wishes. The *Guardian* of 29 October, 1984 reported that Don Kibbler had said that 'the plan isn't final and it could well be put on us if it is displayed publicly . . . Once we've had it on display I don't think it will matter what we do; I think we will be stuck with it'. Ab Oliver sought to proceed with exhibition, but also to have an addendum to the plan to explain that it did not entirely reflect

Council's views. Bruce Golsby, Col Newton and Neville Pengilly were reported by the *Guardian* to favour proceeding with exhibition, Neville Pengilly saying '... the main contentious issue seems to be the subdivision of land. I don't think we can put it in a better form than what we've got until the people of Cowra and district have their say'.

Events were to indicate value in both standpoints; the public response put weight behind the Council's opposition to the minimum subdivision size at the same time as it indicated an assumption that the plan was final and immutable. Don Kibbler's view, which was shared by Harold Upston (and judging by later events, other councillors also, including Jack Mallon and Stephen Bell) indicated that the farmers' wishes were anticipated by some, and may at least have been considered favourably to some extent by all on the Council.

The first shots were fired even before Ab Oliver announced exhibition of the draft plan on 3 December. A local real estate agent spotted the minimum subdivision clause and alerted other town businesses which had an interest in land development. The *Guardian* ran a page one headline on 12 November: 'Disaster for Rural Areas'. The article continued:

> The spokesman [for a group described as 'concerned residents'] said the plan would have a dramatic effect on residents' lifestyles especially in the rural areas of the shire. 'Council would have almost complete control over land and its usage. We are concerned that this plan will be a vehicle for further environmental retentions on farming. It would almost stop dead development in the rural zone in the shire. The plan gives complete power to a few council officers who have never had to make a profit and manage their own business ... These clauses give council staff and bureaucrats the right to make decisions affecting our lifestyles without any consultation or regard for our personal preferences or tastes. The LEP puts concentrated power in the hands of academics'.

This article and a response from Bruce Golsby indicate the agenda of the debate. Bruce's response appeared in the *Guardian* of 14 November:

> The spokesman of the residents said 'We will be beholden to two or three officers of Council and where control is centralised it could create an atmosphere conducive to graft and corruption in years to come'.
> Who do they think makes the decisions now?
> If any ratepayer is unhappy with the treatment they receive then all they have to do is contact one of the councillors...

The 'people's corporation' image had been blown away as the rhetoric focused on a threat from within: an autocracy of bureaucrats. The threat was not the minimum subdivision provision in the plan as much as anticipation of how it would be applied. This is consistent with, but not so apparent in, opposition to planning expressed by farmer organisations, seeking reduction of government intervention in land use decision-making (Dick, 1986a; Livestock and Grain Producers Association (LGPA), n.d.). In Cowra it appeared that some people at least were lacking faith in their elected representatives to look after their interests, against what they saw as a flowing tide of government intervention, personified by local government officials. Some people saw local officials under the thumb of State Government. A letter published in the *Guardian* of 15 February reminded electors that they had 'elected the councillors to protect [their] interests in this area and they need support to avoid a 'takeover' by some city based department', in apparent ignorance of the devolution aspect of the planning legislation which would operate after the plan was established. Power of officials became the issue.

A group consisting of a solicitor, a real estate agent and a surveyor, having been alerted to the undesired plan, pre-empted the Council's programme of public consultation by calling a public meeting. The meeting was to be held on 4 February, 1985. The *Guardian* of 1 February reported that some farmers had been delegated to contact others in order to urge attendance at the meeting. On the day of the meeting the *Guardian* published a letter from the local representative in the New South Wales Parliament, also urging attendance.

The meeting was a great success. On 6 February the *Guardian* reported on page one that more than 500 people attended and 'overwhelmingly showed their support to dramatically change' the plan. 'Although there was huge support to have the plan thrown out altogether it was explained that the only avenue open to the meeting was for individual submissions to be made to have the plan changed.' The *Guardian* described the crowd as 'largely hostile to the Council'. The meeting elected a committee which opened an office on Saturday mornings in an empty shop in the main street to help people make submissions.

Meanwhile the Council arranged the first of three public meetings. Jim Finnimore was quoted in the *Guardian* of 15 February (p. 1): 'the more people that participate at the meeting the better'. He need not have worried, for it attracted 600 people, and was a stormy affair. On 22 February the *Guardian*'s page one headline read: 'Angry LEP Opponents Face Councillors at Fiery Meeting'. The Council (on 27 February) debated withdrawal of the plan before the second public meeting had occurred, but despite opposition from Don Kibbler, Stephen Bell, George Noble, Jack Mallon and Harold Upston, resolved to continue, and formed a committee to guide the progress of the plan. The Council's public meetings continued the earlier success of the protest leaders, reminiscent of the observed tendency of public meetings to be dominated by one group (Melotte, 1983), and in doing so made the farmers' interests, and their professed association with development, very prominent.

Other groups commenced agitation. The Chamber of Commerce discussed the plan and called its own public meeting (*Cowra Guardian*, 18 March). It sought more industrial land in the town. A meeting was convened in the village of Woodstock, attracting eighty-four people, and was addressed by members of the original protest group (ibid.). Concern arose about the plan's placing what they felt to be the precincts of the village in a rural zone, thereby constraining development. Committees were also formed in West Cowra and the villages of Gooloogong and Billimari to express similar concern.

In terms of submissions received, some 819, the public consultation process was also a great success. It was undoubtedly helped by the 'Concerned Citizens Committee' office in the main street where many people took its submission forms, and the similar activities of the Woodstock group. The villages and the rural areas were most demonstrative, the rural areas accounting for almost half the submissions from individuals. The number of submissions received from rural areas equalled about fourteen per cent of the size of the rural population; those from villages about twenty-five per cent. Mulyan and Taragala made fewest submissions. That is somewhat ironic, given that the air pollution problem in Taragala, which had not at that time been solved, was a product of a planning decision, and also that the Chamber of Commerce was pushing for industrial zoning in part of Mulyan. Only one submission complained about industrial pollution nuisance in Taragala. Among all submissions from individuals (except those from Woodstock and Billimari which resembled petitions, being worded as recommended by local committees concerned about zoning), the fear of power in the hands of bureaucrats was the most popular point, being made by twenty per cent. Another nineteen per cent were concerned about constraints on development. The third most popular point was lack of consultation, made by fourteen per cent.

Many submissions showed fear of power in the hands of people who were not thought competent to wield it, based on an assumption that power would be placed in officers' hands, in apparent denial or disregard of the Council's procedure of not allowing officers to reject development applications before consideration by the Council. A letter to the *Guardian*, published on 25 January, 1985 (p. 2), asserted that 'history shows that the vast majority of demands by bureaucrats to control agriculture have been costly failures'.

The issue aroused moral indignation at the prospect of growing bureaucratic power. The public submissions made such assertions drawing on property rights, and expressed the belief that the councillors were irrelevant to the decision making process. Some submissions pointed out that the Council officers may have no long term interest in the development of the Shire. Others even suggested that the officers may use unfair tactics to pursue their own vested interests. This latter aspect should not be overstated. No specific accusations were made, nor, to my knowledge, were there any grounds for making such allegations. The point is that some people anticipated the possibility of such grounds arising.

Other submissions depicted the plan as part of a broader socialist conspiracy into which their council, what might have been the 'peoples' corporation' of their image, seemed to have been swallowed. This threat was, perhaps, suggested to them by the plan's apparent regulation of the private alienation of land. Some people who made submissions put a view which resembled some expressed in the course of the building regulations debates: the plan proposed regulation which would strangle freedom of enterprise and constrict market forces. The desire to maintain freedom of market forces was expressed as the basis of the farmers' case in the LEP issue at a meeting of the LGPA held in October, 1985.[1]

At its meeting of 1 April, the Council accepted its LEP Committee's recommendations to defer consideration of the plan for rural areas until it had been revised in the light of consultation with interested parties, including the protest committee and the LGPA. The *Guardian* editorial of 24 April implied the poor condition of the 'people's corporation' image: 'It appears that Cowra's draft LEP has taken the prize as the most divisive issue in this town's history ... councillors had faced residents at an open meeting at which debate was permitted ... [It was] a salutary lesson to councillors that they were not universally liked.'

For some of the councillors, the authority which the 'people's corporation' bestowed was hard to relinquish, and their attempts to retain it were seen to exacerbate the conflict. After a public meeting in June, 1985, the *Guardian* (14 June, p. 1) reported that a councillor had not helped discussion by saying to participants: 'You have been pretty lucky really ... the councillors and the committee did not have to justify themselves to anyone'.

It implied that such a comment may have further concentrated attention on the councillors and their appearance of collusion with bureaucrats. A clash between Councillor Harold Upston and Shire Clerk Neville Armstrong at the April Council meeting served to focus attention on the councillor and officer dimension of the issue. Ab Oliver, as President, had threatened Harold Upston with suspension from the Chamber. The *Guardian* editorial of 24 April continued:

> It seems difficult to believe that [Ab's] incredible patience was tried to such an extent that he threatened a councillor with dismissal from the meeting. Again the incident arose from the draft LEP. Are some Council officers out of favour with the community? ... Are some Council officers out of favour with some of the councillors? ... Are voters disappointed by the performance of any of the Councillors or the council as a whole?

The editorial went on to suggest that an unrealistic view of the Council's powers, implicitly with respect to State authorities, was abroad, and that

The politics of development 103

this may help to explain the failure of the Council as a 'people's corporation'.

Its failure did not, however, release a flourish of pluralism. The sources of submissions, and the increasing concentration on the councillor-officer conflict further narrowed the issue around the pursuit of the interests of business and farming by effectively smothering a potential point in the public participation process in which the issue may have widened to include, for example, the Taragala air pollution problem, or social planning matters and related local aspirations. Virtually all planning matters other than the minimum size of rural subdivisions, zoning for residential growth in West Cowra and the villages, and the provision of industrial zones in the town, were non-issues. The Chamber of Commerce's bid for industrial zoning in Mulyan was rejected by the Council, on the grounds of the potential effect on residential amenity, without the residents who would have been affected taking any part in discussion. The farmers had formed the body of the protest movement and their concerns attracted much sympathy. Although the originators of the protest were not farmers, their success was largely a product of the passionate support of the farmers. The farmers may not have started the issue, but they made it significant and they made it largely their own. The other players were minor and largely obscured.

The urban component of the plan was adopted by the Council in June, 1985 (*Cowra Guardian*, 26 June), but the rural plan made no further progress, and even regressed, in continuing negotiations among the Council, the LGPA, the protest committee and the Departments of Agriculture and Environment and Planning through 1985 and 1986. The Council failed to gain the permission of the Department of Environment and Planning to exhibit a revised draft of the rural plan. The local victory had been won, but subdivision and development consent remained a sticking point, because of the power it was thought to give to bureaucrats.

The farmers gained complete removal of the minimum subdivision provision from the Council's draft, and it was accepted by the Department of Environment and Planning. This was a substantial achievement, but it was not all they sought. They wanted deletion of the consent requirement altogether. This view, which indicated a desire to remove from the plan a provision which would increase the Council's development control powers, was put most forcefully by Harold Upston with strong support from Jack Mallon, and a sympathetic opinion voiced by Don Kibbler. The Council rejected it, and forwarded a revised draft to the Department of Environment and Planning. The Council also rejected a move by the same councillors to refer the issue back to the LEP Committee. That issue was raised (at the June, 1986, meeting) after the Department declined to approve the draft. This time it was raised by Jack Mallon and Stephen Bell with support from Harold Upston and Don Kibbler. The same councillors raised the consultation issue again at the July meeting after a compromise had been reached with the Department of Environment and Planning (later to be rejected by the Department of Agriculture). The councillors' move was a response to a request for consultation from the LGPA.

The point of contention in the Council turned to the Council's role, focusing on both its functions as leader in the 'people's corporation' image and as regulator. The Council was divided between those who denied both, that is, believing that it should defer to opinions expressed elsewhere and should not regulate (Jack Mallon and others), and those who felt that the Council had a responsibility to lead and exercise powers to regulate beneficently. The latter views were expressed by Tim West at the June meeting when he suggested that the Council may be seen to be 'abrogating its responsibilities' and by Cyril Treasure at the July meeting when he said: 'In my long experience I never saw a Council attempt to obstruct that which a person wanted in rural development ... All you have to do is get Council's consent and so-help-me-Bob no council will refuse subdivision for a family'.

The farmers had brought the 'people's corporation' into doubt and even disrepute. The LEP had furthered the development of a particular ground of conflict, that between councillors and officers, as the councillors who supported the 'people's corporation' were seen to be supporting the officers. The farmers had the resources not only to win a substantial local victory, but also to threaten the apparatus of domination when they felt that it threatened to dominate them.

The decline of the railway

Like the early stages of the LEP process, the decline of the railway industry in Cowra did not become an issue to the extent that one could expect until farmers and the 'people's corporation' found their mutual interests threatened. After recognising that the decline of the railway service may indirectly place a cost burden on the Council, some councillors attempted to defend it. At the same time some farmers found the service withdrawal plans of the State Rail Authority (SRA) to threaten their interests also. Like the LEP, this put the Council with the farmers in opposition to the State Government, but unlike the LEP, the Council had an independent view to push in its 'people's corporation' role. It was pushing the farmers' interests because it was agreeing with the farmers, and could look after itself at the same time. The issue arose during a long period of decline in rail service and consequent decline in rail employment with loss of income to the town. That, however, had not gained such prominence as an issue.

The issue which did arise, to become known as the 'Option Three' debate, was first mentioned in Cowra Shire Council at the meeting of 22 September, 1986. Neville Pengilly, referring to press reports (such as Dick, 1986b, which anticipated opposition from local government) about

SRA plans, asked the President (Cyril Treasure) if any of the railway lines in the Shire were to close. Cyril replied that the Council had not been notified, and Council resolved without debate to ask the SRA about its intentions. The SRA replied, indicating that branch lines may close, but decisions to do so would only be made 'after detailed consideration and discussion with all parties involved in the storage, handling and transport of grain' (SRA letter to Cowra Shire, on Council Agenda for 24 November meeting).

At the 24 November Council meeting, Ab Oliver commented on the SRA reply, pointing out that cost savings to farmers would be admirable, but cost burdens incurred by Council due to increased road damage by grain-carrying trucks would be undesirable. Bruce Golsby felt that rail had served well for a long time and there was no reason why it should not continue to do so. Don Kibbler spoke as the Council's representative on the Lachlan Regional Transport Committee (a committee of local government, private transport firms and rail unionists set up initially to counter any elimination of rural passenger services and co-ordinate such services in the Lachlan Valley). He said that Committee was very concerned about potential damage to roads and intended to speak to the Transport Minister. Council resolved to reply to the SRA indicating concern, and asked Engineer Jim Finnimore to report to the Works Committee on the implications for Cowra Shire. Jim reported that the SRA had added the 'third option' to its range of plans, which unlike its predecessors, indicated the roads to be affected. For Cowra the traffic growth was to occur on the main highway through the Shire, so most of the additional maintenance cost would have been incurred by the State Department of Main Roads.

The SRA convened a meeting in Cowra on 20 January, 1987 to consult local opinion, and found that farmers were opposed to the plan because it threatened to raise costs for some of them. It included closure of parts of the branch lines to Eugowra and Grenfell and all of the line from Cowra to Blayney (Crutchett, 1987). The last mentioned had been the main route to Sydney until the little remaining traffic on it had been diverted through Harden from mid-1986. This would have made Cowra a railway backwater. Cyril Treasure, as Shire President, called a meeting with the Chamber of Commerce. The *Cowra Guardian* of 2 February (p. 1) reported that he was campaigning to encourage use of rail transport by business, and that the Council was using rail exclusively.

Cyril's raising of the implied loss of jobs and associated economic damage to the town was the first mention of this factor in local political circles for thirty years, despite steady decline in railway employment in Cowra over that period. This was confirmed by my reading of the *Guardian* and conversations with a long-serving councillor, a senior railway employee and a long-time member of the Chamber of Commerce. With 205 employees in 1954, the railway's permanent labour force was about the size of that of the Edgell vegetable cannery, those two being the town's biggest employers. By 1986 the railway had declined to about one third of that level of employment.[2]

The period of steepest decline in railway employment, 1954 to 1961, was also a period of local political agitation in support of the railway. By 1956 awareness of change was abroad in Cowra. The *Guardian* of 19 June (p. 7) reported that a councillor had suggested a role for the Council in maintaining Cowra's railway industry. He was quoted: 'I ask that question [whether Council is to act against railway decline] in the firm belief that this Council has a definite role to play if it is going to preserve the progress of the town and not allow it to be forced into some secondary role of a ranch line backwater'.

Leo Lynch supported this view. The *Guardian* of 3 August (p. 14) reported a debate between Lynch and Mayor Whitby, in which Whitby said that the railway service was declining due to loss of patronage because its trains were 'feebly slow'. Nevertheless, he and the Waugoola Shire President made a joint appeal to the Railway Department for a better passenger service (*Cowra Guardian*, 21 September, 1956). This activity proceeded during the following year. Whitby wrote another appeal to the Railway Department, following a request from Lynch (*Cowra Guardian*, 27 August 1957). The matter was raised again in the Council in December 1957, by Lynch with further support from the alderman quoted above. Whitby was reported to have agreed, saying 'they should go out and look for business' (*Cowra Guardian*, 6 December, p. 10). It seems unlikely that these appeals had a substantial long term impact, but the issue of declining railway employment had been raised in the local political arena as an issue of general local concern, as a valid matter for the agenda of the 'people's corporation'.

The local quiescence of the issue for thirty years cannot be attributed to local ignorance. Plans to replace steam locomotives were reported on at least five occasions between 1959 and 1967. The *Guardian* of 12 December, 1969 announced that five sidings on the lines radiating from Cowra were to close, twelve having been closed in the previous two years. On 21 August, 1970 it reported that fourteen platforms on these lines were to close. Between 1970 and 1975 ten stations within Cowra Shire were closed (Ryan, 1986). Rail passenger services to Grenfell and Eugowra ceased in 1974 (ibid.). On 20 September, 1974 the Guardian's page one headline read 'Rail Cuts Hit Cowra Hardest'. The article went on to say that Cowra could lose one million dollars of annual revenue. When the overnight passenger service to Sydney was eliminated the Municipal Council 'expressed concern' at the loss to the Minister for Transport (*Cowra Guardian*, 11 March, 1975, p. 1).

The railway staff tried to tell the people of their locality that it was losing an industry. On 14 January, 1969 the *Guardian* quoted a statement from a union leader that another town had lost business to the value of $100 000 per year as railway employment had declined. A meeting of rail unions with the Cowra Chamber of Commerce was held in 1974. A union representative at the meeting was reported by the *Guardian* (16 August, p. 1) to have said that 'the meeting decided to make the people of Cowra aware of the amount of money to be lost by the town through closure of the branch lines'. Similar pleas were heard in 1985 when closure of the Cowra Freight Centre was rumoured. The *Guardian* page one headline of 29 March read 'Town Will Lose Millions'. The editorial was supportive, finding rail cuts to have 'staggering effects' on towns. The rail unions were trying very hard to make people aware of the loss, but apart from an unsuccessful 1980 Shire election candidate stating that he wished to encourage use of rail services, the issue did not arise in the local political arena until 1986–87.

As in the LEP issue, farmers then demonstrated a capacity to raise an issue, which in the case of the railway decline was helped by the Council seeking to defend its corporate interests. The 1986–87 railway decline issue did not need prompting from the railway employees. The railway unions' attempts to create awareness of railway decline in recent years may have indirectly helped to motivate those who stimulated the issue, but they did not precipitate it. The issue was not raised by railway employees defending their interests.

Conclusion: councillors, officers and ideologies

Two features are prominent among the issues related above. One is the conflict between the Council officers and councillors, as found in 'Spatial Politics', and the other is the quiescence of non-business and non-farm people, except when their interests were expressed as ratepayers' interests. In the 'people's corporation' the only legitimate interests are those which are seen to be congruent with those of the entire locality. Councillors found it easy to relate farm, business and ratepayer interests to those of the entire population, but did not so readily make this connection for railway employees, and they set local interests far apart from what they perceived to be a malevolent bureaucracy.

The perception of a conflict between bureaucratic and local interests structured development politics. This was evident in development regulation matters, and most obvious in the LEP issue where opposition to bureaucracy swept other issues aside. Bureaucratisation provided the main point of discussion about the relation between planning and development. The participation apparatus required by planning law was designed to obviate the potential unfairness produced by bureaucratic procedures, of the kind observed to defuse actual or potential spatial political issues. Farmers were so strong that they were able to quash the procedures without help from the legislation. When they saw the bureaucratic procedure going awry, farmers were able to commandeer the apparatus. Their 'coup' had wide, although not unlimited, public support. Moreover, the identification of the farming interest with the locality interest was not questioned, other than implicitly by those councillors who sought to defend the 'people's corporation'. The issue split the Council into two ideological camps: those councillors who retained the 'people's corporation' image and those who believed that the image had been, or may have been about to be, corrupted by bureaucratic power.

The railway employees could barely manage what came easily to the farmers: raising their interests to the level of a general local concern. They could not call on the ratepayer interest, as non-business and non-farm people had done in the Tourist and Development Corporation matters. No belief system, like those which associated farming and business with a general local interest, was available to them. The onus was on them, as it was for the people of Taragala in the air pollution non-issue, to provide evidence, which they attempted to do. Unlike the Taragala people they could reasonably claim to be defending a unitary local interest: income to the town. Their argument, however, failed to arouse concern among those who had direct access to the political arena for a long period, during which much damage was done to their cause and their material and personnel resources were depleted. When railway employee interests were raised they were mentioned as a question of declining status for the town, as in the statement quoted above by the alderman who supported Leo Lynch, or were mentioned defensively, as in a *Guardian* report of 2 February, 1987 (p. 7): 'Councillor Treasure said the SRA employees would of course be looking after their own interests as it meant their jobs and homes if the rail lines closed. He said they would be stupid not to protest'.

This presents a contrast with the words of those councillors who opposed development and building regulation without feeling a need to justify the actions or complaints of those whose interests they were defending. Development issues offer evidence of substantial ideological resources available to farmers, but meagre resources other than the ratepayer interest as a principle available to non-farm and non-business groups.

Notes
1 The bureaucracy was also seen to be attacking the personal connection between farmers and their land. As Rose et al. (1976) showed, this personal connection and its 'natural' rightfulness are emphasised among farmers, while the productive function of land is downplayed. Many farmers not only anticipated that they were to be told what to do by people who were not qualified to do so, but also feared that their personal property was to be appropriated and their rights infringed.
2 Cowra's Locomotive Depot was the largest source of employment among the branches of the railway service. My conversations with two retired Cowra railway employees indicated that they felt that the Depot's decline had started during the 1930s. It had its largest number of staff (125) in 1924, but in the late 1940s was still busy. The *Cowra Guardian* of

23 December, 1949 (p. 3) reported that the railway was the busiest it had been 'for years' with heavy traffic in coal, and passengers for the migrant camp. The coal traffic originated at Lithgow and went to Victoria to fuel that State's locomotives. It was significant enough for the *Guardian* (19 September, 1952, p. 1) to report its decline, and an anticipated associated loss of jobs at the Cowra Locomotive Depot, which serviced the locomotives on the coal trains. That was the first post-war sign of change.

Decline in rail services and the replacement of steam with diesel locomotives loomed in the early 1950s, and these factors together eventually brought substantial loss of railway employment. But it was the diesel locomotives of Victorian rather than New South Wales railways which first threatened the Cowra Depot by reducing demand for the coal that moved through Cowra. Diesel locomotives were not used around Cowra until the mid 1960s, when the depot had about ten steam locomotives. In 1967 it had just one locomotive and two rail motors, all of which had been lost by 1982, along with need for servicing facilities and staff (Ryan, 1986). From the mid-1950s until the present, passenger as well as goods train traffic declined steadily (ibid.). It was this decline, rather than any sudden impact of introduction of diesel locomotives to Cowra, which brought down the level of railway employment.

7

Gender, race and human services

Restricting political analysis to issues surrounding property and development services would ignore people in whose interests human as well as, or rather than, property services may lie. In Cowra, such people include women and Aborigines, as they may potentially be served by local government, and as their interests may occasionally be pursued in the local political arena. Serving such interests implies an element of redistribution of local resources along a social dimension. Moves to broaden local government's functions into human services would also necessitate action to deviate from tradition and challenge property interests at the same time. Such challenge would have to, implicitly if not explicitly, raise the functions of local government as an issue. People expressing non-property interests may face a substantial task in raising an issue, when the 'people's corporation' sees its corporate interest best served by staying clear of non-traditional functions. Non-decision, within the property services tradition, is a decision to confine services to the property kind.

Human services provide contrast with property services but do not imply an economic redistribution role. Local government is unlikely to take on income or wealth redistributional objectives on its own as long as its revenue is derived from rates, for, as Jones (1977) explained, a council which rated the rich so heavily as to enable significant redistribution to the poor would fear encouraging the rich to move elsewhere. Rating, being based on property values rather than income, can be regressive taxation (Mowbray, 1984), especially among the elderly whose homes and land have appreciated while their incomes have declined post-retirement. Local government may, however, take on administration of the redistributive functions of the other spheres of government, and therefore acquire policies which are seen to be redistributive. Moreover, the popular labelling of human services as welfare, and their image in the perspective provided by a conservative ideology, imbues redistributional connotations. Those connotations are implicitly prominent in the rhetoric of councillors.

Cowra Shire is one of many rural councils which have been reluctant to offer human services (Secretariat to the Joint Officers' Committee of the Local Government Ministers' Conference, 1980). Some metropolitan councils embarked on human services programmes of their own around the time of World War II, pushed by a very small number of female councillors (Sinclair, 1987). However, local government in Australia showed little enthusiasm for human services until the 1970s (Office of Local Government, 1987). Councils are free to decide, or not decide to provide them (Elliffe, 1987).

As entry into human services implies an expansion of the organisation, it may seem curious that the 'people's corporation' does not seek to do so. Colebatch and Degeling (1986) pointed out that council executive officers may not want expansion into areas that they might not find easy to control. In addition, some may see deviation from traditional functions as a potential drain on council resources, and consequently, a threat to the resources of their existing departments. Councils' reluctance to take on a human service role cannot, however, be attributed to organisational inertia. Such inertia may be important, given the influence which council officers can have over council affairs through their control of information flows, but the ability of councillors to raise and successfully push the human service provision issue has been evident in the work of Sinclair (1987) and Wills (1985). As Camasso and Moore (1985) found in the United States, rural people tend to favour minimising government intervention in what is seen as welfare activity. Nevertheless, even in rural areas, if a powerful group wants human services, it can get them. Without such a group, and as long as human services remain an 'optional extra' for local government, they will be avoided.

Women, interests and human services

The interests of women may be served by local government taking on a human service role. The human services provided by local government are largely of the caring kind: child care and help for the elderly such as 'meals on wheels'. Such services reduce the caring burden which falls heavily on women. The ideology which gives domestic caring responsibilities to women is strong in rural Australia, and it is associated with the reluctance among rural local government to adopt human services which many of its male members would see as women's responsibility to their families. The association between these phenomena, by suggesting that women are ideologically placed in the home, and kept there in small part at least by local government non-decision making, suggests local government to be an instrument of oppression. It was a source of frustration for some Cowra women, because while the ideological climate is conducive to maintenance of women's domestic caring role, the caring tradition turns the attention of some women keen on civic service towards the possibility of such a role for local government, only to be turned back by a different ideology which is just as firmly set in the rural ideological climate.

The literature on gender roles in the rural context focuses sharply on relations based on family farm agriculture, and reveals several contradictions. Poiner (1979) describes the historical origins of rural women's pervasive domestic role model, but as she implies, it is an incomplete picture of the role of women in family farming, because, although the ideal place for women is in the home, they are often to be found contradicting the domestic image by working with machinery and animals around the farm. Demands on women for such work may be increasing as economic conditions for farming decline (Austin and Marshall, 1985). Even where women perform the same tasks as men, however, role differentiation is still seen by male employers who prefer women because they adopt a more caring attitude to animals (Masson, 1986:13).

The ideological allocation of caring responsibilities to women has a real counterpart in Cowra Shire. Women in Cowra are more likely than men to anticipate an obligation to care for an aged parent or relative, and family members, who are likely to be women, take a substantial share of caring responsibilities (Gray, 1987a). There are demographic grounds for suggesting that the caring burden on women will increase disproportionately, due to gender differentials in morbidity and life expectancy, and the effects of population ageing in terms of numbers of people involved in caring are likely to be greater in rural areas and small country towns than in large urban centres (ibid.).

The ideology of the domestic, caring role for women, and the demands placed upon them, combine in a climate in which female employment and acquisition of skills and responsibilities have become commonplace. The change which has occurred in female labour force participation since World War II along with the continuation of concentration of female employment in commerce and service industries may have had two effects: strengthening awareness among women of their potential beyond domesticity, and with the persistence of the domestic ideal, creation of tension when expectations of domestic service and income generation outside home and farm collide. Women are showing their interest in family problems outside their own homes, and a willingness to speak on social issues, making caring a public issue.

Given the power relations between men and women in rural situations (as discussed by Dempsey, 1990; James, 1982 and Poiner, 1990), the undervaluation of women's farm work (Reimer, 1986), and their financial dependency (Dempsey, 1987), it would seem unlikely that many women are relieved of caring tasks by their menfolk. In this situation it would be reasonable to expect women to seek to help with essential caring tasks, and to seek careers in which the caring role is maintained. Relief from some of the caring burden, and their socialisation and expanding labour force role in service industry, place human services by government among the political interests of women.

Women on Council

While women in local government have steered its functions towards human service activity, the issue of furthering women's interests through local government is broader than concern about numbers of women representatives. Indeed, the ideologies of councillors regardless of sex may be a more important factor, as there is no necessity for men to follow the traditional property service path exclusively, nor will all women always pursue human services. Nevertheless, women's interests are more likely to be represented by women.

This point should not direct research back to the individualistic emphasis of the elitist-pluralist debate. That could lead to circularity, as implied by Bokemeier and Tait (1980) who explained an increasing local political presence of women in terms of institutional movement into areas of traditional concern to women, in which female leadership is acceptable. Certainly women elected as representatives are in a better position than others to move local government into human services, and a human service role for local government would be likely to attract attention from women who are likely to use the service, but explanation of gender power relations at the local political level is best approached by treating the matter of representation separately, and as background to the more fundamental problem of realisation of interests.

Women councillors in Australia have grown steadily in numbers since the early 1970s, having been very few prior to the 1970s, although the first was elected in 1919 (Sinclair, 1987). They are, however, still a minority, and many councils have no women members. All-male councils have been more common in rural areas (Burdess, 1981).

The status position of women and its associated processes help to explain this situation. Dempsey (1986a, 1990) analysed a process of social closure in which men successfully excluded women from community decision making, greatly assisted by a prevailing belief that men are better suited to leadership than women. This accords with the picture of Australian rural communities developed through Wild (1974a), Rew (1978), and Poiner (1990), in which women and their local organisations and activities are placed in a back-stage position.

Other factors must, however, be added to this picture. Women do operate the status system, and as shown by James (1979) can do so more effectively than men. Many women hold managerial and professional positions which command respect, even around the male bastions of agriculture such as farms and research establishments. In Cowra, several successful main street businesses were run by women. I recollect a farmer telling me that his wife's business was making more money than his farm.

The Cowra Chamber of Commerce elected a woman to its presidency for the first time in 1985. The important point is not that women are in an inferior status position, but that when they enter local government they are entering an institution constructed by men which was not designed to serve the interests of women, and which operates in an ideological climate more conducive to the interests of men.

Cowra Shire Council in 1986 had one woman councillor, Barbara Bennett. Barbara was first elected to the Municipal Council in 1971, and served until her retirement in 1987, including five years as Mayor and three years as Deputy President of Cowra Shire. Barbara was one of two women elected to the Municipal Council in 1971. The other served two terms before standing down at the 1977 election. Both women espoused women's interests, and they were instrumental in the establishment of a women's rest centre offering short term child care in the main street.

Nomination of two women for the Council in 1971 created headlines in the *Guardian* of 27 August (p. 1), which went on to illustrate a male perspective on women's service in local government:

> Both women are mothers and housewives who admit to being in their forties. They say it is only at this time of their lives with the children less of a full time problem, that they can spare the hours necessary to become involved in council work. While confessing to being tyros as far as that is concerned, they say it is time that the woman's point of view was represented in what is after all the town's biggest and most vital industry. The fact of being the first women in history to nominate for the Cowra Council is not important, they say, since women are now involved in the highest levels of government.

I found Barbara to be a caring person who was keen to return something of value to the locality in which her family had prospered for many generations. She and her family had a long history of participation in local service organisations. To that extent, and to the extent that she had become free of child-raising responsibilities, she resembled Sinclair's (1987) most common female rural shire councillor, but unlike that type, Barbara did not nominate to substitute for her husband or another male. She saw it as an extension of her own service career.

Barbara brought substantial resources to the Council, helped by her business activities and her consequent association with business people. She was well in touch with local affairs, helped in the past by participation in the *Guardian* as well as her period as Mayor. She was also prominent in the Tourist and Development Corporation. During 1986, Cowra Shire Council did not operate as the exclusivist male elitist club, so often typified as local government, which would find it very easy to exclude women. Barbara had sufficient resources to resist exclusion, and moreover, the conflict atmosphere described in the previous two chapters was not conducive to unitary male exclusivist tactics. She was able to play a role in local politics, without such heavy constraints on information and interaction found by Rew (1978) and Sinclair (1987) to be placed on women councillors. This does not, however, mean that women's interests were put to the fore, and it certainly does not imply fertile ground for acceptance of human services, as Barbara was part of a council and a locality which operated in a rural ideological climate.

Human services in Cowra Shire

Human services were provided in Cowra Shire, but Cowra Shire Council had very little to do with their provision. They came from State and Federal Government and local voluntary agencies. The Council made money available by way of grants and loans to local projects, such as facilities for the care of children and the elderly, but it had avoided any on-going commitment. This means that human services were a non-issue in two senses: in that there was no manifest lack of them such as one would expect to precipitate howling demands, and in that the Council had largely kept any such demands off the local political agenda. Bureaucratic apparatus (this time that of the State and Federal Governments) had produced a reasonable level of service, so minimising discontent, but at the same time not realising maximum potential local benefit.

The history of child care facilities in Cowra, as related by Williams (1986), provides a good illustration of the roles the Council had, and had not, taken on. The first child care centre was conducted in the Salvation Army Hall, which was used by a group of mothers who co-operated to care for each other's children during the early 1950s. The group grew, and in 1956 decided to borrow money to establish its own centre. It did so, and the Municipal Council donated land for the building. The first trained teacher was employed in the late 1960s, financed by service charges and State Government subsidies. Around this time the building was becoming inadequate. In 1970 a block of land was set aside by the State Lands Department for a new centre. In 1975 the committee applied unsuccessfully to the State and Federal Governments for funding for the new building. By 1976 the space needed was seen to have grown, so a larger block of land was sought and obtained from the State Government. In 1978 the Municipal Council's Health Surveyor drew up plans for a building, but again grant applications to government were rejected.

After a public meeting in August 1978, the Municipal and Shire Councils decided to offer grants, and in doing so changed the course of events. One of the leaders of the committee told me that this support had a powerful effect on the prospects for obtaining State grants. In 1980, the project received a grant of $80 000 from the State Government to add to $35 000 from the Shire and Municipal Councils and $25 000 raised by volunteers. Cowra obtained a child care centre, which in 1986 was still run as a co-operative caring for about 275 children each week. Local government had made a substantial contribution, but had not made any continuing commitment. The commitment it did make confirms that council support can be very important to local organisations, and it suggests that if substantial support from local government had been on-going from the beginning, or if a council had taken on responsibility for child care, the larger centre may have been established earlier. That, however, is speculation. But it does reinforce the point that it was in the interests of women to obtain Council support and the observation that the Councils did not provide on-going support.

Two matters arose in the Council in 1986 which illustrate resistance to supporting human services among councillors, and the means of subduing related issues. One concerned a proposal for a vacation play centre for school children, and the other arose over accommodation for the Cowra Neighbourhood and Information Centre.

The former matter surfaced when thirty-eight residents asked the Council to set up a vacation play centre in conjunction with the State Department of Sport and Recreation. The Finance Committee adopted Clerk Neville Armstrong's recommendation 'that Council not conduct vacation play centres and the petitioners be advised that Council does not consider such to be its function nor does it consider funds are available for conduct of such centres' (Cowra Shire Council agenda, 24 February, 1986). This position was confirmed by the full Council without debate.

The *Guardian* reacted with a page one headline: 'No Discussion on Play Centres, not council's function – Clerk' (28 February, 1986), and an editorial on page 2 (its editor was a woman) which began: 'It is becoming very difficult to determine those issues which will be considered by Cowra Shire Council as important or worthy of discussion. In a democracy it could be said that those matters brought before government by the people have a certain priority ...'. The page one article directed its wrath at the Clerk. It reported that he had told the Finance Committee that a vacation play centre had been held by the Municipal Council fifteen years previously, and that it had been terminated due to lack of patronage. The *Guardian* further quoted Neville Armstrong:

> 'In other areas where the council employs a Social Worker, Youth Worker or some similarly titled person, the organisation of such a centre is possible ... No such officer is employed by this council.
> No financial provision has been made for the conduct of such a centre ...'
> Mr Armstrong said should the committee be interested in pursuing this matter, inquiries could be made.
> He asked if that was the case then which department of the council would be responsible for further investigation and conduct.

Neville sought a decision which could have had substantial long term policy implications. The last paragraph could reasonably have been inferred by the councillors to mean that a suitable officer, like those listed, would have had to be employed. Discussion might therefore have raised a major issue which would have been difficult to push, and could have opened a 'can of worms'. Neville opened the door to the issue, and left the councillors to decide, or not decide, to walk through it. They chose not to. The editorial turned its attention to the councillors:

> Not one councillor questioned the fact that current information [on assistance from the Department of Sport and Recreation] was not provided [by the Clerk to Finance Committee]. Not one councillor asked that the matter be further investigated. Not one councillor felt that 38 local people who had taken the trouble to prepare a petition were entitled to better treatment ... The people have a right to a reasonable hearing and a result, even if negative, which is at least researched and discussed. (*Cowra Guardian*: ibid.).

The petitioners eventually obtained their play centre, with funding from the State Department of Sport and Recreation through the Council, but, importantly, without discussion in the Council. The funding employed the necessary staff. Arrangements were made in discussions among Neville Armstrong, Cyril Treasure and representatives of the petitioners. The resulting play centre was a great success. The matter did not again surface on the Council's agendas, and was not raised by a councillor. So another 'human service' had been provided, despite the Council's reluctance to initiate and carry it, and human services stayed off Cowra Shire Council's agenda.

The *Guardian* of 28 February also reported another human services non-issue. On page 3 it commenced an article: 'Cowra Shire Council will again tell the Cowra Community Information and Neighbourhood Centre Committee that at the present time council has no space available for them'.

The Community Information and Neighbourhood Centre (or Neighbourhood Centre) was established at a public meeting in June 1984 to provide a joint facility for voluntary and government welfare agencies and a 'drop-in' information centre. The public meeting, which attracted about seventy representatives of such organisations, elected a committee and resolved to apply for funding. Women were a majority at the inaugural meeting, and have maintained a majority on the Centre's committee. Indeed, in 1986 there was only one male on the executive, who was the local hospital social worker, and only one male among the ten volunteers who staffed the Centre. The Centre offered attractive, although unpaid, activities for women in a town in which employment opportunities were few. Some of the women were professionals, such as community nurses, and most of the men, like the social worker, also became involved through professional interest. They came from a range of occupational backgrounds, from farming to factory employment.

The Centre Committee's first tasks were to obtain funding and accommodation. It obtained $500 from the State Government, and approached the Council for help with accommodation. The first rejection by the Council came in August 1984. The Council adopted a Finance Committee recommendation that more information be sought from the Centre about 'the operation of similar centres in other areas before giving final consideration' to the request (Minutes of Council Meeting 27 August, 1984). Fortunately the committee obtained use of an old rectory in the main street in mid-1985 for six months, and the Centre was able to open (Centre President's and Co-ordinator's *Annual Reports*, 1986).

Late in the year the Centre Committee approached the Council again. When the matter came up at the October Council meeting there was some discussion, but it did not proceed beyond Harold Upston's statement that the request looked like the 'thin end of the wedge'. The Council again resolved to seek more information. The Centre Committee made its third attempt, as reported in the *Guardian* above, in February 1986. Its letter arrived too late for the Clerk to cover it with a recommendation in his report. He reported verbally that a prospective tenant had appeared to show interest in the empty space in the Council building which the Centre sought. Harold Upston moved and Col Newton seconded a successful motion to reject the request.

The Centre Committee again obtained free accommodation, this time from a shop owner who had vacant space next door to his shop. That was also a temporary situation, and when the shop owner suggested that it might be more permanent if an arrangement could be made in which the Council waived his rates, the Committee approached the Council. Again the Council's response was negative, reached after no discussion of the motion from Harold Upston to reject the request. The Centre's tenuous situation was later stabilised by an offer of a house by the State Department of Housing. The Centre prospered after occupying that house.

In all three of these human services non-issues it would appear very likely that Council support could have launched projects that proved to be very successful ones into operation much earlier, with much less expenditure of money and energy by local people. Had Council staff included a person with human services responsibilities, these issues may have surfaced and been considered in the way that the *Guardian* editor wanted the Vacation Play Centre discussed. Such an officer would have assessed the Neighbourhood Centre request, having the kind of information that the Council repeatedly requested, and presented a recommendation to the Council. Employment of such an officer would of course have implied that a decision to enter the human service field had been taken, and as Clerk Neville Armstrong's report to Finance Committee about the Play Centre illustrated, that was the contentious issue that the Council was avoiding.

The councillor perspective

Application of Dye's (1986:42) belief that 'community elites have an interest in keeping redistributional questions out of local politics since their resolution may jeopardise members' wealth and income' cannot be directly applied to Cowra Shire, because human service provision by local government is unlikely to bring about, or even be intended to bring about, redistribution of wealth or income. Dye's proposition does, however, have some application, because the possibility of redistribution was on the minds of councillors. It was expressed in terms of potential cost to ratepayers, as implied in Harold Upston's reference to 'the thin end of the wedge' in the Neighbourhood Centre non-issue. It was expressed in the Council only by Ab Oliver, in terms of local self-defence against imposed costs, in his valedictory speech before standing down at the 1987 election, as reported by the *Guardian* (23 September, p. 1): 'His departing advice for the new Council was to keep away from the field of social service to the community. He said a number of councils had endeavoured to provide community services and had found the Government had been all too willing to foist a large part of social services on to them'. This view was also expressed, but less directly, at an earlier meeting of the Council by Jack Mallon in calling for a return from other activities to the 'three Rs' (roads, rates and rubbish). Jack's speech was a reaction to a letter to the Council from a ratepayer criticising the Council for spending on what the ratepayer felt to be five unnecessary items, none of which were human services, and three of which were road maintenance. A need to minimise expenditure was raised many times, most notably by Bruce Golsby in a successful motion that the Council aim at a zero rate increase in 1986.

In my conversations with councillors only one expressed any interest in raising the issue, but the cost factor had dissuaded him. He had taken the idea only as far as discussing it privately. He felt that:

> Council should have a social conscience. But I can see the difficulties involved, because it is very hard to define the parameters of social conscience because they are ever expanding. As the Clerk pointed out in discussions, we haven't a person on the staff who is into those sorts of issues so we would have to find someone, and then you would have to give them a car so they can get out and about. And then they'll need an office. So I had to pull the curtain down on that one ...
> The fear of a lot of councillors is that once you let one through the door you'll have them all lined up. It's a big field out there.

Other councillors expressed fear that human services might be imposed. When Neville Armstrong presented a particularly healthy financial report to the Finance Committee during the estimates process, Don Kibbler asked if the Council might 'have to clean out some hollow logs' in order to maintain levels of Commonwealth grants. Neville replied that there was no such threat. Another councillor expressed the view to me that there was too much duplication of human services and Council involvement would only exacerbate the situation. Yet another believed that Cowra was a 'self help town' and that the Council should not interfere with successful organisations.

The councillors were not uncharitable people. They looked sympathetically upon individual cases of hardship in matters of revenue collection and administration. Their resistance was aimed at institutionalisation of 'welfare'. Their rationalisation drew on a range of ideologies, the most prominent of which were the ratepayer principle and the localist ideal. A distaste for the welfare state in general was evident in Cowra. A local welfare professional, who had also worked in city situations, told me of a stigma attached to seeking help. The survey reported in Gray (1987a) also encountered resistance.

In the 1986 non-issues described above, women had the *Guardian*, which was undoubtedly an important force on their side in the matter of the vacation play centre. A larger number of women on the Council would help to secure such outcomes, as the *Guardian* did. This assumes, however, that women who successfully seek election recognise and pursue the objective interests of women, a bold assumption in a climate conducive to the maintenance of patriarchal role relations at the ideal level at least. The *Guardian* note on Barbara Bennett's nomination suggests that women councillors may still have been judged by the electorate in terms of their traditional roles, rather than as representatives of women. This implies no pluralistic threat to the 'people's corporation' image. Women councillors, moreover, would after election still have confronted the same resources, as they sought to preserve their legitimacy as councillors who do not accept demands for welfare.

The Aboriginal non-issue

Aboriginal welfare was not just off the agenda of Cowra Shire Council, it was for historical reasons bound to State Government policy, far removed from the agenda. There have been recent signs, however, that in the more enlightened policy climate of the late 1980s, Aboriginal people are taking more interest in local affairs, and exerting their rights to participate in local politics. This was manifest in the nomination of an Aboriginal for the first time in the Council election of 1987. This beginning of local political activity has shown no immediate signs of putting Aboriginal welfare on the local political agenda, but it was a step towards bringing Aboriginal interests to local attention in the political arena. This section looks at those interests in terms of current needs, after discussion of the history in which Aboriginal interests were detached from local concern.

Many of Australia's Aboriginal people continue to suffer poverty and dependence in situations of geographic, social and economic isolation.

'The history of while colonisation in Australia is an account of the transformation of semi-nomadic hunters and collectors into sedentary unskilled labourers and of freely self-determining individuals into degraded dependents' (Middleton, 1987: 344). The last twenty years have seen some progress in recognition that the living conditions of the Aboriginal population are unacceptable to both white and black Australians, and that white government policies and actions have contributed to many Aboriginal social problems. Aboriginal people have started to affirm and develop a consciousness. Nevertheless, 'being black in Australia has always meant ... precarious control over one's own existence' (Cowlishaw, 1988: 2). These aspects of recent Aboriginal history have been visible in Cowra.

The historical background which follows is drawn almost entirely from the work of Read (1983, 1984, 1988), supplemented by information collected in conversations with Aboriginal people at Erambie, the Aboriginal settlement on the outskirts of Cowra (see map 2) and elsewhere in Cowra, and my reading of the *Cowra Guardian*. The conversations added little to the information provided by Read's work, but they contributed greatly to my understanding of the Aboriginal perspective.

State Government policy from 1909 to 1968 separated the Aborigines from the town and the concerns of the townspeople. It intended the opposite. Governments attempted to force Aborigines to assimilate into white society, something which both Aboriginal people and the white people of Cowra did not want and which they resisted. White resistance in Cowra was one of the factors which hampered implementation of State Government policy, thereby helping the Aboriginal resistance. The Aborigines were, however, caught in the middle.

By 1909 many Aborigines who had survived the white invasion lived on reserved lands which were entirely the responsibility of the Aborigines Protection Board. The Board retained that responsibility until 1969, so that although their settlements would have been subject to local government regulation, the Aborigines under the 'protection' of the Board were substantially insulated from local affairs. In practice under the Board they were alienated rather than insulated. Cowra local government could easily afford to exhibit the lack of interest in Aboriginal people observed among local councils by Rowley (1971) and Sanders (1984).

Legislation enacted in 1909 aimed in the short term to increase control over the people on the reserves, and in the long term to 'reduce their populations and in the end close them altogether' (Read, 1984: 2). The legislation gave the Board vast powers, which enabled destruction of some reserves, but failed to destroy Erambie. Read (1984: 4) attributes the failure to the absence of a manager, and the lack of interest shown by local police who were delegated responsibility for enforcement of the Board's regulations. Erambie's population grew quietly until around 1920, but by the early 1920s the Cowra whites had become disgruntled with the lack of management at Erambie. The Board relented under local complaints, and put in a manager. That decision saved Erambie, for although the manager 'set about ejecting as many residents as he could' (Read, 1988: 71), the effects of economic depression in the 1930s, which made conditions difficult for moving people, and Aboriginal resistance from the 1940s, which made people difficult to move, preserved the settlement.

Erambie survived, but its management created tension and suffering. Read (1988) placed fault with the Board's employment policies. Complaints about managers were heard and apparently responded to among the white people of Cowra. The *Cowra Guardian* of 16 September, 1949 reported that three members of the local Labor League (one of whom was Leo Lynch) were to investigate allegations by Aborigines that the manager had withheld rations. Later in the same year, the *Guardian* (8 November) reported that the local State Parliament representative (Labor) had called for an inquiry into Erambie's management and that a new manager was to be appointed.

It is not surprising that in this troubled climate, racism aside, attempts by the Board to move Aboriginal people into town were resisted by the whites. Read (1988: 111) found that rumours of such plans brought a response from the manager of the Edgell Cannery, perhaps because it was rumoured that houses for them were to be built in Mulyan. He wrote 'to his State MP, asking if Chief Secretary Evatt [to whom the Board was responsible] would like Aborigines living in his home: why then should Cowra people have "this nuisance" inflicted on them?' Mayor Whitby joined in.

> We should object . . . The Council should protest against this move to bring these people to live among the white people . . . The Government should take these people down the river where there is plenty of land and water and give them areas where they can produce for themselves. But to bring them into the town would be like putting oil in water . . .' (*Cowra Guardian*, 9 January, 1953, p. 3)

Cowlishaw (1988) reported a similar instance of obstruction when the State Government sought a house in which to establish a refuge for drunks, an alternative to police cells, and Brindleton's council interpreted the proposal as a means of foisting Aboriginal problems onto local whites. Cowra's Municipal Council made further difficulties for the Board by ordering the destruction of two river camps in 1953, inhabitants of which the Board had to accommodate, and eventually only four houses were built in Mulyan. After the tumult in 1951, the Board again relented and announced that it would build twenty-one houses at Erambie. The whites of Cowra had unwittingly helped the Aborigines secure what they wanted: the survival of Erambie, their place.

After the Board's demise in 1969, responsibility for Erambie fell upon the State housing and welfare departments. By then, however, a referendum had passed responsibility for Aboriginal affairs to the Commonwealth Government, and after the election of the Whitlam Labor Government in 1972, significant changes occurred. In 1973 Erambie people formed the Koori Housing Company, and with Commonwealth assistance, started to improve living conditions after incorporation in 1975. Around that time houses were built in the town for Aborigines and made available to those who wanted to live there.

There was much work to be done at Erambie. Many domestic facilities, including water supply, had had to be improvised, and there were health problems. The changes of the mid-1970s brought the situation of Cowra's Aborigines to the attention of its white people through the pages of the *Guardian* in a revealing manner. The Government had abandoned the assimilation ideal but the *Guardian* had not, despite all the clamour and resistance that assimilationist housing policy had created among the white people of Cowra. When the Erambie housing programme was announced in 1975, the *Guardian* said in an editorial that the plan 'turns its back on the slow but sure process of assimilation' in building at Erambie rather than in town. While not expressly opposing the plan, the editorial went on to affirm that the Aborigines could not expect anything for nothing from the white townspeople. 'It is up to the white population to support this project and it is equally up to the Aboriginal population to support it. Because, let there be no mistake, the community does not, by itself, support the concept of wholesale handouts . . .' (*Cowra Guardian*, 16 September, 1975, p. 3)

The connection of sewerage to Erambie raised another storm in the pages of the *Guardian*, providing the closest point that Aboriginal welfare has come to being an issue before local government in Cowra. The *Guardian* of 1 July, 1977 (p. 1) reported that the Municipal Council had invited the Commonwealth Aboriginal Affairs Minister to see for himself 'large pools of sullage lying under homes' because of delays in construction work. The issue was not so much the Aborigines' living conditions but 'bureaucratic bungling' by the Commonwealth Department of Construction over the sewerage work (*Cowra Guardian*, 22 July, 1977, p. 1). (Cowlishaw (1988: 138) discusses the bureaucratic problems which were associated with such housing programs.)

Recent legislative changes have created an issue for Cowra Shire Council, which although related to Aboriginal Welfare, was not related to need for human services. State land rights legislation allows Aboriginal groups to claim any public land which is not required for a public purpose, placing the onus on government to show that it needs the land. When such a claim was made in Cowra, some councillors took exception to it, feeling that it was discriminating against white people. One councillor was reported in the *Guardian* (27 March, 1985, p. 1) to have said that 'he did not see how they had the hide to do it', and, wishing to reject the Council's apparent weakness before the legislation, 'what they basically said is we want this land, well, I want to know what for ... They may have a real reason for wanting it, which may not be as important as ours'. A letter to the *Guardian* (5 April, 1985) from an Aboriginal representative accused the Council of stirring racial tension and reminded it that the Aborigines were not obliged to state their plans for the land. It was not within the power of the Council to make the issue a local one, for the matter would have been resolved in Sydney in administrative or legal processes over which Cowra Shire Council would not have presided.

The interest of Cowra's Aboriginal people in having a human services function in the Council was not so apparent as the similar interest of women. A human service role for the Council would have been beneficial for women not because it would have redistributed local resources toward them on a large scale, but rather because it would have allowed greater access to local resources, and more importantly, facilitated access to State Government resources. The continuing history of specialised administration of Aboriginal affairs through the Board and the Commonwealth Department of Aboriginal Affairs left local government separated from this chain of responsibility. Nevertheless, Aborigines had problems which could be addressed at the local level, and local government involvement for liaison purposes may have been beneficial to them.

While the living conditions of Cowra's Aboriginal people had improved greatly during the previous ten years, and the worst days of racial tension and victimisation (as depicted in Merritt, 1983) by local authorities had passed, enormous social problems remained. (Some of these are analysed in Gray (1988a), a study in which the questionnaire developed for the earlier project on community care (Gray, 1987a) was administered among local Aboriginal people.) Alcohol consumption, a problem among children as well as adult Aborigines, was probably the worst.

Given the long history of the detachment of Aboriginal people from local government, and the hostility between their so-called protectors and Cowra Municipal Council, it is not surprising that Aboriginal welfare had not become an issue. There had been no need to keep it off the local political agenda, because there had never been any suggestion that it might be put on the agenda. Aborigines were therefore a long way from furthering their interests through the local political arena. They had, however, since the demise of assimilationism, begun to accumulate resources. But as Read (1988) points out, the wounds suffered in what he describes as one hundred of years of warfare over assertion of the right to exist will take a long time to heal. When they do heal, and Aborigines eventually acquire substantial local political resources, they may confront the same ideological obstacles encountered by women, as illustrated in the *Guardian*'s 'you don't get something for nothing' editorial quoted above. Even in Cowlishaw's (1988) Brindleton, where Aboriginal people were a much larger proportion of the population than were the Aboriginal people of Cowra's, and where an Aboriginal was elected to the council in 1983, the only issues which appeared likely to arise, other than matters related to the council's provision of basic services to Aboriginal residents, were the continuation of allegations by whites of black misbehaviour. Unless Brindleton's council anticipated a possible benefit for the whole town from Federal money for projects, intended for the benefit of the Aboriginal population, but which the council would put to wider use. Such projects could then become issues.

Conclusion

Human services had barely touched Cowra Shire Council's agenda, leaving property concerns superior, and those in whose interests property services lie in a powerful position. Their superordination had not been questioned in the local political arena. This point needs some qualification, because many people, including women and Aborigines, who had property however small, had an interest in property services, and everybody in the Shire had some interest in local government services. The point is that women and Aborigines may have reaped greater benefit from a Council which also provided human services.

They were, however, in a double bind, for a human service role for local government would inevitably have involved some cost to ratepayers, if the Council was not to be merely another administrative arm of the State by spending specific purpose grants under State regulation. Even if all revenue to be spent on human services was obtained through untied grants, the decision to spend it would have involved forgoing some property service activity, and given the nature of local government priorities in general and particularly those of Cowra Shire Council, property service activity would not have been forgone lightly. Entry into human services was likely to call for some popularly unwanted addition to rate collection, which may have worsened an already regressive taxation regime. The double bind was built-in. That is a problem which women and Aborigines, and any other people who seek human services from local government, inevitably face. It is not surprising, therefore, that councillors were unwilling to face it. Their capacity not to face it was reinforced by their ideological resources which gave it a particular interpretation, and which legitimated an anti-welfare and patriarchal stand.[1]

Reference to Saunders' (1979) non-decision making filter aids comparison between the gender and Aboriginal non-issues. The gender non-issue was formulated by women who were aware of their interests, and so passed the first of the three stages; was articulated by women who were not dissuaded by anticipated reactions; but was not resolved due to negative decision-making, a process which Saunders (1979: 29) depicts as 'situations where dogs may bark themselves hoarse in the night but nobody listens'. It was similar in this regard to the non-issues of the West Cowra water supply, Taragala air pollution and the railway decline.

The Aboriginal issue was different, because, although I heard some dissatisfaction with the Council's property services expressed by Aboriginal people, just as I heard it from whites, the non-issue of human services appeared not to have been formulated. When welfare services had for so long been provided by State and (more recently) Commonwealth authorities, it is not surprising that Aborigines did not look to local government, especially when Commonwealth funds had recently helped great improvements in living conditions, and State legislation had enabled acquisition of what they wanted most of all: the return of some land. The need for human services among Aborigines was probably greater than that among any other people in Cowra, but nomination by an Aborigine at the 1987 Council election was not aimed specifically at obtaining human services. Her election manifesto printed in the *Guardian* (18 September, 1987, p. 10) said that she would represent the interests of other people as well as Aborigines.

In distributional, as in allocational and developmental policy areas, the range of issues which gained currency was constrained to those which impinged on either the operational efficiency of the 'peoples' corporation', or the financial interests of ratepayers. The issues which did gain currency were those which were seen to impinge on property interests, in particular, those of farming and town business.

Note

1 Two women who had been involved with the establishment of the child care centre told me that while women were trying to set it up they encountered the belief that women should stay at home to care for children, and, therefore, there should be no need for a child care centre. They attributed the early lack of interest of the Council to this belief. I did not see evidence of this in the political arena in 1986. I found no suggestion of such a rationale being applied in the Vacation Play Centre matter. While it is impossible to discount the possibility of this ideology having some effect at a covert level, there were signs of recognition by men of the value of non-domestic roles for women, especially where off-farm income was essential.

8
The making of local politics

Local politics in Cowra Shire were specialised. The non-issues over matters which had a substantial bearing on the life chances and living conditions of Cowra residents implicitly pose the question of what did or could become an issue. Issues certainly arose. The Council split into factions and councillors engaged in spirited debate. Such debate, however, was precipitated by conflict between the councillors and the Council's senior officers, which dominated Council affairs. This distracted attention from matters which were allowed to become, or were turned into, non-issues and, moreover, helped to maintain a popular definition of local politics which enhanced the political resources of people with business and farm interests while denying resources to others.

Perspectives on councillor–officer relations

Two interpretations of relations between elected representatives and the bureaucracy are particularly prominent in the literature. One assumes that bureaucracy is an independent and powerful actor in political relations. The second suggests that bureaucracy and a business elite form a unified powerful force. There are other possibilities: pluralism, with bureaucratic and other interests opposed but balanced; and a democratic ideal in which the bureaucracy is not a significant power actor. These are rendered unlikely by the elitist tradition of local government and the prominent role which bureaucracy has played in it.

Bureaucracy poses fundamental problems for the operation of democratic government when it is viewed as an independent actor in power relations, by decreasing the likelihood of the democratic ideal in which the bureaucracy is independent but insignificant. Bureaucracy is, as argued by Etzioni-Halevy (1985), essentially undemocratic at the same time as it is essential to the operation of democracy, because it is supposed to be both independent and subservient at the same time. In such an interpretation of a citizen's perspective, incompatible goals are held to be desirable. People want the services of professionals at the same time as they want to retain some influence over the actions of professionals. They are, however, also aware that influence over officials can lead to corruption and inefficiency.[1] Hence they want an insulated bureaucracy (Alford, 1969).

Bureaucracy need only act to further its pursuit of the demands made upon it to illustrate the contradictions. That is, acting in its own interests while acting contrary to others may amount to no more than pursuing one of the contradictory demands placed upon it. As I illustrated earlier, bureaucracy's urge for efficiency may be sufficient to place it counter to the interests of citizens by stifling opportunities for pluralistic bargaining.

In so far as this view proposes that bureaucrats act in the interests of the bureaucracy which they serve, it is parallel in its Weberian approach to that of the managerialist school in urban sociology. Without pluralism this perspective becomes a 'technocratic view' (Etzioni-Halevy, 1985: 54), which is sometimes expressed as 'dictatorship of the official' (by for example, Newton, 1976: 145 and Stoker and Wilson, 1986: 287). This interpretation found strong expression (by for example, Davies (1972) and Goodman (1972)) in reactions to imposition of planning decisions and regulations in the late 1960s and early 1970s, where bureaucracy was seen to be powerful, irrational and malevolent. Such ideas moved planners toward acceptance of public participation, such as that intended for Cowra's LEP formulation process. Empirical evidence for 'the dictatorship of the official' in Australian local studies is inconclusive. Pandey (1972) and Vandeloo (1983) found officers to be of at least substantial potential influence in local affairs, but Oxley (1978) found that bureaucrats were subservient to councillors while councillors were subservient to their constituents.

The other potentially fruitful interpretation of the councillor–officer relationship places bureaucrats in a 'joint elite' with councillors who represent a propertied ruling class. The traditional role of local government as provider of property services and the elitist dominance of councils by those with property interests render elites with interests other than property unlikely. The relationship between councillors and officers is seen with this interpretation to be one of close co-operation.

The rules of local democracy, although changed from the traditional property franchise to an adult resident franchise, have not stimulated pluralistic demands and expectations which might politicise the arena and logically imply a need for an independent bureaucracy. Moreover, in the image of the apolitical 'people's corporation', the potential problem of corruption does not arise, because the members are elected to be trustworthy representatives of an all-encompassing mutual interest group. Hence there is no need for an independent bureaucracy. Parker (1978: 390), however, points out that councillors' intimate role in administration opens opportunities for them to obtain favours for faithful voters. If there is a bureaucracy, its alliance with property interests would be quite acceptable to electors, or indeed essential for efficient operation of the 'people's corporation'. To the extent that the 'people's corporation' does not need democracy, the local government tradition is not democratic (Purdie, 1976: 26). The joint-elite model might therefore be readily applicable, and the prospects for pluralism would be nil.

Evidence from British studies neither conclusively supports nor refutes the joint-elite model. Alexander (1982), Cockburn (1977), Green (1981) and Saunders (1979) all identified a joint-elite, but Stoker and Wilson (1986), citing instances of conflict between councillors and officers in which councillors rejected officers' recommendations, claim that a joint-elite consensus should not be assumed. Madgwick et al. (1973) and Bell et al. (1976), in rural situations, found councillors in disagreement with officers. Bell identified 'stout resistance of many councillors to any bureaucratic development' (41). Alexander (1982), while finding a joint-elite, also suggested such conflict, in so far as some councillors feared dictatorship by officials, and this had some effect on their relationship.

Chapman and Wood (1984) found Australian evidence to indicate that councillors and officers want to work in partnership, despite legal responsibility for council affairs lying with councillors, and 'the real informal action is one of mutual agreement between councillors and clerks' (64). Such mutual agreement was illustrated by the relationship between the Mayor and the Town Clerk in Wild's Bradstow (Wild, 1974a). These two cemented an elite, taming the aldermen to the extent that the duumvirate maintained control of the council's agenda. But like the British, the Australian literature also offers contradictory evidence. Sinclair (1987: 79) reported that on some councils, members are not allowed to speak to the staff, treating staff as enemies. That does not, however, imply pluralism, as only two interests remain represented in the arena.

A joint-elite in Cowra?

The evidence of farmer and business domination of Cowra Shire Council's agenda is not amenable to pluralism, nor does it suggest that the bureaucracy is an insignificant power actor. It does not, however, encourage application of the 'joint-elite' and 'dictatorship of the official' models either. The 'dictatorship of the official' model is not readily applicable because officials suffered defeat several times. The Shire Clerk's plans to decrease the size of the Council and introduce differential rating for 'hobby farms' were rejected; the Shire Engineer's options for supplying water to West Cowra were bypassed and the Draft Local Environmental Plan was drastically changed; and the Health Surveyor's recommendation about fire-rating for the Japanese Garden building was altered. The councillors could and did ignore the wishes of the senior officers and made independent assessments before making their decisions.

One might, however, suppose either that the elite existed but was not very cohesive, or that as Saunders (1979), Green (1981) and Wild (1974a) found, the elite consisted of senior councillors and senior officers only. Both of these suppositions are difficult to sustain because the lack of cohesion was profound, and there was no on-going working arrangement between the senior officers and the elected members, or senior elected members and senior officers. This is not to say that there was no close association between Clerk Neville Armstrong and President Cyril Treasure. They worked in consultation, but did not dominate the Council. Indeed their relationship precipitated debate in the Council, when some councillors were tempted to see it as a conspiracy.

I observed two instances of councillors rebuking Cyril Treasure for what they felt to have been bilateral action with Neville Armstrong without the Council's endorsement. After Cyril had written to town businesses explaining the Council's decision about fire-rating, Stephen Bell asked him at the next meeting to 'please inform the Council' about his action, suggesting that someone could move endorsement. Ab Oliver responded that endorsement was not necessary and there was no further discussion. On the other occasion Jack Mallon protested that he had been excluded from a meeting which the President, Engineer and Clerk had held with the 'Concerned Citizens Committee' and the LGPA to discuss the LEP. Jack also objected to the recording of the minutes of the last Council meeting. His motion to have them altered was successful. Such debate certainly does not fit the joint-elite model as it was exemplified by Wild (1974a). Moreover, Cyril could reject the advice of senior officers, as he did in the West Cowra Water Supply matter.

It was not only in 1986 that conflict was apparent between senior staff and councillors. The Health Inspector was criticised as a 'joke' by Mayor Whitby (*Cowra Guardian*, 12 January, 1951, p. 1). Whitby and Leo Lynch clashed with the Engineer about the condition of a street (*Cowra Guardian*, 4 March, 1955). The *Guardian* of 17 October, 1958 reported an argument between a Waugoola councillor and the Shire Engineer after the Engineer offered an explanation for the condition of a road. These may have been isolated incidents, but they do suggest that if a joint-elite has been present, it has been unstable.

Council meetings of 1986 provided many illustrations of conflict among the would-be joint-elite over relatively minor matters in addition to the more important ones discussed above. A compromise proposed by Cyril Treasure replaced Neville Armstrong's recommendations for distribution of Bicentennial grants after the latter's plan precipitated public opposition. Neville's rejection of a request to extend the opening period of the town swimming pool was overturned by the Council. A request from the Health Surveyor for leave for one of his subordinates to attend a work-related conference (at the subordinate's own expense) was rejected by Council. Another recommendation of the Health Surveyor, this time for adoption of regulations for the installation of domestic fireplaces and solid fuel heaters, was also rejected. They were also willing to criticise officers' management of Council activities, alleging, for example, that the Council's trucks did not always cover loads, that accounts were misleading, that residents had not been advised of road work, and that Council staff had been discourteous and exerted undue pressure on residents. The councillors did not look upon themselves as 'rubber stamps'.

Failure to criticise where they felt it warranted would have been dereliction of duty to the 'people's corporation', whose bureaucrats could, if left unyoked, become enemies of the people whom they were employed to serve. The perceived need to keep the bureaucrats under control, and keep the 'corporation' for the 'people', turned councillor–officer relations toward the relationship of enemies referred to by Sinclair (1987). Councillors restrained bureaucrats from what might have been seen as assumption of undue privilege. Desire to see the Council obey the same stringency and regulation as it imposed on others was expressed by Harold Upston and Jack Mallon when Harold asked the Health Surveyor if the Council had applied to itself for permission to modify the front door of the Civic Centre. Jack seconded Harold's unsuccessful motion that the Council be required to submit an application.

These disputes were not minor quarrels among otherwise united allies. The major disagreements over the LEP, the West Cowra water supply and the other matters analysed in earlier chapters discourage such an interpretation. Informal networks linked senior officers and councillors as Wild (1974a) found, but evidence that such links effected co-ordination among councillors and officers was not available in Cowra. Neville Armstrong, Ab Oliver and Don Kibbler were all prominent members of Rotary, but that contact did not produce perception of universal common interest among them. All councillors were likely to encounter each other and the senior officers on social occasions, but all valued isolation of social relations from political life. Some councillors expressed concern that the divisions created by contentious issues in the Council were being maintained outside. A councillor indicated the value placed on isolation of political vendettas inside the Council: 'There is some dissent [inside Council]. But you do get good results when there are different points of view provided that those who are beaten still play. One of the worst things is to have a decision go against you and then tear them to pieces down the street'. Another saw the Council being divided by personal vendettas which were carried outside. 'Personal vendettas are appearing, among councillors as well as between staff and councillors. Not every decision [in the former Municipal Council] was unanimous but we were able to sort things out without bearing grudges. Now people form grudges in Council which are taken outside'. Rather than informal networks maintaining an elite in the Council, conflict in it was destroying, or at least was felt by some to be destroying, informal networks.

The joint-elite model is difficult to impose on the local political arena in

Cowra, not because Cowra had deviated from tradition into a pluralistic democracy, but rather because of strains in the would-be elite relationship. Some signs of a joint-elite, however, emerged. They were most obvious in the human services non-issues when all Councillors concurred with Neville Armstrong's view of the Vacation Play Centre and Neighbourhood Centre matters, but were also apparent when the Policy Register was applied to West Cowra's drainage, the response to the complaints about air pollution from Taragala and the railway decline non-issue. Why a joint-elite would emerge over these matters and not others is discussed below. For now, the important point is that a resilient joint-elite, as Wild (1974a) found, was not apparent in Cowra, despite some apparently largely favourable conditions.

We are left, therefore, without an appropriate model among all four of those proposed above. The bureaucracy was significant but not all powerful, and it was neither part of a persistent joint-elite with councillors nor a participant in a pluralistic arena. The 'technocratic view' (Etzioni-Halevy, 1985) was, however, useful as an interpretation of the view of councillors rather than for its illumination of the power structure. They saw bureaucracy as independent of them and pursuing its own interests.

Institutional explanations for councillor–officer friction

A recipe for councillor–officer friction is built into local government, and is reinforced by relations between local and State Government. The 'people's corporation' image, without the usual governmental need for service from an independent bureaucracy, places the bureaucracy in an ambivalent situation. It seeks independence at the same time as elected members seek, and to some extent have, intimate relationships with it, in line with the 'people's corporation' image. The bureaucrats are free to think, advise and speak, but are not so free to act. The 'people's corporation' places responsibility for its efficient management in the hands of the people's representatives. Conflict arises because an 'unnecessary' independent bureaucracy does exist, it does take an independent stance, and its actions are sometimes seen as unacceptable.

Local government operates a committee system rather than an executive system of government, placing councillors close to administration. All Cowra's councillors shared in decision making. All Cowra Shire's senior bureaucrats usually attended the meetings of all three committees, and were available to be questioned as well as offer advice. They did both quite freely, especially at committee meetings which were less formal than Council meetings. They also entered debate in Council meetings, and could do so to provide information as they felt necessary, not just in response to a councillor's question. This was highlighted by the incident during the LEP controversy in which President Ab Oliver asked Harold Upston to leave the chamber. The *Guardian* (24 April, 1985, p. 1) reported that the commotion had arisen after Harold claimed that Clerk Neville Armstrong's report of a meeting was inaccurate. The *Guardian* continued:

> The Shire Clerk commented that he had been present at the meeting and Councillor Upston was not making any sense to him. He indicated he thought the decisions Councillor Upston was referring to were only private comments. Councillor Upston retorted that the Shire Clerk didn't make much sense to a lot of people either.

Harold's refusal to apologise for this comment precipitated, as reported in the *Guardian*, Ab's request for his absence. Neville and Harold soon exchanged apologies. The *Guardian* report continued with a quote from Harold:

> At the meeting I made history by being the first Shire Councillor ever to be asked to leave. However, I am not sorry for my remarks. The Shire Clerk is a paid employee of the Council and I am sick of his remarks. Councillors are only allowed to make one comment on an issue and yet in my opinion, the Shire Clerk is constantly making his remarks. My understanding is that he is supposed to speak when he is spoken to and last night I decided I'd had enough and would pull him into line.

Harold was referring to a standing order which prohibits councillors from speaking more than once on a motion, other than in right-of-reply.

Councillors could develop an intimate knowledge of the operation of the Council. Indeed their own interpretation of their job as councillors, as well as their formal responsibilities under State legislation, required it. Some examples of matters raised in the Council illustrate the councillors' closeness to the administration of its affairs: a councillor queried the condition of the compactor machine at the rubbish tip; the decision to allow, or not allow, officers to attend conferences was made by the Council rather than by officers alone; councillors sought and made detailed input into the setting of priorities for work on small items such as culverts. Such intimate involvement has been recognised in other councils (Parker, 1978). It was illustrated by the annual tour of the Shire made by members of the Policy and Resources Committee, on which I accompanied them in 1986, to take a close look at the condition of roads and other facilities before determining priorities for forthcoming work. I was struck by councillors' detailed knowledge; one was able to tell which employee had done some grading work on a section of unsealed road by looking at the road, applying knowledge of Council management and considering the standard of the work. Long serving councillors could see Shire Clerks come and go, especially as local government officers move among councils to gain promotion, and some knew as much about the Council's employees as the senior officers.

Councillors as well as officers were judged by the Council's performance and the legal responsibility for management affairs rested with the councillors. They were intimately involved in all Council activities, down to day-to-day matters such as equipment purchases, staffing, detail of location and design of water reticulation systems and recreation facilities, and many more. There was plenty of room for dispute when two groups were given different definitions of the same task.[2] A contest between councillors and officers for control of a council's activities was recognised by Cowlishaw (1988) in Brindleton, as both groups felt that they should be making the relevant decisions.

Most State politicians and bureaucrats treat local government as a State department (Wiltshire, 1985). As Wild (1983) illustrated, State government can take what is seen locally to be an arrogant stance against local interests, and bring great pressure to bear on local government. State governments make regulations and pass them on to local government for enforcement. The LEP and fire regulation issues were raised after officers had been obliged to bring up matters which offended what councillors perceived to be local interests.

The councillor–officer relationship is one between amateurs and professionals, and, moreover, one in which the professionals not only have information but can control its flow. An officer could 'exert biases in favour of his own demands and at the same time feed the [council] negative information about the demands of his opponents' (Pettigrew, 1972: 202), but should do so tactfully because council 'should always feel that it has itself made the decision' (Richards, 1975: 131). As Chapman and Wood (1984: 64) point out, 'councillors must trade off the desire for more information with trust in the staff'. They do not have time to acquire knowledge as their full-time professional counterparts have. This was the 'fundamental complaint' found by Heclo (1969: 198) among British councillors. While I saw no manipulation of information, I heard expression of concern among councillors. Criticism of the Caravan Park accounts by Harold Upston implied that he felt that Clerk Neville Armstrong was not providing adequate information.

All Cowra's councillors indicated dependence on the senior officers for the information upon which to base decisions. Many told me that they used other sources, especially local contacts and newspapers, but with a large pile of agenda papers to be battled through before each meeting, their capacity to learn from other sources was limited. They were well aware of this deficiency, just as they were aware of the senior officers' greater information resources.

Three institutional features: the committee system, inter-governmental relations and councillors' dependence on officers for information, build strains into the councillor–officer relationship. These strains, however, did not bring about a state of continual war between the two groups in Cowra. Other ingredients entered the recipe for overt conflict, one of which was ideological: the technocratic view of the relationship. The three institutional features appear to have fostered the technocratic view, in that officers' resources were obvious to councillors in the intimacy of their working relationship, at the same time as officers' regulatory roles handed down from the State Government took on the appearance of an undesirable imposition on councillors. Officers could appear to be building an empire which appeared to the councillors as an end in itself, while the officers were finding that they needed greater resources to perform their tasks. Institutional factors, however, were only part of the process in which resentment at such apparent empire building came about.

Councillors and officers making local politics

Councillor–officer relations were implicated in the most divisive, perhaps the only internally divisive issues to confront the Council in 1986. Local political issues, as against non-issues, all contained a strong councillor versus officer element without which a joint-elite model could emerge. That is, perception by one or more councillors of the bureaucracy pursuing its own or foreign interests, in conflict with what they felt to be the general local interest, was a prerequisite for action to raise an issue. The bureaucracy could act bureaucratically without precipitating a reaction, as it did by applying the Policy Register, and as it did in the Taragala air pollution non-issue, or it could put a negative point of view as it did in the Play Centre and Neighbourhood Centre matters, but in all those cases, no councillors, or insufficient councillors, saw the bureaucracy to be pursuing a hostile interest. Hence such matters did not become issues in the way of, for example, the LEP and the Japanese Garden lease.

The adversary element entered local politics when bureaucrats were seen to be pursuing interests which enough councillors saw to be threatening. It seems that only bureaucrats could raise threatening issues without being smothered by joint-elite action; they had sufficient resources bestowed by the institutional factors discussed above. The problem so implied is one of defining the conditions in which adversarial or joint-elite actions are pursued.

The adversary element may have existed more in interpretations by councillors than in the overt appearance of the issues. For example, while the rural rating and representation issues had an element of defence of rural interests against urban, some councillors felt that the issues were created by Clerk Neville Armstrong in his desire to further his organisation's strength in terms of revenue and its ability to influence councillors. Similarly, the conflict over the Tourist and Development Corporation's lease of the Japanese Garden site was interpreted by some councillors to have been set up by Neville, his motivation being defence of the power of Council. There is some substance to that interpretation in that Neville stated in discussion about Corporation-member councillors' voting rights that he wanted to ensure that the Corporation did not take over the Council, but some councillors appeared to interpret that to mean that he wanted to maintain his own individual power.

Their technocratic view was clearest in the LEP issue. The councillors who opposed the plan took their stance because they believed that giving the Council the right to demand its consent for subdivision really meant giving bureaucrats the right to say no to development, even though bureaucrats could only recommend to the Council that consent be denied. The power to reject subdivision applications would have belonged exclusively to the elected representatives, under the provisions of the plan, and all councillors knew so. Yet the plan's opponents consistently read it differently, inferring that the councillors' power would be undermined by the officers' technocratic domination, even though the LEP itself had provided a good example of defeat for the officers. The LEP became so notorious that it helped people to make sense of other issues. It legitimated the councillor–officer power issue by suggesting that other issues could be seen that way, and by showing that the officers could be defeated.

The building regulation problems illustrate a similarly technocratic view in that the issue was: whose interests were to be catered for, business or bureaucracy? There was no assumed coincidence of authority and competence, to paraphrase Davies (1972: 227), and apparently little recognition of the Health Surveyor's attempts at compromise. The West Cowra water supply issue was an attack on officer legitimacy in the role of Council's adviser, rather than on officer competence. Tim West and Cyril Treasure designed a system, believing that they should be accorded a legitimacy equal to Jim Finnimore's in the designer role. The West/Treasure bid for legitimacy was contentious, and while it is not possible to say categorically that it was successful when the outcome was a compromise, it certainly created an issue.

All councillors shared the adversarial interpretation of their relations with the bureaucrats, but some reacted more strongly to it. A councillor who took a relatively mild view made the following observation:

> Some councillors have come onto Council who ... saw their main concern as too much power being vested in the officers. They were concerned with that aspect more than some of the other issues. They were going to take on the Council officers, which brought another tension to an already tense situation.

While some councillors were going to 'take on' the officers, all were willing to criticise when they felt it necessary, and all indicated to me that they felt an undercurrent of friction between the councillors and officers, exemplified by the expression: 'kick'em when they need to be kicked'. One who made very few criticisms of officers feared that those who appeared to launch vendettas against officers were making themselves vulnerable,

The making of local politics 137

because they could not remove the ingredient of subservience in the councillors' position.

While the councillor–officer relationship split the Council it did not form anything like a government–opposition division. Rather, it created issues, and they were its important products. Coalitions were formed in the course of issue resolution. While they were temporary coalitions, some councillors, more consistently than others, took a position contrary to the officers (table 1). In order to differentiate between those councillors who oppposed the officers and the others, the former will be called the Adversary group and the latter the Alliance group.

Table 1
Councillor Grouping on Major Issues Discussed During 1986

Issue	Alliance groups' members	Adversary groups' members
West Cowra water	Pengilly, Noble, Golsby	Treasure, West, Upston (who persuaded the remained)
Rural rates	Treasure, Bennett, West	Kibbler, Noble, Mallon (who persuaded the remainder)
Tourist and Development Corp. matters	Treasure, Newton, Golsby, West	Oliver, Upston, Kibbler, Noble, Pengilly, Mallon, Bennett, Bell
Building regulation	Treasure, Golsby, Noble, West, Bennett, Newton	Upston, Kibbler, Mallon, Bell, Pengilly
LEP	Treasure, West, Oliver, Bennett, Pengilly, Golsby, Newton	Upston, Kibbler, Mallon, Bell, Noble

Notes
Names are listed when they made a significant contribution to debate.

Some judgement has been used to generalise councillors' positions from the way they voted and their contributions to debate. This does not mean that all the 'Adversary group' spoke against the officers' recommendations. Stephen Bell, for example, in the building regulation matters, made a significant contribution to debate by seeking information from officers about Council's rights and responsibilities. His position overall indicated a desire to come to a decision, independent of the officer's recommendation, which would protect the interests of the businesses concerned. His move for independence was a contribution to the 'Adversary group' stance.

By 1986 farmer interests had largely won their LEP victory. Hence the large 'Alliance group' for the LEP shown in the table does not deny that the outcome of the issue favoured an earlier 'Adversary group'.

Some names appear consistently, but not always, in one group rather than the other, indicating that some councillors are more likely than others to have 'taken on' the officers. Harold Upston, Don Kibbler, Jack Mallon and Stephen Bell do not appear in the 'Alliance group'. Cyril Treasure, Bruce Golsby and Col Newton do not appear in the 'Adversary group'. This is not to say, for example, that Bruce Golsby always supported the officers. A farmer in the visitors' gallery at a Council meeting indicated to me that he had anticipated Bruce's support for the Clerk's recommendation on a matter related to the LEP, and a local professional told me that Bruce always supported the Clerk 'because they are good mates', but such a generalisation is not warranted. Bruce may have been seen to be in league with the officers because he supported their position on the highly visible issues like the LEP. From time to time he was critical of Council management, such as the occasion mentioned above when he suggested that Jim Finnimore had badly timed some repair work on the main street. The same could be said of other councillors. The appearance of a name in the Adversary group does not mean that that councillor opposed the officers just in order to trim their power. It was possible, for example, for councillors to oppose the Clerk's recommendation on matters relating to the Tourist and Development Corporation because they wanted, as they saw it, to defend the Corporation. Table 1 indicates that some councillors (Upston, Kibbler, Mallon and Bell) were less likely than others to take the officer 'alliance' position, and hence contribute to the making of issues. Of those four only Stephen Bell had been elected prior to the last election in 1983, having served since 1977. The longer serving councillors also took a technocratic view, but tended to choose a less active approach to its application.

The Council did not factionalise, even to the extent revealed in table 1, on any matters in which a councillor–officer conflict theme was not identifiable. All issues other than West Cowra's water supply were seen to affect the interests of farmers and business people. The West Cowra water supply was purely a councillor–officer affair, over the management of the 'people's corporation', in which no interests were apparent, except the legitimacy of performance of technical roles. In all the other issues, farmer and business interests were identifiable, and contrary to what were seen to be the interests of the bureaucracy and the bureaucrats. Other interests were not precipitating issues while the councillor–officer relationship was creating strife, even when undue officer influence was publicly implied, as it was by the *Guardian* in the Vacation Play Centre matter. The councillor–officer conflict loaded the political agenda, or was available for the agenda to be loaded with it.

There being no joint-elite does not mean, however, that the relationship did not further particular interests. The products of the relationship may have been the same as one would expect if there was an identifiable and persistent joint-elite. If we think of a joint-elite in terms of its impact on

The making of local politics

the power structure rather than as individuals and their relationships, a joint-elite becomes visible. An individualistic joint-elite model has the same shortcomings as those power studies which seek to explain power relations seen only from Lukes' (1974) one-dimensional view, in that it does not admit consideration of agenda setting and the effect of ideology.

The relationship between councillors and officers which produced the conflict might be described as a 'would-be joint-elite'. That is, it could reasonably be hypothesised that a joint-elite would have been identifiable if the institutional and ideological factors behind conflict had not been present, or if they had been present, a joint-elite would have existed if councillors had not chosen to act in a way which those factors directed. Councillors' choice to raise issues could be explained structurally by the interests which they sought to defend against bureaucracy. Politics in Cowra were elitist in that a narrow range of interests was accommodated by the political agenda, but the political structure was not elitist in terms of control by a small cohesive group.

To analyse this production of politics, it is useful to call on some conceptualisation of triad behaviour. Most issues and non-issues precipitated one of two types of coalition between a majority of councillors and the officers; what Mugford (1979: 261) describes as 'facilitative coalitions' (when alliance groups had a majority) which were likely to produce non-issues, and 'obstructive coalitions' (when adversary groups had a majority) which produced issues. Identification of the membership of a singular powerful group would be impossible and an attempt to do so would be pointless, partly because membership of the coalitions changed, but, most importantly, the interests served by coalition formation did not. 'Facilitative coalitions' to further the interests of women and Aboriginal people were not formed. The joint-elite may have failed to form because councillors and officers found themselves to have opposing interests, but their opposition became a large part of the political agenda.

An understanding of coalition behaviour requires introduction of the third element forming the triad (Mugford 1979). 'Obstructive coalitions' are formed to defend what their members perceive to be a general interest. In this case the third element is the electorate, whose interests the coalitions were interpreting, and in the case of obstructive coalitions, defending against the bureaucracy. Focus will now turn to the factors external to the political arena which stimulated local politics.

Town and country: deference in politics

Tension in town and country relations has been identified in earlier studies. Cowlishaw (1988: 152) found townspeople to offer 'a certain deference' to graziers. Agricultural producers believe that towns are dependent upon them (Bell et al, 1976; Montague, 1981), and see towns enjoying insulation from the vicissitudes of weather and foreign markets. Oeser and Emery (1957: 19) found that while town interests owed their existence to farmers, the farmers were dependent on town businesses for supplies, and town businesses could adjust prices and credit terms, or engage in 'sharp practices'. Dempsey (1990) found an anticipation among farmers that town businesses would extend credit during hard times. This was not well received by business people. Oeser and Emery (1957) and Montague (1981) pointed out that towns are decreasingly dependent on farmers as industrial, government and other service employment has grown.

From the town perspective, the farmers' belief in townspeople's dependence on them can look like aloofness and snobbishness (Oxley, 1978). Some Cowra town business people expressed dislike of what they saw as farmer arrogance, and criticised the then current protest action by the LGPA against the policies of the Commonwealth Government. 'They're all just bad farmers', one business person said to me. Another explained business people's dislike of farmers, and reluctance of the latter to support the town:

> They've been taught and trained the value of farming. So why be interested in anything else? That's their attitude ... The farmers' attitude is that they do us a favour by doing business with us. 'We don't need you. We can go to [a larger town about 100 kilometres distant].' They carry this attitude into community activities. On committees, they always like to think that they know more than we do.

A town-dwelling employed person told me that the farmers thought themselves to be 'lords of the manor', and that they had a general contempt for people in the town. A retired farmer living in town felt that town business people have a general contempt for farmers, seeing them as slow-witted. 'They go to business people who smile and pat them on the back; make them feel very important; make them feel that they are good blokes.' Such statements are better taken as illustrating a tension than indicating hostility.

Farming people also expressed the tension. A farmer pointed out to me that rural people see town businesses prospering while avoiding the brunt of the ups and downs of agriculture. One who grew up on a Cowra district farm said: 'Ever since I can remember there has been a feeling of us and them between country people and the townies ... You always got a feeling that there was a definite barrier between farmers and townies.'

I became aware of town and country differentiation, or at least the potential for it, at an interactional level. A conversation which I overheard in a shop reminded me of the farmers' perspective. As a woman whom I knew to be a farmer approached the counter the attendant smiled and said 'nice day'. The customer muttered 'even better if it rained', to which the attendant replied 'Yes, I like listening to the rain on the roof while I'm in bed at night'. That reply caught my attention. It was midwinter at the time and there had been no significant rain since midsummer; farmers feared that they would not be able to sow their crops for the next harvest. While rain is either pleasant or inconvenient for town people, it is essential for farmers. This is not to say that town people are unaware. In April 1981 the Cowra clergy organised special church services to pray for rain (*Cowra Guardian*, 29 April).

Town and country differentiation was acknowledged, and farmers defended their interests. In the rates issue farmers used the weapon of impending farm decline and consequent town business contraction, as they had done successfully during earlier drought years to keep their share of rate collections down. As Bruce Golsby said in arguing for expenditure restraint at the February, 1986 Council meeting, 'if the rural part of the Shire is suffering, we are all suffering'.

On occasions the Council readily deferred to farm interests. During discussion about a motion to increase parking time in the main street from one hour to two, a farmer councillor said bluntly that 'farmers need two hours'. There followed some laughter upon a comment from a town councillor that 'they've got no money to spend anyway', whereupon another town councillor replied: 'That's what we're here for, so let's make it two hours'.

This is reminiscent of the 'deferential dialectic' (Newby,1975; Bell and Newby, 1976a; Newby, 1977). Farmers sought to retain a perception among town people of a unity of interest in farming among town and country people: a view of farming as 'an 'organic' partnership in a cooperative enterprise' (Newby, 1975: 150). But in doing so they confronted the popular perception of hierarchical differentiation. Perception of hierarchy hung tenuously on the old belief in town dependence and popular aspirations and reverence for the farming life. Farmers maintained their belief that the town was largely dependent upon their economic well-being and argued that action which threatened their economic health was a threat to the economic health of the whole district. This view was expressed in one of the submissions to the LEP, which said: 'I cannot understand how the members of a rural council can be so ignorant concerning the management of the area which actually keeps the town (Cowra) in existence'. Another submission stated: 'This district derives its main income from the earnings of agricultural pursuits and indeed survives only because of the agricultural effort'.

To maintain a deferential relationship, they managed the tension inherent in the contradiction between identification and differentiation, in circumstances in which identification was threatened as farming had lost much of its dominance in the district's economy. As Newby (1975) suggested, an element of localism is, however, still available. Irony is apparent in the observation that some issues which inflamed much conflict on Council were those raised by farmers who felt that their relative contribution to the Shire's revenue was excessive; when they used an ideology of localism to argue that their contribution to local collective wealth was too great. It was farmers' perception of spending on town facilities which precipitated conflict over rural rates. Farmers were able to take advantage of both identification and differentiation.

Farmers' willingness to raise the rates issue may have been reinforced by lack of knowledge of their relative contribution to Council revenue, and reminders every time they go to town that rates helped to make life easier for the town people, who had sealed streets and reticulated water among other blessings, while farmers may have had to negotiate potholed and corrugated roads to get home to find a dry tank. This was evident in the letter from a farmer to the *Guardian* about the water augmentation scheme discussed in chapter 5. It was also evident in the following statement made by a farmer, which I believe indicates a popular view:

> A lot of rural ratepayers are dissatisfied because they contribute such a large proportion of rates. This comes back to this business about us being considered wealthy because we have property ... I think it's something like seventy per cent of Council's income is contributed by rural landholders and yet we are only thirty per cent of the Shire population. I forget the exact figures. A lot of people see that as unfair. We don't get representation proportional to our input. It's a bit like taxation without representation.

Farmers' rate bills could consume a substantial part of their income, but the rural part of the Shire contributed only about one sixth of Shire income in 1986.

The amalgamation of Waugoola and Cowra Shires created the potential battle ground over rating and representation, but the amalgamation alone could not be blamed for the persistence of the issues. One councillor felt that the amalgamation had created adversary conditions which had subsequently waned:

> It's taken away the closeness and the acceptance of things because of certain issues ... The problems are firstly the councillors who came across from the rural council never wanted the situation. They were saying it wasn't our idea. That was number one. Number two was 'we are here to make sure that the people of the old Shire are not disadvantaged by this exercise so we are going to do all we can to make sure that our interests are guarded'. That dominated proceedings for some time. I don't see that as so strong now.

Waugoola Shire and Cowra Municipal Councils appear to have been good company, falling out only occasionally, but possibly significantly in local minds, as incidents were related in the *Guardian*. In 1956 Waugoola supported the Municipal Council in a protest to the State Government over arrangements for a loan. In 1965 the Municipal Council made its building inspector available to Waugoola. The two Councils negotiated an agreement on responsibility for the cost of the Civic Centre (1967). However, when the Municipal Council asked Waugoola for a contribution to the cost of reconstructing the swimming pool, Waugoola declined (1976), and when, in 1963, Waugoola announced that it was going to build its own saleyards not far from the existing yards operated by the Municipal Council, the aldermen were upset (Armstrong, 1988 and *Cowra Guardian*, 25 October, 1963). A quotation from Shire President Oliver (Ab's brother) on the *Guardian*'s page one could have been interpreted as paternalistic: '. . . The Shire Council had always accepted the policy and responsibilities of Local Government in regard to bettering the town and district, and the Shire Council considered that Cowra was as much the Shire Council's town as it was the Municipal Council's town.'

The amalgamation was a marriage based on a difficult relationship and no courtship. Farmers were accustomed to the notion that their use of town facilities gave them a right to some say in town affairs. This was illustrated when the Municipal Council received opinions from farmers during a debate over parking restrictions in 1974, during which one correspondent to the *Guardian* wrote: 'The fact that the [Municipal] Council is pleased to receive suggestions and opinions from the country people is most gratifying . . . it is difficult to understand why Shire residents should have no say in Municipal affairs'.

The country people considered the town to be shared property. But at amalgamation, they realised that the town people would have more representatives on Council while they made a similar, or in the minds of some, a greater contribution to rate income. From the country perspective it was like a husband, in what had been a traditional patriarchal marriage, finding out that his wife had acquired most of the domestic political resources. The wave of amalgamations which hit Cowra was generally unpopular among town and country people, but it was more unpopular among country people (Musgrave et al., 1983, 1985). There had been tension between the two councils before amalgamation. Its persistence since that event is hardly surprising. It has added to the politics of councillor–officer relations, because the rural people were quick to see bureaucratic expansion, as they did in the LEP and rates issues, and demanded protection by their elected members.

Ratepayer defence

Local politics largely arose from attempts to defend what were interpreted to be the interests of ratepayers. Property owners were expected by councillors to demand fair value for their rate contributions. As local government has been constrained to property service, emphasis has been placed on rate minimisation rather than service maximisation. That is the essence of the 'ratepayer ideology', as described by Dunleavy (1980) and Halligan and Paris (1984). It was used in Cowra against business interests in the Japanese Garden issue and by business interests in the human services non-issue.

The important feature of the ratepayer ideology is that, in situations like Cowra, where people of diverse occupations and incomes have a property interest by way of home ownership, it sweeps along a large proportion of the population regardless of other class characteristics. That is how it creates popular politics in a situation which, as will be discussed below, politics are ideologically barred. As Rose et al. (1976: 703) showed, the universality of property interest, regardless of differences in kinds of property such as between those used for production (factories, farms etc) and those used for consumption (houses, motor cars etc), can be used to demonstrate a universal interest in maintaining the status quo. Privatisation and allegiance to property interest through home ownership, which Kilmartin and Thorns (1978) found to have a pacifying effect on suburban populations by suggesting a common interest in urban space, can, however, arouse protest which crosses class lines when that common interest is seen to be threatened. Other studies, including those of Painter (1974), Bell et al. (1976), Oxley (1978) and Wild (1983), have revealed a willingness to protest about rating, or at least a concern to keep rates down.

Such concern was expressed long ago in Cowra, when in 1898, a Ratepayers' Association was formed under the chairmanship of the inimitable J.C. Ryall (*Cowra Free Press*, 5 May, 1898). In recent times ratepayers' associations have come and gone. A rise in rates is likely to ignite protest, as it did in 1986, but rises are also likely to be avoided by the Council if it feels that it can do so. In early 1986, Bruce Golsby successfully moved that there be no general rate increase that year. This occurred in a gloomy rural economic climate in which farmer moves for rate freezes were reported in the rural press (Petrikas, 1986).

Waugoola Council often avoided rate increases, but when it raised rates it sometimes attracted vehement criticism and disruptive protest in the form of withholding. The pages of the *Guardian* indicate that it did not raise its rate in 1950, 1954, 1955, 1956, 1958, 1960 and 1968. It actually reduced its rate in 1952, 1957, 1965 and 1971, but in 1951, 1962, 1964, 1969, 1970 and 1972, its rate rises attracted opposition. The opposition could be vehement and close to home. The *Guardian* of 21 March, 1952 (p.1) reported that at a Farmers and Settlers Association meeting 'the 20-odd members present pounced on the councillors for the recent increase in Shire rates'. A former Waugoola councillor told me that another farmer had challenged him to a public fight at one of the annual village shows after a rate increase. As Bell et al. (1976) offered a reminder, otherwise friendly rural neighbours can become mortal enemies, and rates offered a point for falling out.

The 1986 water rate protest arose after accounts were received by ratepayers. The accounts were larger than many people had expected but in line with Council policy for augmentation of the water reticulation system. The increases had come about through a reduction in the amount of water allowed under a fixed fee before it has to be paid for according to quantity consumed. A prominent local businessman called a meeting to re-form the Ratepayers Association. The Association attracted about 250 members. That meeting and other problems which arose over the water augmentation prompted a Special Council Meeting at which water rating policy decisions were made. The Council resolved to apply the 'user pays' principle more stringently in domestic water rating but, among other matters, to continue to subsidise the town's large industries.

I heard appeals for application of the 'user pays' principle several times at Council meetings, and on one occasion a direct reference to the property value enhancement effect of Council works. At a Policy and Resources Committee meeting, Tim West raised the matter of charging adjacent property owners for footpath paving. He claimed that the policy was unfair because people living further down a street made greater use of the footpath, and the charge was a burden on pensioners. He further argued that the cost should be met from general rate revenue because footpaths are a public asset. Don Kibbler and Bruce Golsby replied that footpaths increase property values and the discussion ceased.

A prominent member of the Ratepayers' Association told me after the water rates issue had dissipated that the Association had tried to change the Council's ways, but it was not optimistic about eliminating what it saw to be inefficiencies and inequities in Council administration. It was important, the member said, for the Association to have representatives from a variety of occupations. (Its executive included employed as well as business people.) 'The wealthy don't even notice an increase in rates. When the rates go up [a prominent business person] just increases the rent; [another prominent business person] raises prices, but the little bloke goes without.' This Ratepayers' Association member may have doubted the Association's viability, but did not doubt the rightfulness of its objectives, nor the legitimacy of its protest. The rating issue arose again in 1986, when a councillor examined the accounts presented by the Clerk at estimates time, and concluded that the Council's reserves were larger than necessary. The councillor moved to use the reserves to finance a rate reduction. He was not successful, but it is interesting to note that the matter was again thoroughly discussed in the Council, and nobody inside or outside the Council publicly suggested that the reserves be used to provide additional local facilities. There is plenty of room for those who want to raise the issue, but the politics of rates are removed from the potential issues of class, race and gender.

Status politics

The issues surrounding the Tourist and Development Corporation contained an individualistic element, introduced by the presence of Don Kibbler as Corporation President. Don's presence made the status system a resource of his opponents in so far as his personal background denied him resources which may have been available to others.

Australian community studies, notably those of Wild (1974a) and Oxley (1978), have provided extensive analyses of status systems. Oxley in particular pinpoints the possible hazards of climbing the ladder into high local office. 'Social climbing is watched for and disapproved of. Anyone who fraternizes too much with people of a higher stratum risks criticism from his own' (97). Don, however, did not just aspire to friendships among high status people in order to social climb. He achieved business success. His parents had migrated from Britain and established a building firm in Cowra. Don continued the building business but later went into others including a hotel, a newsagency and real estate. He received much local publicity, mainly through his work as President of the Tourist and Development Corporation and sponsorship of the Cowra Sportsperson of the Year Award. A photograph of him with Prime Minister Bob Hawke appeared on page one of the *Guardian*. The photograph was taken when the Prime Minister was in Japan on an official visit, and Don was there to discuss the Cowra Japanese Garden with Japanese dignitaries. Don had made a substantial contribution to the Garden project, but unfortunately for his experience in local politics, he collided with the Australian manifestation of Lloyd Warner's dictum: 'Successful social mobility in the American mind is a magnificent performance but is never as good as being born to the group of those who already belong' (1949: 295).

British rural community studies have also found such traps for self-made people. Littlejohn (1963) found that people who associated with others of a higher class were apt to be stigmatised, and Newby et al. (1978: 309) found that both farmers and farm workers distinguished the 'nouveaux riches' from those who were ascribed the qualities of traditional high status.

Don Kibbler had challenged what Gramson (1985: 610) might call 'the working consensus' on the personal background desired for Cowra leadership, a challenge which could take on, with what were perceived to be Don's clearly displayed ambitions, 'the character of moral transgression' (ibid.). Four people close to the Corporation told me that they believed that opposition to it was a manifestation of the 'tall poppy syndrome', and merely a personal attack on Don. This personal aspect, however, did not surface in debate as the ratepayer principle did. The point is that the Corporation's affairs might more readily have become an issue when it was possible for its President's credentials, albeit status credentials, to be questioned.

There was therefore some potential for status warfare in local politics, with, broadly speaking, a lower stratum fighting the middle. The lower stratum came to the fight armed with the principles of egalitarianism embedded in the status system while those at the top were made invulnerable by tradition based on property. It could be likened to the symbolic politics discussed by Gusfield (1963). For Gusfield, the politics of temperance symbolised protest against status; in Cowra, protest over public support for the Tourist and Development Corporation in part at least symbolised a struggle to retain the old status structure with its reinforcing ideology of egalitarianism. To the very limited extent that the Tourist and Development Corporation issues were status politics, they lacked the councillor–officer dimension present in all others.

Conclusion: coalitions and interests

The overt politics of Cowra Shire arose when councillors perceived a need to defend their electorate, sometimes erroneously equated by many people with the ratepayers, against the bureaucracy. In the Tourist and Development Corporation issues the 'real' matter of contention was seen in each instance as power being placed in the hands of senior officers. The water rate billing issue was seen to be a contest between the Shire Clerk and the ratepayers. The Council formed a 'facilitative coalition', standing by the officers and effectively turning it into a non-issue, because councillors believed that they and the officers were pursuing ratepayers' real interests. The rural rating and representation issues were seen differently: as problems of bureaucratic empire building. The Council formed an 'obstructive coalition', as it did in the Tourist and Development Corporation issues, with a majority of councillors opposing what they interpreted to be the Shire Clerk's wishes. As 'facilitative coalitions' produced non-issues, such as Taragala's air pollution and the general non-issue of human services, the formation of 'obstructive coalitions' virtually became visible local politics.

Perception of the rightfulness of defending a third party, which in Cowra was the ratepayers, was the important factor in formation of 'obstructive coalitions'. Ratepayers were believed to need protection from 'experts' and bureaucrats who could not be trusted to design water reticulation systems, who might have got away with pursuing their own interests, who might have strangled development and personal freedoms with rules and regulation, or might have thrown the Council into an expensive exercise in human services which was not its own idea and was beyond its traditional bailiwick. The councillors believed that they were protecting what the ratepayers valued; that they were expressing not just their own values but those of the people they served. The constriction of politics into obstructive coalition formation was enabled by the desire of ratepayers to have their interests defended, and the interpretation which both ratepayers and councillors placed upon those interests. Ratepayers' desires for defence constituted resources which were used by, and hence empowered, business and farm people.

Notes

1 Nineteenth-century reform in the United States established independent local bureaucracy in order to replace influence with efficiency (Viteritti, 1982).
2 A phantom distinction between councillors as policy makers and officers as administrators has a long history. Stanyer (1976) found its origins in an American attack on public corruption in the late nineteenth century. Stoker and Wilson (1986: 287) described it as a 'hoary cliche', which had been superseded by the 'dictatorship of the official' hypothesis. These views are supported by the absence of stated policies among councillors. Blowers (1977) and Jones (1981) suggested that bureaucrats may be able to exploit a political vacuum. Elliott and McCrone (1982) and Laffin and Young (1985) found increased partisanship in British local government to have decreased the power of officials.

9
Ideologies and resources

Business and farm interests dominated local politics in Cowra Shire as their proponents defined the political agenda. Such domination reflected the values and beliefs of councillors and was seen by the people of the Shire to be legitimate. Domination was enabled by this perception of rightfulness. These observations call for explanation as the politics created, while popularly legitimate, contained expression of the interests of some people of the Shire, but either ignored or obscured the interests of others. They suggest that domination was at least in part a consequence of the wishes of those who were dominated.

The antecedents of this power structure can be seen largely in terms of ideological resources. That is, those structural products of the social system which were manifest in beliefs and values, and which were expressed by councillors in the course of local politics. They were available as resources and were used consciously or unconsciously by political actors, because they were widely shared among both the more and the less powerful. While legitimacy may be a property of rulers, it is a product of the ideas of the ruled. The legitimacy of rulers need not be a product of their own efforts. The concept of resources breaks the connection. The ideas of the ruled can be resources of rulers without either party making conscious attempts at creating, altering or maintaining them. Attention is, therefore, moved from the local political arena to the system of interrelated beliefs and values which legitimate political action, and the ways in which those beliefs and values accrue to actors and are used as resources in the local political arena.

Rhetoric

To explore the beliefs and values of political actors, it will be useful to apply an analysis based on Bailey's (1983) concept of 'assertive rhetoric':

> In short, assertive rhetoric inescapably must proceed by begging the question: by simple assertion of the correctness of one answer to the question at issue. There is no other way of arguing about intrinsic

values, for these are ends in themselves. The speaker asserts a truth by identifying the true believers who 'happen' to be those who believe that truth. Accordingly it is inappropriate to ask whether an argument advanced in this form of rhetoric is valid or invalid, and to test it by the rules of logic. The proper question to ask about assertive rhetoric concerns effectiveness. It is intended to provoke attitudes of approval or disapproval, to compel assent, to bring people over to one's side. For doing so what rhetorical devices are thought to be effective? (1983: 135)

The West Cowra water supply issue offered examples of councillors asserting their right to challenge opinions of formally qualified technicians. Several councillors challenged 'expert' opinion, and claimed that consultation with them was unnecessary. Harold Upston could claim qualification to make technical judgements. He said that he was 'amazed at some of the things that had been said about water', and suggested that 'councillors should come to my place out the back to learn about fluids'. Tim West criticised the design of the water works, saying that it would never work correctly. 'We've been sold one of the greatest lemons any council has ever had.' He could claim that the river bank pump vibrated so badly that 'the bails fall off the stumps' at the nearby cricket ground. These councillors believed that engineers and technicians did not have a monopoly on design skill, and that the judgements of councillors who had no formal technical qualifications would be accepted as legitimate.

The comment by a passing politician about the Taragala air pollution problem asserted the value of the polluting factory to Cowra. Bruce Golsby's comment about the effect of rural economic 'suffering' was a similar assertion. Both assertions contained a belief in a communal identity for the Cowra district.

The Japanese Garden issue provided opposing assertions. While Stephen Bell implied that the bureaucrats were furthering their own interests, Col Newton implied that business was furthering its interests. Ab Oliver, in the debate about 'in-committee' sitting during discussion of the Garden issue, appealed to perceptions of a wider public interest. None of these assertions contained an extended argument to support the interpretations they espoused. They appealed rather to value placed on what was seen to be fair and mutually beneficial dealing.

Don Kibbler and Harold Upston asserted that planning policies were undesirable because they required regulation. Don argued that planning policies were bad because they discouraged development. Harold asserted that the LEP should not have included a statement that there are no types of prohibited development because there should be no need to say so. Ab Oliver appealed for maintenance of the exclusive property service function of Council on the basis that other functions were represented by external threats. Jack Mallon made the same appeal with reference to tradition. All such appeals assumed a consensus of values.

Each assertion was made, at least implicitly, as a defence of ratepayers. West Cowra people would have been better off without an 'expert' to design their water supply system. The polluting factory was good for Cowra's economy, just as suffering farmers would have been bad for it. Profit by the bureaucracy, and business risk-taking at public expense would have been bad for ratepayers, but development of the project would have been in the general interest. Attempts by bureaucrats to formalise and regulate were bad for ratepayers, as were excursions into non-traditional functions which were all the ideas of outsiders.

They were often effective. The West/Treasure plan for West Cowra's water supply was accepted, albeit in modified form. Taragala's air pollution took ten years to be removed. The farmers were protected from rate increases. The Tourist and Development Corporation won the local battle for the Gardens. The LEP was drastically altered, and human services stayed off the local political agenda. The effectiveness of the rhetoric used to obtain these outcomes can be explained with examination of the ideological climate in which the issues arose.

Rural ideology

Although several sets of beliefs and values may be identified among the people of Cowra, they may be generalised into a peculiarly rural ideology. Although similar ideologies have been identified in studies of urban local government (Dunleavy, 1980; Halligan and Paris, 1984), each set of beliefs and values among Cowra people has a particular manifestation and perhaps a special intensity associated with the rural situation. Rural ideology was introduced earlier with references to Poiner's (1990) use of a concept of a 'rural idyll', and encountered again as the historical agrarian ideal invoked as 'assertive rhetoric' by proponents of land reform. Both are expressions of an ideal of rural life perceived from an urban perspective, but being associated with what rural people see as positive aspects of rural life, they are also components of the rural belief system. It is, however, useful to separate the 'rural idyll' from the ideologies of farmers. Origins of the 'rural idyll' lie in British tradition, the core of which attributes harmony and virtue to rural living and disorganisation and alienation to city life (Newby, 1977).

In the Australian context, farming is seen not only as a good lifestyle but as an ennobling vocation, in that it consists of honest hard work in a situation in which self-reliance is essential and enterprise is rewarded. Farming produces many of the essentials of life for urban as well as rural people, and in Australia it provides a traditionally very important contribution to economic prosperity by way of production for export. The better lifestyle component of the ideology is shared by those urban dwellers who idealise rural living, some of whom have chosen to move to the country to take up farming or some other small business, but it is the other components which give agricultural society its distinctiveness.

At a behavioural level, agrarianism has been credited with helping to sustain the small family farming system in Australia (Craig, 1983; Craig and Phillips, 1983). Poiner (1990) found that rural people share a genuine commitment to rural life. The role of ideology in family farming in the Cowra district has been considered in Gray (1988b), a study in which sixteen local farming couples were interviewed on matters relating to ideology and intergenerational property transfer. The study identified two sets of values among farming couples, 'one set oriented towards the peculiarly rural aspects of farming and the other looking more like a business ethic' (25). The ideal of family persistence in agriculture through inheritance was found to be stronger among those expressing the former set of values. Both sets of values had one feature prominently in common; they both included emphasis on independence and self-reliance, even among those respondents for whom the uniquely rural aspects of farming, like being part of a rural community and the opportunity to work close to nature, were not so important. Agrarianism is more complex than the belief in the virtues of rural living of the British tradition and the land reform rhetoric. It contains rationalisations of persistence and survival in trying circumstances, which are so trying as to be threatening the future of family farming (Lawrence, 1987).

Self-reliance is an important component of rural ideology. As Marshall (1985) wrote of farmers: 'They have claimed to possess the characteristics of independence and individual initiative, identifying them with all that is best in the "national character" (24). Belief in self-reliance can have direct political ramifications as aversion to welfare. Rural ideology also has a gender dimension. The woman in the home is a central feature of the image of rural bliss. Reality for farming women is, however, often very different to what the domestic tradition would have us suppose (Davidoff et al., 1976; Little, 1986).

Perception of contrast, even opposition, between country and city is another component of rural ideology. Such perceptions are often called 'countrymindedness', which Verrall et al. (1985) define as consisting of belief in '... the special elevated virtue of rural living, and the 'mission' of rural people to defend embattled faiths and 'standards'...' (21). Aitkin's (1972) research on the Country (now National) party found it to have adopted a 'countrymindedness' ideology which had changed little through the history of the party (17). Aitkin found the ideology to be based on belief that farmers' interests should be fostered by government because Australia's economy is dependent on them, and farming is a worthy occupation which brings out the best in people. The latter aspect rose to moral convictions which gave farmers much political vigour.

'Countrymindedness' produces differentiation at the individual level.

Ideologies and resources 153

Dempsey (1983: 119) found that having country origins helped to make newly arrived ministers in a rural parish acceptable as an 'insider' rather than an 'outsider'. It also leads to contradictions which create tensions for country people. While they want to retain the country lifestyle and its valued attributes for their children, they know that city education and careers offer potential for relatively high income, which appears increasingly unlikely on the farm. While they value hard work and self-reliance, they envy the facilities and associated comfortable lifestyle of the cities. And while they see themselves as the backbone of the Australian economy, they see their share of exports having declined and the future for their international markets appearing bleak.[1] Cowra people have seen their autonomy succumb to city advances. Rural ideology is both a set of beliefs and values which elevates rural living and helps to sustain rural settlement, and a means for comprehending the hierarchical relationship between city and country. Both these features have ramifications for local government.

Subjugation of bureaucrats

Local government generally operates in a climate in which, as Dunleavy (1980: 145) found, 'ideological forms ... produce generalised or stereotyped responses to decision problems'. In Australia, three ideologies: the ratepayer principle, political neutrality and localism have been found to affect local political relations (Halligan and Paris, 1984: 60). The characteristic which ratepayers are assumed to want most of all from their councillors is willingness and initiative to subjugate their bureaucratic servants, who, from a popular technocratic perspective, threaten to become masters. In so far as it seeks to promote the welfare of ratepayers by constraining excesses within councils, it is related to Halligan and Paris's ratepayer principle. In Cowra the popularity of this view around the electorate was made clear to me in many conversations, some of which have been reported above, and others in which Harold Upston was praised in his absence with reports of attempts to curtail the supposed ambitions of the bureaucrats. The point was made to me by a candidate at the 1987 election, who said that the one thing which everybody, to whom the candidate had spoken, had asked was: 'Are you going to stir up [the officers and those councillors who were thought to readily join 'alliance groups']?' The assumption that there was something about Council officers that made them need either mobilisation or restraint for the good of the people was the most direct ideological stimulus for 'obstructive coalitions'.

There were three aspects to this view. One was an assumed need for quite direct defence from objective threats in the form of unfair or unreasonable regulation and policing. Another stemmed from the belief that bureaucrats should not be powerful, either because they were inept, or because it was morally wrong for them to be powerful. The third arose from fear of less direct effects from poor management due to the assumed inherently stultifying effects of bureaucratisation on council management practices. In its demand for efficiency, the third could be seen in part to be an application of the ratepayer principle.

Regulation was sometimes assumed to open the door to potential bureaucratic malpractice. This view, expressed in the LEP controversy, contradicted the reasoning behind the establishment of independent bureaucracies which emphasised the risk of elected representative malpractice. The Council has a policing role which can give it an authoritarian public image. It occasionally prosecuted malefactors, who, for example, had failed to remove their noxious weeds, rubbish or material which constituted a fire hazard. The officers' perspective on this role was depicted in the *Guardian* after the New South Wales Government had decided to move responsibility for administration of the Dog Act from the shoulders of the Police Force onto local government:

> Nothing will make the heavens tremble like the outcry, wailing and vituperation of someone who has lost their pet dog and if it has disappeared forever into the maw of the Council's pound there is no weapon the sufferer will not lay his hands on to bring the miscreant official to the dust. He will have the sympathy of all other dog owners, relatives and friends – which comprise a sizeable portion of the community.' (*Cowra Guardian*, 21 June, 1966, p.2)

The Council could find itself unable to please anyone, or could be used by some ratepayers to resolve their feuds with others. At a 1986 meeting of the Works Committee, the Health Surveyor reported that a ratepayer had asked a solicitor to write to the Council asking it to serve notice on a neighbour to remove manure placed beside trees along the common boundary. The Shire President and the Health Surveyor investigated and found that action by the Council was not warranted. The Health Surveyor added the following to his report: 'It is well to mention that over the past five or six years inspections at [the neighbouring houses] have been made for the purpose of investigation of alleged nuisances by four Health Surveyors, in some cases, several times, two Shire Presidents and the Health Department.'

Councillors could seek to restrain this aspect of the Council's operations. At another Works Committee meeting a councillor spoke against agreement to a request from the Health Surveyor that special constable status be sought for the Ordinance Officer (who was effectively the Council's policeman), despite assurances from the Health Surveyor that most such officers in local government were special constables and that it was largely a convenient formality. The objecting councillor believed that such a move would be 'contrary to the mood of the electorate'.

Allegations from councillors of bureaucratic ineptitude were made in the context of conflict arising from feelings among both councillors and officers that each was usurping the others' roles. There were many illustrations, especially among the LEP submissions, of the fear of giving bureaucrats responsibilities of which they were not worthy. The LEP also aroused moral indignation and fear of 'socialism' among farmers. They saw planning as a threat from bureaucracy to the vital features of their business ethic, noted in Gray (1988b) to place great value on self-reliance, initiative and independent decision making. A candidate at the 1987 Council election included in his manifesto, published in the *Guardian,* the statement: 'There is a great danger that big government and creeping bureaucracy will rapidly absorb all the rights of local people, particularly their right to control their district through their own elected representatives and shire officers.'

These sentiments were reflected in Council debates on other issues, notably in the positions taken by Harold Upston and Don Kibbler in building regulation and other planning matters when they were used significantly as resources, even if those who used them could only obtain compromise. They were decisive resources in the wider arena opened by the public meetings, as they were used to arouse mass support for the 'concerned citizens' protest.

The third aspect of the view that bureaucrats needed mobilisation or restraint favoured mobilisation. This is an expression of the desire for efficiency, keystone of the ratepayer principle. Bureaucrats lacked access to an important legitimating factor in Cowra's rural ideological climate: they were not subjected to the economic and physical environments' imposition of hard work and self-reliance. Farmers could consider themselves to be efficient, because the logic of the physical environment and the market place told them that they must be if they had survived so long. Farmers believed that they were entitled to efficiency among their local government servants. Moreover, farmers themselves had to survive without ready availability of expert advice, often having just their own skills and perhaps those of family and neighbours, or both, to draw on. Faith in personal abilities was perhaps best expressed in the Council by the West/Treasure plan for West Cowra's water supply.

As well as leading to debate which clouded the distributional aspects of issues, the desire for efficiency further clouded distributional aspects of local non-politics by ratifying administration practices. In this way 'facilitative coalitions', and associated non-issues, were created, rather than the 'obstructive coalitions' which formed over West Cowra's water, among other matters. The 'facilitative coalitions' were formed because the efficiency of the administrative apparatus, as operated by the bureaucrats, was to be defended for the sake of the ratepayers. The apparatus rather than the 'squeaky wheels' was seen to be benign.

Efficiency of administration had popular appeal. This may have been associated with Cowra's large number of self-employed people and employers, who may have taken a particular interest in, and valued efficient administration. Among Cowra election candidates, minimisation of rates was used as a platform, rather than more abstract references to efficiency. Although a candidate at the 1977 municipal election claimed to seek both minimal rates and efficiency, another emphasised his 'extensive training in business management', another wanted the 'best use of ratepayers' money', another wanted to maintain a strong financial position and provide facilities, and yet another believed that 'Cowra's future lies in steady continued growth based on sound management techniques' (*Cowra Guardian*, 16 September, pp. 4, 6). In 1980 four candidates mentioned management in their brief manifestos published in the *Guardian*. In 1983 a candidate planned to 'assist in sound and responsible administration' (*Cowra Guardian*, 7 September, 1983, p. 2). In 1987 two of the eighteen candidates mentioned management, and another used a metaphor I heard many times, and saw in a *Guardian* (3 October) editorial prior to the 1986 by-election: describing the Council as a large business.

Rural people sought a council which was worthy of the ideals they cast upon their social environment as the font of freedom, enterprise and honourable living. Unfortunately for the bureaucrats, these features were either lacking in or threatened by their peculiar bureaucratic environment, in which organisation must prevail over individualism. Points of compatibility between the two systems were few, but were at least found in the search for managerial efficiency. Unfortunately that search also provided grounds for councillor-officer friction over their respective roles, so exacerbating the dominance of councillor-officer conflict over Cowra's local politics.

Political neutrality

Maintenance of local government free of politics is the second of the Halligan and Paris (1984) ideologies. It accrues as a resource to those who seek to maintain the status quo by denying legitimacy to those who might pursue opposing interests.[2] Non-partisanship has been written into Australian local government, institutionalised in a volume which has been a councillors' 'bible' (Stuckey, 1975). This publication declares in a heading that 'Sectional Interests Have No Place in Local Government', and goes on to exhort councillors to turn their energies to looking after their whole municipalities and shires (6).[3] Loveday (1972), Painter (1974) and Bowman (n.d.) all reported the ideology, as did Aitkin (1972), Pandey (1972) and Wild (1974a), in rural situations. Loveday found that criticism of politicisation was always aimed at the Labor Party. Bowman found that conservatives tended to gain by being seen not to present a threat to entrenched interests in local government.

Wild (1974a), applying an individualistic approach, showed how a mayor drew on the value which the aldermen placed on maintaining consensus within the Council to sustain his personal power. Wild found his direction of the agenda to be carried out in a 'forthright' manner. When debate arose he cut it short either by asking for an alderman to frame a motion, or by stating what the motion would be, from which point the motion would be quickly put to the meeting and carried. Wild interpreted this as direction of a 'voluntary consensus' (141), implying that the Mayor used the aldermen's wish to avoid conflict to gain his will. Such power, however, need not depend on conscious action of this kind.

Any view of politics as class-based is obscured in a climate of 'country-mindedness'. As Aitkin (1972) commented, farmers do not take a hierarchical view of society. Rather, they see divisions in terms of city and country, and economic sectors. In addition, as Oeser and Emery (1957) reported, there can be such hostility to the Labor Party that its activities are discouraged, reinforcing the local power of farmers. Oeser and Emery stated that the farmers 'can enforce a rigorous censorship on the public expression of political views' (1957: 32). They did so to keep political discussion out of local currency. 'Politics are seen as mainly concerned with national or state issues, not local, and as mainly an activity for parliamentarians or would-be parliamentarians (except for the three-yearly intervention of the electors). Thus defined, politics have no place in the local community' (ibid.). Pandey (1972) also identified a belief that there was no local place for politics, and showed how this belief was voiced by rural interests. It was widely accepted, and had kept the Labor Party out of an overt role in local government.

Hostility is, however, not necessary, because, as Rose et al. (1976) reported, Labor is itself shy of politics in local government. Dempsey (1983) pointed out that political conflict can make life uncomfortable in small rural settlements where frequent interaction is common, adding undesirability of conflict to the perceived lack of necessity for local politicisation. Dempsey (1990) found 'Smalltownites' to see themselves as loyal to each other, preserving an image of community harmony and solidarity. I encountered a general distaste for conflict in Cowra, people seeing it as unnecessary and distracting, and associating it with political parties. The reluctance of aspirants to local public office, and the reticence of the Labor Party in local politics would be sufficient to rule out class-based politics.

Labor has been a viable political party in Cowra. There are unions representing employees at the three large factories, the railway, the banks, the hospital and the high school. The railway may have been especially important. Verrall et al. (1985) found that the decline of the railway had contributed to the decline of the Labor Party in rural areas, along with the decrease in numbers of rural workers. A Cowra member of the Party told me that local Party membership had fallen, but it was still able to attract around half the Cowra town vote at State and Federal elections.

In the 1987 House of Representatives election the ratio of first preference votes was 2 240 for Labor to 2 968 for the National candidate.[4] That is, the ALP attracted forty-three per cent of the vote for the two major parties across the polling booths in the Shire (Australian Electoral Commission, 1987). It attracted forty-five per cent at the town booths, rising to forty-eight per cent at the village of Woodstock, and falling to eight per cent at each of two rural booths. If local politics operated and behaved electorally as State and Federal elections have done, the Labor Party could reasonably have expected to gain about as many representative seats as the National or Liberal Parties, other things, such as division of the electorate, having been equal.

The Labor Party members went as far as forming a group on the ballot paper at Shire elections, but maintained that they were standing as independents. Col Newton was quoted by the *Guardian* (19 September, p. 2) before the 1983 election to have said: '... even though councillors were standing as groups, they were really standing as independents'. It seemed that the councillors who were members of the Labor Party felt that being labelled as 'politicisers' would be politically damaging for them. For this reason, and another to be mentioned shortly, I did not pursue my initial wish to attend Party meetings, as it seemed that members may have been concerned that my presence would create links in people's minds between the Party and the Council, which I was known to be studying.

There is some irony in this fear of political stigma, because, while the councillors who happened to be members of the Labor Party found that they had to defend themselves from anticipated allegations that they were politicising local politics, they made no attempt to pursue class politics when on the Council, despite what appeared, to all voters but the few who might have been totally ignorant of local affairs, to be their appearance on the ballot paper as a Labor Party team. I heard suggestions, from people who expressed fear of politicisation, that, despite their denials, the Labor councillors really did caucus and communicate in order to block vote at meetings. I found no evidence of that, which is not surprising, given that there was only one issue that even remotely resembled class politics (the controversy surrounding the Tourist and Development Corporation).

Party politics were excluded from Cowra Shire. That is the other reason for my not pursuing the party organisations. I knew two of the councillors to be, or to have been, associated with the National Party and to have held higher political ambitions. But that had no necessary relevance either. The Council may have operated as though it was dominated by the National Party, in that it served business and farm interests, but in Cowra's ideological climate, it could probably have done so with or without National Party member councillors. Conversely, there was nothing to suggest that the Council would have had more 'issues' on its agenda if a majority, or even all of its members were Labor Party members, such was the elimination of class politics from the agenda, except in so far as ratepayer defence was class politics, by the perceived necessity for constituent defence. The electorate largely ruled out overt class-based politics.

The threat of politicisation worked for Stephen Bell at the 1983 election. All candidates except Stephen and Jack Mallon decided to form or join a group on the ballot paper. Consequently Stephen and Jack were placed together, with one name above the other, on the ballot paper. They looked like another group. Stephen challenged the Clerk's decision to 'group' him with Jack, and the consequent fuss in Council made front page headlines in the *Guardian* during the week before the election. Stephen loudly proclaimed his independence, which gave the electorate the impression that he and Jack (Stephen was the one in the limelight) were the only independents. Stephen polled well, being elected fifth, behind four more experienced councillors (Ab Oliver, Barbara Bennett, Col Newton and Neville Pengilly). The *Guardian* reported (26 September, p. 1) that 'Cowra people ... clearly demonstrated that they voted for people and not groups'. For example, Don Kibbler was placed second in Group A but was elected sixth, as he received many first preference votes.

The grouping at this election also attracted a letter to the *Guardian* which indicated a popular view, associating ballot paper group formation with politicisation:

> At the last Shire election it was obvious that party politics and sectional voting had been introduced ...
> When viewing the 1983 proposed ballot it appears that most of the candidates have considered it necessary to follow suit.
> At the local government level most candidates and their abilities are known by the electors and I would have thought the organizational ability of political parties and perhaps biased views of sectional groups was unnecessary. We as electors of this diverse electorate need councillors with common sense and balanced views elected on their merit and not the effectiveness of a campaign. (19 September, p. 2)

I encountered similar views in interviews and conversations:

> 'Grouping is the worst thing that has ever happened to the Council.' (Farmer)
> 'There are few in it – I don't know how they got there – on these political tickets I think.' (Town-dwelling employee)
> 'A lot of people said: I wouldn't vote for a man in a group no matter who he was.' (Former Waugoola Councillor)

Some believed that grouping on the ballot paper did not just mean tickets; it meant party political tickets. 'I believe that country towns used to be apolitical. Locally up until the last two elections there was no party politics. Every person stood on their own merits. It never entered people's thoughts as to what affiliation they were ...' (farmer). Expressions of the fear of politicisation extended to devising methods to combat its symptoms. I heard a suggestion from a farmer that the ballot paper be circular so that grouping would be impossible. The seating at Council meetings was randomised around the table to discourage co-ordinated action among councillors.

Not surprisingly, and with the exception of aberrations like the 1983 election (to be discussed further below), candidates presented themselves as independent of political parties, and/or claimed to represent the whole town and district. This suggests an explanation for the slow turnover of councillors. Electors were seldom offered policies which would upset the status quo, and when such policies were offered they were likely to be rejected. At the 1980 election, two candidates each proposed to improve facilities in parts of the town (Mulyan and West Cowra), and were not elected. At the 1987 election only one group was formed, other than the usual one of Labor Party members. There was little prospect of a return to the old pluralistic spatial politics of the 1950s, because the administrative apparatus discouraged group ventures, but moreover, because fear of politicisation eliminated electoral prospects for groups seeking to pursue a spatial interest.

In terms of forming groups as teams, the Council was politicised overtly and successfully at the 1983 election. A group of candidates called the 'Advance Cowra Team' was advertised in the *Guardian*. The group of four included two successful candidates, Harold Upston and Neville Pengilly. While stating that 'it was felt that Cowra's business sector, which pays 27% of the Shire rates should have representation on the Council', Harold Upston, who was described in the article as President of the Chamber of Commerce, said 'if elected the team would serve as independents without affiliation to any party or organisation' (*Cowra Guardian*, 6 July, 1983, p. 1). Ab Oliver and four other candidates produced a joint manifesto for the 1974 election without giving themselves a title. I recall a conversation with a group of three farmers at a social function in which one farmer suggested to another that he stand in the next election as a farmers' representative. Nobody baulked at the implied politicisation. The Farmers' Association placed an advertisement in the *Guardian* (23 September, p. 15) recommending two candidates. There was a tendency among farmers and business people to believe that only Labor could politicise, and that any participation by it as a party must inevitably have that effect. There may have been an element of truth in that if one assumed the existence of a conservative autocracy in which all politics were a non-issue, but as implied above, Labor would have had to introduce class politics: a most unlikely scenario.

Belief in political neutrality was a resource available to conservative forces which they could use, if they chose, to maintain their dominance by keeping conflict off the agenda; conflict, that is along class, gender, race or spatial lines. The ideology could be useful to conservative interests in its denial of resources to those who might potentially have wished to pursue opposing interests and disturb the status quo. While denying legitimacy to opposition, however, it did not deny legitimacy to the pursuit of maintenance of farm and business interests. In that way it was similar to the ratepayer ideology.

Localism

The desire for political neutrality extended to elimination of all 'sectional interests', unless those interests could also be portrayed as common to everyone in the Shire. The interests of farmers and business people were portrayed as such, while other interests were rarely presented in the local political arena. The narrow definition of legitimate political interests was enabled by the ideology of localism, which supported the belief in the necessity of political neutrality by fostering perception of a social whole to which all local residents belong, and moreover, by proposing a unique common interest. In that way it became, and was used as, a political resource for business and farm interests.

Strathern (1984a: 44; 1984b:182) defined localism as 'a set of ideas about the significance of place'. Poiner (1990) found an ideology of localism which she described as 'locality consciousness' (87). Dempsey (1990) found the people of Smalltown, regardless of class and other divisions, to espouse a feeling of attachment to their locality. Analysis of such sentiment may appear straightforward, despite the proximity of the concept of belonging, as used by Dempsey, to the perennially troublesome idea of community. Complexity does arise, however, when localism is found to have been given positive connotations, as it is in public policy discussion related to devolution (discussed in, for example Power, 1984 and Self, 1987), and put to political use. The concept of localism can also be extended by introducing a characteristic of 'community' which local inhabitants bestow upon it: 'the positive affect' of 'communion' (Willmott, 1985). This describes a conceptual scheme related to the community, communion, society historical process model used by Wild (1983), and retains the positive tone common among proponents of devolution.

Localism, however, can be seen from a darker side. Willmott (1985), for example, recognised significance for localism beyond Wild's scheme by noting the distracting effect which communion can have on class consciousness, through offering an alternative avenue for group identity formation. Bell and Newby (1976b) showed how localist ideology, as expressed in the ideal of neighbourhood communion, leads to misunderstanding of the local social system and distraction from its other attributes. Brook and Finn (1978) discussed localism as a spatially divisive attribute of working class images of society. Bryson and Mowbray (1981) and Mowbray (1985) discussed the ways in which the reified community has permeated public policy to the benefit of conservative interests. Attacks on localism usually focus on its tendency to obscure local class relations.

Localism should not, however, be depicted as a symptom of conspiracy. In the context of a locality study, Pearson (1980) noted that images of local community legitimated local power relations, but he also noted that such images emanated from a power differential between a locality and elsewhere. Indeed, growing interest in locality studies has been associated with observation of the increasing significance of inter-local or inter-regional relations amid international economic change, and the recognition that the relationships between class and locality deserve exploration (Hall et al., 1984; Rees, 1985; Urry, 1981). The concern so aroused has turned attention to examination of characteristically local forms of class relations and political expression in the extra-local political arena. But while local class relations may be significant to political communion as it affects relations in the wider arena, so communion which directs political energy in the wider arena may be significant to local political relations, because such communion may become a local political resource. It is necessary to disentangle both local and extra-local referents for localism in analysing its availability and use as a local political resource.

It is also necessary to establish whose resource localism is. As with communion, localism may offer the promise of liberation from internal and external conflict. Williams (1983: 196) looked to Welsh mining valleys which had long suffered conflict and repression, but propinquity and freedom 'from external ideological definitions' had fostered perception of common interest and social identity that brought real hope. The difference between localism as repression and localism as liberation lies in identification or obfuscation of interests. Those whose interests are identical with a common local interest, as presumably were those of the people of Williams' Welsh mining valleys, have localism as a potential resource, but so too do those who are able to use localism to distract local opponents from the latter's objective interests. Such distraction need not be conspiratorial. It may rather be an unintended consequence. Nor may it be appropriate to think of it simply as imposed from above, a point which Strathern (1982) made about Newby's (1977) suggestion that farmers had imposed localism as a class model upon their employees. A model which describes imposition may explain domination but it would not explain how such domination came to be enabled.

The point of departure for empirical exploration of localism remains, as it has traditionally been in community sociology, the process of identity formation in which local people form an attachment to their locality. One might apply the concepts of community and communion to the farmers' action over the LEP commotion in the way that Wild (1983) applied them to the waste dump issue in Heathcote. Local 'communion' was the farmers' political resource, among others, as they succeeded in raising support from beyond their own ranks. There was, however, no such sustained communion working for, and available to, Taragala residents over the air pollution issue. That issue provided a threat to local interests which was more readily and objectively definable, yet those threatened could not even sustain support from among their own number. The analysis to follow uses the model of Hall et al. (1984), which proposes that any one or all of three sets of relations, being those of *property, propinquity* and *kinship,* can be a basis for localism. They will be considered separately before introduction of a fourth element, *countrymindedness.* This model extends analysis of the processes of communion formation into the latent factors behind the manifest processes.

Property: The LEP issue brought forth communion, aroused as defence against threats to property. The point was made neatly in one submission which simply stated: 'The plan will affect the sale of property thus affecting the development of Cowra and thus the future of all residents'. Property brings more into local government than the common interest of ratepayers. It is also a focus of aspirations and a principle to be defended, as it was for those who feared socialist incursions and made submissions to the LEP process. To those people, the institution of private property was essential to Cowra's continued existence. This is an extension of the process through which Poiner (1990) found the rural idyll to develop into rural ideology. The process appears to rely heavily on social value universally placed on the acquisition of property. Under the 'rural idyll' and its associated status structure, property symbolises that which is good and can be achieved by hard work and perseverance.

Propinquity: Boundaries and social organisation were found by Hall et al. (1984) to be propinquity's important concomitants. The binding forces of social organisation in terms of local clubs and societies are not so problematic as boundaries, for the latter may not necessarily have physical referents. As Strathern (1984a) proposed, perception of a permeable and normally permeated boundary can co-exist in the same set of ideas as recognition of effective local limits.

Cowra people encountered each other at a frequency which most city dwellers would not have experienced, offering symbolic help in the construction of boundaries of their locality. When people passed each other in the street, they acknowledged one another's existence by at least saying hello, regardless of whether or not they were formally acquainted. I quickly became accustomed to greeting everyone I met while walking about, except in the more crowded parts of the main street where it would be impossible to do so.

They also shared local knowledge, particularly of its spatial features and its prominent personalities. This is an aspect of Cohen's (1985) symbolic construction of community: that which provides local people with symbols 'to think with' (19). They used place names which did not appear on maps, just as they used nicknames for prominent people. Bellevue Hill (map 2), for example, was known locally as 'Billy Goat Hill'.

This mutuality can appear more profound when it is instrumental, as demonstrated in instances of neighbourliness. I found that out on the evening I moved into my accommodation in Cowra. As I started to unload the van which had carried my furniture from Canberra, two of my neighbours, whom I had never seen before, came out of their homes to help me. Later, a farmer told me that after he had lost his home and virtually all its contents in a fire, townspeople led by the service clubs, rebuilt his house. Neighbourliness can also be intensely expressive. Early in my fieldwork period four young Cowra men were killed in a road accident. The tragedy had been prominently reported in the *Guardian* and was a frequent topic of conversation. So too was the vast expression of sympathy. I heard people say that the church 'overflowed', and the town 'stood still' during the funeral. Neighbours were not, however, always friendly, as conflict over rate rises indicated, but neighbours could still be important parts of each others' lives.

Cowra had many local organisations in which many people participate. The 1985/86 directory compiled by the Shire Council listed 180. Of the 509 Cowra Shire respondents to the community needs survey, reported in Gray (1987a), sixty-four per cent stated that they were members of organisations whose meetings they attended, and thirty-seven per cent were members of more than one.

The collective local sense of 'social self' is 'informed by implicit or explicit contrast' (Cohen, 1985: 115). Living in a town or rural area offers an identity in its differentiation of its people against those of other towns and rural areas.[5] Inter-town rivalry was noted by Aitkin (1972) and Wild (1983). Aitkin (1972: 96) likened inter-town school sport to 'inter-tribal ritual warfare', something which Cohen (1985) might interpret as symbolic construction of community.

Local organisations illustrated the local-non-local dichotomy by being fiercely parochial. While setting up the data collection in the project reported in Gray (1987a), I addressed meetings of a men's club in Cowra and two nearby towns. One of the latter clubs' members expressed a competitive relationship with the Cowra club, boasting that their club had poached members from Cowra's territory, promoting identity with the locality as much as with the organisation itself. I was a member of an organisation, the Historical Society, which implicitly saw its task as preservation and maintenance of local identity. I unfortunately missed observing a good illustration of local solidarity in the context of inter-town rivalry, when I left a meeting early in order to attend another. During a crowded lunch hour gathering at the Neighbourhood Centre, called to publicise an adult education program to be conducted there, a representative of a neighbourhood centre from a nearby town said that that town had a very progressive committee co-ordinating welfare activities.

A representative from the Cowra Neighbourhood Centre proudly announced that Cowra had such a committee and that it was conducting a community needs survey. My informant told me that the reply drew a resounding cheer, and my informant convinced me that the incident aroused a bond of sentiment among local people.

The *Guardian* from time to time contained expressions of concern for the locality. At the time the LEP controversy was brewing, it ran an editorial calling for 'all Cowra and district residents becoming supporters and promoters of their area' (2 January, 1985, p. 2). On 15 March 1985, it published a letter from a resident who was worried because he feared that Cowra was not attracting light industrial development as rapidly as a nearby town of similar size. Parallel concern prompted Waugoola Council to refuse permission for a motelier to erect a sign in the Shire advertising a business in the same town (*Cowra Guardian*, 21 March, 1961). In 1948 the Municipal Council refused a request from another shire for electricity, on the grounds that its 'first duty is to cater for the residents in the Cowra Municipality and Waugoola Shire' (*Cowra Guardian*, 19 November, p. 11). The *Guardian* explained its support for the conservative opposition parties during the 1959 State election campaign in terms of arousing support for local defence, claiming that if the Labor Government was returned Cowra would lose control of its water and electricity reticulation and would lose its stock slaughtering to a regional abattoir. On 24 June, 1955, the *Guardian*'s page one editorial was headed 'Support the Local Man – He Supports You', and went on to alert readers that 'outside organisations' were coming to Cowra and deflecting business away from local firms.

Councillors felt that supporting the town and district was an important task for them. They readily considered their performance as leaders by comparisons with other towns. One councillor reported frustration because he felt that the Council could do more for the town.

> Unfortunately clouds come across our passage to the extent that we fail to see where we're going. That has always been disappointing because if you live in a town that you feel has some potential and you see other towns around about doing their own little things and yet you never see your own town doing it.

The Shire Council's role as supporter of its locality extended to favouring local organisations over others. For example, it decided not to give a donation to the Royal Life Saving Society because it was not local, and refused a request to waive the Civic Centre hire charge for a non-local charity. The Council tried to support local business with its contracts for purchase of goods and services, and on one occasion some councillors expressed disappointment when a local firm did not tender. When a travelling market organisation applied for permission to set up on the outskirts of town, several councillors unsuccessfully sought means of preventing it from doing so, foreseeing unfair competition with local businesses. Brindleton's council did prohibit such traders (Cowlishaw, 1988). Such actions are products of, and help to foster perception of, a local identity which represents an interest to be pursued. Dempsey's (1990) Smalltown shows a very similar phenomenon: people with a strong sense of local attachment, and identification of a community interest, with indicated boundaries between themselves and those who belong elsewhere, based on propinquity.

Kinship: In family farming areas where kinship networks may be locally concentrated kinship is particularly salient (Hall et al., 1984). Size and density of local social networks may be related to both propinquity and kinship as bases for local identification. Dempsey (1983) found that locally powerful families had extensive local kin networks. He was referring to networks as directly manifesting a power resource, rather than doing so as a basis for an ideology of localism, but his finding indicates both possibilities. Such solidarity around a set of values would be likely to promote ideals related to maintenance of the group and its identity. Aitkin (1972) attributed the relative political conservatism of the country to limited social contact and isolation from new and different ways of thinking. Newby et al. (1978) drew a parallel implied contrast between country and city in terms of social networks, illustrating a basis for localism in the narrow range of contact among farmers.

Strathern (1984a: 46) found that the villagers of her study agreed upon a model of their village as consisting of 'locals' and 'outsiders', but while the model was consistent among villagers, application of it by villagers to individuals was not. Birch (1959) and Strathern (1981, 1982, 1984a, b) associated kinship with ideas of belonging to a locality, of being an 'insider' which could be contrasted with being an 'outsider'. Being local is a product of family background, however vague the criteria may be. Strathern (1981) found that definitions of localness depended on family origins rather than place of birth. They had precision in the minds of local people from acceptance of the idea that there were 'insiders' and 'outsiders', even if as mentioned above, there was no universal agreement on which individuals fitted which category. Some local people were 'real' locals, separated by the idea of a boundary rather than a real boundary which would have relevance to everyday life.

Many people in the Cowra district had kinship networks which were concentrated locally, and many had similar friendship networks. Forty-one percent of the 509 Cowra Shire respondents to the community needs survey (Gray, 1987a) stated that either most or all of their 'good friends' lived within about fifty kilometres of their homes. Forty-six per cent said that either most or all of their 'friends' who lived within about fifty kilometres of their homes knew each other well.[6] This left many people whose networks were neither locally concentrated nor locally dense, but it showed that for many others, their locality was an important base of social contact.

The same survey prompts similar conclusions about kinship networks, although the proportion of respondents having most or all of their relatives within fifty kilometres is smaller than the figure for friends, at eighteen per cent. This is also fewer than the twenty-seven per cent who said that they had no relatives within about fifty kilometres.[7] But again, for many people their locality contained a concentration of kin. Thirty-seven per cent of respondents stated that about half or more of their relatives lived in their locality, when defined as the area within a fifty kilometre radius of the respondents' homes. Many also had a dense network of friends and relatives. Thirty-one per cent of respondents said that most or all of their local friends knew some or all of their relatives, a similar finding to that of Dempsey (1990). It should not be assumed that kinship is associated with intimacy or even contact, as kin may also be enemies or just irrelevant to everyday life. As Hall et al. (1984) proposed with regard to New Zealand, it appears likely that kinship relations played a relatively minor direct role in the structuring of localism.

Cowra people, nevertheless, had a model of local identity which implies an important role for kinship in association with longevity of family residence. This model defined 'locals' in a similar fashion to the definition 'insiders' discussed by Birch (1959) and Strathern (1981, 1982, 1984a, b). A business person who had moved to Cowra from Sydney about eight years previously said to me that he had noticed two differences between life in Cowra and life in Sydney: 'First, people live here slowly. Second, you have to be a "local local".' He suggested that being a 'local local' was a prerequisite for acceptance, relating a story about a club committee which was desperate for an additional person to serve on it. In its predicament it allowed someone to serve on it after living in Cowra for ten years, but didn't listen to him. A farmer who took a more cynical approach to this said: 'You know we haven't been here very long. I mean, my father only bought the place thirty three years ago. You have to be here a lot longer to be a local.'

The farmer explained that newcomers could be isolated because farming people found it difficult to become accustomed to having strangers in their neighbourhood, and was pained to assure me that nobody wanted or tried to make newcomers feel unwelcome. I am sure that nobody tried to make me feel unwelcome, and if people did, they failed. I heard a telling comment from a woman who had lived in Cowra for thirty years. She was at a social gathering, among a group of people who included a member of a family which could trace its ancestory back to early settlers, discussing some fine points of local history, when she said that although she had lived in Cowra for thirty years she did not feel that she was part of the town as some of the older families were. Whereupon the member of one of the 'older families' said with tongue-in-cheek: 'You mean you don't feel that you really understand Cowra'. She agreed. The town was sometimes portrayed as one big family, such as when one notably successful expatriate was described as 'a Cowra girl'. This is reminiscent of the image called upon by aspirants to Council seats at election time, mentioned above as service to the 'whole' community. This wholistic view was used by one of the submissions to the LEP, which said: 'The principal aim of a Local Environmental Plan should be first and foremost to promote the growth, development and prosperity of the Shire as a whole'.

Countrymindedness: Perception of the locality in its external relations, fostered in a climate of countrymindedness, also contributed to the formation of localism. The dependence of Cohen's (1985) symbolic construction of community on reference to other localities extended to contrast of the rural identity of the district with the cities which local people have seen to threaten them. Identity formation may draw on models which range geographically, demographically and politically beyond the locality. Dempsey (1990) found negative depictions of Smalltown's enemies by its leaders to be an important factor in development of belonging.

Country people have long been aware of their subordination to city interests, and indeed have seen growth in their own localities hindered by 'Sydney tyranny' (Aitkin, 1972: 13). Kennedy (1981) found that Broken Hill people were bound by anti-metropolitan sentiment which had a substantial bearing on the city's history. Wild (1983) found a similar binding sentiment. Fear of the effect of decision-making in the cities for the cities is still expressed in rural political discussion, with good reason (Jones, 1987; McPhedran, 1987). At an individual level, Dempsey (1983: 119) found, as quoted above, that newcomers were more likely to be accepted as 'insiders' if they had characteristics which they attributed to rural people. Perception of a relationship between a locality and other places which are in some way different, a relationship in which interests are not mutual, adds perception of interests as motivation for action to property, propinquity and kinship as bases for localism, and interpretation of action generates localism as a political resource.

Strathern (1984a), Bell et al. (1976) and Cohen (1982b) offer reminders that local idioms can also be interpreted as characteristic of a wider geographical reality. Understanding Strathern's villagers requires interpretation of their Englishness as well as their village situation. Bell et al. (1976: 42) found among locally powerful individuals an ideology of community in which anti-urbanism was an essential factor. On a similar theme, Cohen (1982b) saw local perceptions of an external reality to be important. His islanders saw themselves and their locality as peripheral, drawing on images of incompetent outsiders who are willing to meddle with and even trample on local interests. One might expect such images to emerge in Cowra Shire, given its history of local vulnerability and perceived external interference.

Hall et al. (1984) considered a different process: one in which sentiment surrounding local institutions develops identity with, rather than against, a larger entity, such as a local war memorial fostering nationalism. The opposite is also feasible. Countrymindedness may help local people make sense of their situation in the locality, by suggesting explanations of local events which are often products of extra-local relationships. Being 'country', or for that matter being Australian, may be just as salient to an individual's identity as a local person as residence within the Shire. Self-identification as rural people maintains a political resource as it is reconstructed in local discourse. Perception of such an external threat identifies a local interest which allows no internal division, as it motivates political action. It can do so more readily than threats from neighbouring towns, because its rapaciousness appears invincible.

The public submissions to the LEP brought forth clear images of this distant enemy. Many proclaimed that city bureaucrats had neither skills nor rights to plan Cowra Shire. Others thought that the Plan must have been merely adapted from one drawn for a city area. A letter to the *Guardian* indicated a clear perception of threat: '... You elected the councillors to protect your interests in this area and they need your support to avoid a 'takeover' by some city based department' (15 February, 1985, p. 2). This was not a new phenomenon. In 1956, when rumours were spreading that Cowra would lose control of its electricity supply, the *Guardian* asked 'Is the master plan to eventually amalgamate all electricity undertakings into one huge octopus with headquarters in Sydney?' (4 December, p. 14). The need for self defence is sometimes expressed in Council. The *Guardian* of 26 September 1984 reported (p. 3) that the Council had received a letter from the mayor of a Sydney municipality seeking support for animal liberation, and quoted Stephen Bell: 'It's a case of to hell with the people beyond Parramatta; they don't exist'. Stephen went on to suggest that some mice be forwarded with a reply; there was a plague of them at the time.

The Cowra press has not hesitated to infer that city decision makers look after their own territory at the expense of Cowra. In 1918 the *Free Press* (23 March, p. 2) headed an item 'Country vs City – Politicians Always Put the Latter First – The Curse of Vested Interests', and went on to complain that rural railway construction had not been completed, but, curiously, also said that work on a city railway had ceased. During the local housing shortage in 1952, the *Guardian* reported that the Housing Commission had stopped building houses in Cowra because, it claimed, it had run out of money, but it was still building houses in Sydney (25 March, p. 1). When the *Guardian* took sides in the 1959 election campaign under the banner of local defence, as quoted above, Col Newton wrote to it complaining about politicisation. The paper's editorial of

25 March (p. 1) claimed that it owed no political allegiance and supported only Cowra.

Such statements made the threat visible. Seeing one issue that way opened the door to similar interpretations of others. Cowra people had seen their locality succumb to the encroachment of city-based organisations. They had perceived their local autonomy wither under forces directed by people who not only came from distant places, but pursued the interests of those distant places. When Cowra people felt that they had much to share, when it was possible to identify families as living local heritage, and when there was a common enemy that threatened, Cowra was all that mattered.

These events constructed and reconstructed the symbolic boundaries of the locality. The local sense of the virtuous was dependent on the contrast with plundering bureaucrats and politicians from the city. As Cohen (1985) points out, people become aware of their culture when they see it threatened, and to defend it, they state it symbolically by reversing their normal behaviour. The farmers thought the LEP to be attacking the foundations of local tradition: property, and in the family farming tradition: kinship. Instead of supporting their local representatives on the Shire Council, they turned against them, temporarily destroying the image of trusteeship which they usually held of councillors. But in doing so they defended their culture, bringing forth its meaning by showing their willingness to destroy their own image of local harmony. The resulting local political crisis was not a denial of the image of a community devoid of conflicting interests, an image which normally accrues to powerful people as a political resource, because it identified a threat which had infiltrated the locality, disturbing its usual harmony. This identification at the same time strengthened perception of that usual harmony.[8] Vidich and Bensman (1968: 287) provide a contrast. The people of Springdale were portrayed as supplicants to 'mass society', basking in their own self-righteousness, showing few signs of understanding their structural position. Cowra people were well aware of their interests in relation to metropolitan Australia, and have fiercely resisted its dominance, reproducing localism.

Localism has been shown to contain a division between 'local locals' and others, but that division was not perceived to be grounds for a clash of interests. Rather, it served to show that there were people who really belonged, and that concomitantly, the district was more than a geographical expression; it was an identity that people could belong to. The old families may have been looked upon as different, but they bestowed continuity on the locality, and to that extent personified local identity. Such an identity must be unique; it left no room for division. Any individual who tried to demonstrate a group interest within the whole was liable to attract accusation of divisiveness, of failing to recognise that the district

Ideologies and resources

had an identity of its own, and moreover, that identity counted for more than what were popularly described as 'sectional interests'. This was implicit in calls for support for 'the community' from the Tourist and Development Corporation when it sought help from the Shire Council. It was also implicit in one of the submissions to the LEP which read: 'I feel that any councillors that accept this plan are selling out their community and their forefathers who built this area into what it is today'. Hall et al. (1984) admit the possibility that propinquity, kinship and property may be contradictory, but in this locality, it would appear that they are mutually reinforcing.

Localism can be used as a resource, as it was when Harold Upston called, in the Council, for further tourism development for the sake of the local community. Localism could also be used to deny other people legitimacy. A councillor complained to me that the people who had recently been protesting about smells emanating from the garbage tip had only lived in Cowra for a few years. Localism was effective as a resource, not only because it held the promise of arousing communion, as occurred in the LEP issue, but moreover, because it rationalised political neutrality. Localism obfuscated the local political interests of those who were already weak. Herein lies Lukes' third mode of power. While people believed that political neutrality served their interests, they were unlikely to take political action. They were more inclined to leave the political stage vacant for those who were interpreting and advocating neutrality.

The side of local politics which could enlist localism had a great advantage. In the hands of the farmers, the LEP itself came to symbolise the evils of metropolitan dominance. The farmers took advantage of such symbolism by using it to stir localist sentiment into communion, set up by the mutual reinforcement of values related to property, propinquity and kinship, and taken to its heights by perception of an external threat. Localism was such a useful resource that nobody could afford to approach Cowra's local politics without it. This was associated with the tendency for election candidates to be seen to pursue a general rather than only a specific group interest. In this climate there may be a temptation leading to self-contradiction for anyone seeking to pursue a group interest. When, in 1932, formation of the Taragala Progress Association was announced in the *Guardian*, the article stated that the Association had decided to call itself the Cowra Progress Association. In 1949, after completing construction of a sports ground, the West Cowra Progress Association was reported to be in a vigorous debate (in the *Guardian* of 4 November, p. 15) over the name for the ground. Some members felt that West Cowra should not be mentioned, as 'the Association had resolved to work for the progress and development of Cowra and District'. This view was repeated in 1975 when the committee formed to combat the air pollution problem confronting Taragala called itself the Cowra Anti-Pollution Committee. Taragala people twice implicitly denied their interest as Taragala people.

They wanted to be seen to serve the 'whole' town, rather than just their particular area. While pursuing their interests they feared accusations of doing just that. Of course such accusations could readily be sensibly made, moving the invaluable resource of localism beyond their reach and turning it against them.

They were effectively, like female ratepayers, in a double bind, for their interests lay in supporting both their area and being seen to support the town as a whole, when obtaining facilities for their area would deny them to others. Their titling of their organisations 'Cowra' would no doubt have been motivated by a desire to serve the interests of the 'whole' town, but the definition of acceptable ways of doing so was out of their hands, and in the LEP case at least, firmly in the hands of farmers and business.

The Labor Party in Cowra actively supported and reinforced this 'countryminded' definition of legitimate political action. A short time before the 1983 local government elections, a letter from a farmer attacking the Labor Party for supporting the Royal Society for the Prevention of Cruelty to Animals (RSPCA) was published in the *Guardian*. Tim West replied, describing himself as the local ALP Secretary and State Conference Delegate, stating that the Party was not involved with the RSPCA and did not support it. The letter continued: 'The Labor Party has within its ranks many members who, directly or indirectly, have close association with rural enterprise', and concluded that the Party would not do anything to disrupt rural enterprise (*Cowra Guardian*, 26 August, 1983, p. 2). Tim was the first person to write to the *Guardian* protesting about the LEP. He opposed the plan's proposals for environmental protection, which would have seemed to be another threat to farming. Tim was implicitly defending the farmers, although, when the issue became Council's planning power, he opposed them. Tim used the resource of localism in the symbolic manner discussed by Edelman (1971). Through the LEP issue, he could make reassurances that he and, implicitly given his high public profile, the Labor Party were looking after 'local' interests. This action, as Edelman would suggest, may have helped to keep alive the adversary interpretation of Cowra's relationship with 'the city'; it helped to confirm the external threat.

Status

Like localism, status was available as a resource, but unlike localism, it was logically specific to some individuals, leaving no possibility of it being called upon by others. Status, what those blessed individuals possessed, was the perception of others that they had it. Popular perceptions of status among individuals either created or denied a potential, although minor, power resource. Pandey (1972) found that acceptance in social circles bestowed political legitimacy. Status was available for use as an ideological resource in Barretta.

Status is often approached in terms of the stratifying effects of such perceptions, and the attributes of the resulting hierarchy, following Weber (Gerth and Mills, 1977: 186–88). So Wild (1974a:2) used the concept to refer to lifestyles and 'forms of conduct in so far as these provide bases for interaction'. Oxley (1978: 30) used two dimensions of status, being esteem (in terms of achieved characteristics) as well as prestige (in terms of ascribed characteristics). The concept of status as a resource, however, requires further extension of the concept. The concept of status can help to reveal much more, when as Barbalet (1986) and Omodei (1982) seek, Weber is reinterpreted so that status includes access to or exclusion from rights and duties. The popular perceptions, therefore, through which some people gained power resources while others did not, are those which bestowed rights and duties, as well as prestige and esteem, while placing people high on the status ladder.

Those at the top of the ladder were seen to have a claim on rights and responsibilities of leadership. Ab Oliver and Barbara Bennett both enjoyed enormous prestige, being associated with families which had long and successful local histories, and esteem from their records of service. They were both assuredly 'local locals'. Their status was, however, more than that. It gave them a right to a special claim on public office at the same time as it laid down their responsibilities to the locality, which some of their ancestors had also served in local government. When Barbara was elected Mayor for her first term as such, Ab was quoted by the *Guardian* (14 September, 1976, p. 1) to have said: 'Mrs Bennett's background as one of Cowra's pioneer families should stand her in good stead'. For them, status was a resource, and they neither had to create nor consciously use it, although it might be claimed that simply stating their backgrounds at election time was using it. Status may also have been called upon during Council debate, as the supporters of the Tourist and Development Corporation implicitly did when Ab Oliver made an opening speech on the Japanese Garden issue.

For those, the vast majority, who were not at the top of the ladder, status had only indirect relevance and should not be overstated as a contributory factor in elitism of representation. As Chapman and Wood (1984) indicate, however, personal characteristics of prospective councillors can be more important than policies at election time in Australian local government. In a climate of ostensible political neutrality, electors are asked to vote for particular people as 'trustees' (Jones, 1981: 212). It is important, therefore, for election candidates that they be known to the voters (Painter, 1974), and that they be worthy of the rights of office and capable of the duties. Hence election manifestos emphasised experience in community service and often mentioned longevity of residence. 'Local locals' were more likely than others to be able to make such claims. In this way status reinforced, as it reconstructed, the political neutrality ideal at each election.

Australian community studies have constructed status ladders for country districts which would implicitly put Cowra's 'local locals' at the top. The people with the easiest claim on 'local localness' would be those farming families whose ancestry went back to early settlers, simply because, despite the long history of closer settlement, they may still have retained large farms, and they would have handsomely met the longevity criterion. This may be related conversely to the point made by Rose et al. (1976) that ownership of property can gain legitimacy, in addition to that gained from legal criteria, through traditional association with particular families. In Cowra, particular families gained legitimacy through long association with particular properties. Business people may also have longevity, and some, including Neville Pengilly, did so, but town business did not bestow the same legitimacy as rural property. In the rural ideological climate, successful farming is a greater source of esteem than successful business. In any case, three of the four largest town business proprietors were first generation Cowra people, and the family of the fourth qualified as 'local local' through very long and continuing association with farming.

High positions on the status ladder were not monopolised by landed 'local locals', but such people were certainly at or close to the top. The prestige ranking of occupations by Nalson and Craig (1987: 337), which places 'grazing' above 'professions' above 'business entrepreneurs' followed by 'mixed' and 'other farming' which are above 'small business' and 'skilled', is not easily applied strictly to Cowra because some of the highest status 'local locals' derived income from farming in the best country by the Lachlan River. The other rankings still largely held true, although application to specific occupations could bring forth problems, as such classifications often do. Dempsey (1983) found teachers to have lower status than farmers and businessmen. Oxley's (1978) classification of townspeople may be a more useful approach. Oxley identified an upper stratum consisting of professionals, managers, higher spiralists and larger burgesses; a middle stratum of smaller burgesses, junior industry staff and lower spiralists; and a lower stratum of skilled, semi-skilled and other workers.

Such problems do not, however, prohibit analysis of recent local government elections in order to consider an hypothesised bias in favour of candidates with higher status occupations. Comparing the recent electoral performance of skilled and other workers with other occupations shows that they did not perform especially poorly. At the 1987 election similar proportions of the two groups, three of five low status candidates, and eight of thirteen higher status (Oxley's middle and upper), were successful. In 1983, one of three low status compared with eleven of seventeen higher status candidates were elected. In the 1977 Municipal Council election, three of six low status and six of ten higher status candidates were elected.[9] The apparent elitism identified in chapter 4 was a product of the relatively small number of lower status candidates, fourteen against forty higher status at the three elections, rather than failure at the polls.

Status based on occupation (prestige) is not a good indicator of local electoral potential, because people with low occupational prestige may have gained esteem and become known to voters. Col Newton's consistently good electoral performance over a long period was a product of the esteem in which he was held, rather than prestige associated with his occupation. Much of his esteem had been earned through local service, most notably although by no means entirely, in local government. The value placed on local service was exemplified by a quotation from Shire President Cyril Treasure in the context of an appeal for nominations at the 1987 election, published in the *Guardian* of 7 August (p. 1): 'The service clubs in this town have a large number of strong leaders who would be the ideal type of people to stand for Council'. As would be expected, the service clubs had their own status ladder based on occupational prestige, with Rotary at the top, but that certainly does not mean that only Rotarians could earn sufficient esteem to add to what prestige they may have derived from their occupations to bring them to the attention of the electorate. Nor does it mean that participation in a service club was a necessary qualification. But participation may, as Cyril Treasure implied, have helped.

Prestige had greater impact on local politics in the shared perception of 'local localness'. 'Local locals' may have been more likely to nominate for Council, but the abstract nature of the concept rules out the testing of such a proposition. While Ab Oliver and Barbara Bennett were certainly 'local locals', there were, in 1986, several other sitting councillors who might also have been. No hard and fast criteria are available, except perhaps family residence in the district for at least two, or perhaps three, generations.

When combined with property, longevity of residence became the key to the rights and duties of high status. Such rights and duties were not, therefore, available to professionals who might have similar occupational prestige to the highest status 'local local' farm families. Although some professionals whose families had been resident for several generations could claim similar status. I met people who believed that there was a top stratum and others who felt, and expressed annoyance, that they were mistakenly included in the top rank by some who felt themselves lower. Property had an important place in such thinking, a point which was made by Hill (1985: 76–77). A farming woman told me that when people heard that she and her husband did not own their property, they felt excluded from one 'set'; and when it became known that she was employed off-farm, they felt excluded from another. To her disgust, a friend went to one particular club in order to mix with the 'right' people. A town-dweller put the role of property for farmers quite plainly: 'They have pride in their bit of dirt. That's their status'. When I asked a farmer if he thought that town people felt farmers to be aloof, he replied

> I think that existed ... There were grazing families who sent their children away to boarding school and there certainly was a class distinction there. I've often heard us referred to as blue bloods. I've thought of that as an insult. We don't go back to squattocracy. There's been nothing easy for my father or grandfather. I've taken it good naturedly but it's an insult to be called a blue blood because I think that's the way people have meant it.

This farmer had not denied the existence of 'blue bloods', only that he was not one of them. I asked: who would call you a blue blood?

> Just ordinary people. I heard a local greengrocer say 'don't you blue bloods ever go to the picnics [races]?' I said why do you call us blue bloods? How long has your family been here? He said since 1934. I said you're as much a blue blood as me. My grandfather has only been here since 1920. You have got a business in town. Why aren't you a blue blood? A lot of people on the land do think there is something special about them because they have a property.

Perceptions of what the person above referred to as 'blue bloodedness' have more instrumental connotations. When I asked another person to identify the influential people in the district, he replied

> There are certain families who have been here for 100 years, own four or five farms, and there is a tendency in the community to look up to these people. Their opinions are respected, right down to the fact that if one of these families were to say to you that you have a fire hazard, they could expect you to do something about it. If I was to say to you that you've got a fire hazard you'd say mind your own bloody business.

The wife of a town businessman offered another perspective. She related that after they had moved to Cowra and taken on management of a business: 'Some families came into [the business] and thought they could tell my husband how to run it. They had been customers for generations and thought that gave them authority'. While such statements may or may not indicate real behaviour, they do show that people were conscious of a high status group. One would expect that such behaviour, as this person interpreted it, could not attract the kind of esteem enjoyed by Ab Oliver and Barbara Bennett; but perceptions that there were people who may have commanded deference, indicate acknowledgement of rights peculiar to this perceived high prestige group, even if exercise of those rights was not always considered legitimate. Only farm families could possess such rights, and those who were thought to do so had a resource which, at the very least, helped to make them known, and at most may have legitimated leadership.

Its legitimacy, however, was vulnerable, not only because people might see its use as arrogance, but because it had dynastic connotations. A town business person who expressed frustration at what was seen as Council inactivity in economic development, attributed the alleged problem to unnamed conservative councillors whose families had been represented on the Council for generations. Certainly some councillors could find aldermen and councillors in their family trees, but the point was made more generally, like the 'old established families' mentioned above. It was as if a cloud of families was seen to be hanging over Cowra's economic and political life.

Perhaps the greatest effects of status perceptions on local politics in Cowra during 1986 came from the issues surrounding the Tourist and Development Corporation. The people who saw Don Kibbler as a 'tall poppy' under attack were, implicitly, seeing the attackers as defenders of the status structure. Some of them also saw the traditional, supposedly dynastic, system as undesirable. These interpretations came from business people and farmers, who were seeing Don under attack in the name of small ratepayers who preferred not to have their rate contributions risked. That is, they saw people lower in the status structure implicitly defending that structure and reinforcing what they saw as a dynastic system.

Resources and non-resources

The ideologies discussed above were resources available to some groups rather than others while they were maintained by all. The ideals of efficiency, bureaucratic subservience, political neutrality and localism were available to reinforce demands on the political apparatus, as they were used in the instances of 'assertive rhetoric' quoted above. Status ideology was, however, a minor factor when operating in those rare circumstances of traditional deference to highly honoured families, but played a greater role by focusing attention on personal characteristics of election candidates, thereby removing potential threats to political neutrality. Without sustenance from below, however, those resources would not have survived. They were resources only because they were adhered to by subordinate groups. But while ideological resources were dependent on subordinate groups, they may have obscured the interests of subordinate groups, and not have been available for use by them to further their own interests.

The inter-dependence of ideologies can be illustrated by showing how one group, the railway workers, were denied resources, while in the same ideological climate that both groups reproduced, their local political superiors seemed to ignore their own interests. Being able to call logically upon one ideology did not guarantee possession and potential use of a viable resource, because another ideology may have negated the first. At the same time possession and use of resources did not necessarily lead to benefit for those so endowed, because there was no necessity in the rural ideological climate that the powerful would perceive all their own interests.

Local political action to slow the decline of local railway employment was seldom taken until the interests of farmers and ratepayers were threatened. It seemed that perceptions of *the* local interest had not been aroused as railway employment had been falling in recent years, at least not in the way a local interest was perceived in the LEP issue. There are three avenues for explanation of this paradox. One lies in the relationship between the railway people and the rest of the town; another lies in perceptions by others of the railway; and the third lies in the railway workers' perceptions of their predicament.

The railway people were not set apart, but they had their own social surrounds, having some of the characteristics of Lockwood's (1975) 'proletarian traditional' workers. They were a substantial part of the population, there being about two hundred railway employees and hence perhaps six hundred members of railway families (out of a town population of about five thousand) in the early 1950s. They had their own recreation, based on the Railway Institute Library and Hall, and sport teams. A retired railway worker told me that there were three tennis courts behind the locomotive depot that the employees had made themselves, built with loads of locomotive ash. There was also a cricket ground. The railway had cricket and rugby teams. When I asked if the railway people joined the railway rather than other local teams, my interviewee said: 'Yes. It brought the railway people together. It gave us something to do amongst ourselves, instead of everybody going away to do different things. There were very, very few railway men with the other teams'. I asked a retired employee if he kept in touch with his old mates. 'Oh yes', he replied, 'I see a lot of them. We have a yarn. There's dozens of them here. A lot of our friends are railway people.'

Some of the older railway people spoke of it as having been a high status occupation. 'At one time a railway man was always looked up to. The young fellows were always trying to get a position on the railway. Because they always maintained they were somebody. The train driver was every boy's idol.' Some railway families qualified as 'local locals'. Watmore and Roberson (n.d.) identified four families which had provided railway staff at Cowra across several generations. Although railway employees moved about to obtain promotion, they tended to settle after marriage, and two that I spoke to came back and remained in Cowra where they had started. When I asked a current employee if there was a rapid turnover, he replied that one who had been in Cowra for twelve years could be considered a newcomer. This would seem to be fertile ground for formation of a Cowra railway people's identity, and adoption of the power model image of society discussed by Lockwood (1975).

I detected two images of their social situation in the predicament of decline. One was disbelief. 'When you look at it over the years – the way it's deteriorated – when you look at the job in 1925 and look at the staff now, you'd hardly reckon it could happen. It was a booming industry. Thousands of pounds used to come into the town.' The railway had been a deep personal loss. Perhaps the most moving experience I had in Cowra occurred when a retired railway employee reminisced, expressing disbelief that such a loss could have happened.

Some employed railway workers adopted the dichotomous power model suggested by Lockwood (1975), but they placed it in the localism image. That is, they saw the railway decline as a product of urban-rural relations. A member of a long-time railway family told me how the 'big wigs in Sydney' made decisions in ignorance of conditions in the country. Perhaps the most galling habit among them was their practice of travelling by road. This practice, which Vaughan (1984) also found disturbing, looked like treachery to Cowra railway people. Many times I heard them speak of the improvements being made to the metropolitan rail network, at the apparent expense of the country system.

It is not just that Cowra's railway workers were employed by an extra-local authority and responded to that relationship, for they identified with Cowra just as the highest status farmers did, and they saw the railway decline as local decline. A member of the local branch of the Labor Party, which might be expected to support the railway as it did under Leo Lynch, indicated to me that he saw the matter in urban-rural terms also. Unlike Leo Lynch he felt that local political effort would therefore be futile. Decline in rural rail services was indeed another example of decisions made in Sydney to the detriment of the country, but it does not follow that such decision-making is immutable. Rural people are justifiably concerned about rationalisation of rural government services (McKenzie, 1986). It is not that the railway people were unaware of the lack of local action. One employee explained decline as a product of local business ignorance of, and lack of interest in the railway, which he could not understand. Country towns frequently unite in protest, as Cowra did over loss of its telephone exchange and other threats, but not the railway.

The explanation for the failure of localism to produce a viable political resource lies in the relationships between the elements of rural ideology and localism. Had railway people taken their problems to the local political arena, as they did in the time of Leo Lynch, armed with their localist perspective, they would also have been burdened with what might be called an anti-resource. They would have been vulnerable to the ideology which bestowed resources on farmers and business people. The railway was seen among the latter as a bureaucracy, perhaps a bureaucracy of the worst kind. Railway workers did not have the legitimacy bestowed by independence and self-reliance. As Dempsey (1990) noted, farmers and business people can be antagonistic to government workers of all kinds, including those long resident in the locality. The following comment from a long-term resident and business person reveals the railway people's predicament.

> If we had really appreciated their role, what the benefits were, maybe we would have been stirred up and defended it. I never sensed that people had a big hang up over rail. From a businessman's point of view it was probably just the opposite. The image of the railway was to go down there and see a few fellas sitting around and not doing too much. A lot of people thought they could do with less staff, and the fact that they were going to put the sweepers through may have been appreciated, rather than look at the effects it might have had in the town. That's the businessman's point of view but I think there would be support for that community-wise too.

A farmer told me that he had been most impressed by the energy that some of the railway employees put into their centenary celebrations, people who he thought were usually lazy at their jobs. I knew the people he mentioned, and knew them to be conscientious at their work, but the image of bureaucracy, and the same perceived lack of legitimacy suffered by Council officers, had taken over.

The railway people were devoid of local political resources, other than the energies of people like Leo Lynch, and those since, who had fought their struggle for survival in the wider industrial context. This gave them no place in local politics, and nowhere to raise the support which their call on localist sentiment might hypothetically obtain for them, were the counter-ideological factors not operating. The resource of localism, which did so much for the farmers in the LEP issue, was not available to the railway workers in local politics, just as it was not available to the Taragala people and those who sought the Council's entry into human services. While seemingly everybody adhered to the localist ideals, not all local interest groups identified their interests with the locality in a way which was universally accepted, as the farmers did in the LEP issue. Ability to claim defence of a local interest was not enough to ensure legitimacy. Legitimacy of one set of local ideals could be tempered by others, just as political neutrality was redefined by farmers and business people as they injected adversary elements into local politics.

Ideological resources were not the only resources drawn upon in local politics, but they were the least evenly distributed. The material resources required for political expression were not great. The farmers could finance a public meeting to set off the LEP issue, but so too did the Taragala people before Lachlan Industries was established, and the Neighbourhood Centre in its early establishment period. The Mulyan, Taragala and West Cowra Progress Associations had substantial material resources. All of these groups had access to the local media. Even the railway decline could make front page news, but that did not make an issue. They could all find access to senior councillors. Ab Oliver chaired the public meeting that launched the Neighbourhood Centre and was involved with the committee that set up the child care centre. Access to a prominent citizen may be helpful, but it does not guarantee wider political support.

Notes

1 Similar phenomena were identified by Widdows (1974), Bolton (1978) and Share (1987), and political paradoxes by Chatterton (1984).
2 Political neutrality is commonly valued in both British and Australian local government. The British is discussed in Gyford (1976), Newton (1976), and in the rural context in Madgwick et al. (1973), Bell et al. (1976) and Newby et al. (1978).
3 This perspective has, fortunately, been contradicted in Colebatch and Degeling (1986), a more recent and realistic instructional publication aimed at councillors.
4 1987 was not an aberration. In 1954, the Liberal Party obtained 2 314 votes to Labor's 2 002 in Cowra (*Cowra Guardian*, 1 June) at a House of Representatives election. The previous year Labor gained a majority of Cowra votes at a Senate election (*Cowra Guardian*, 12 May, 1953). The 1958 Federal election result was similar to that of 1954 (*Cowra Guardian*, 5 December, 1958). The Country Party won the 1971 election in the Cowra subdivision by only 2 180 votes to 2 099 (*Cowra Guardian*, 16 February). In the 1972 Federal election, won by the Labor Party, that Party polled a majority of votes in Cowra, but in the 1973 State election it could manage only 1 865 to the Country Party's 3 044 (*Cowra Guardian*, 5 December and 20 November respectively). Tim West, as the Labor candidate, polled more votes than his overall successful Country Party opponent in 1981 (*Cowra Guardian*, 30 September).
5 Many Cowra Shire farmers remote from a town or village could claim allegiance to a named area, probably using the name of an early squatter's run.
6 Contrary to what one might anticipate after the finding of Newby et al. (1978: 210) that farmers' social networks are heavily concentrated in their localities, the rural residents of the Shire showed a lower frequency of locally concentrated networks than town and village residents. Twenty-three, forty-four and forty-one per cent of rural, town and village residents respectively reported that most or all of their good friends lived within fifty kilometres of their homes. This does not, of course, contradict the Newby finding that farmers tend not to have many city-dwelling or working class friends.
7 Controlling for place of residence does not suggest that rural people have greater local concentration of kin networks. Twelve, nineteen and twenty per cent of rural, village and town dwelling respondents respectively reported that most or all of their relatives lived within about fifty kilometres of their homes.
8 Cohen (1986) considered the problem of identification of symbols being a matter of interpretation, and while offering no solution, he emphasised the common meaning of actions, like the LEP protest, which ethnographers impute to their informants, and alluded to the persistence of local interpretations of those actions as evidence to support the ethnographic interpretation of symbolic action. Thus the persistence of the city versus country theme through the LEP issue and subsequent local discussion of it offers support to interpretation as symbolism.
9 The 1980 election was an aberration with a large number of farmers nominating following amalgamation.

10

Conclusion: the machinery of power

Local government in Cowra was a specialised political arena, in that it acknowledged, and gave expression to, a particular set of ideals. These ideals were called upon successfully by the business and farming sectors of the population as they pursued their interests. The ideals were not, however, so easily called upon by others, and moreover, they could cloud the interests of others. The business and farm sectors were made powerful by these ideals.

The process of exclusion was not necessarily a product of conscious action on the part of farm and business people, nor was it always, nor indeed often, recognised as such by others. Rather, political actors endeavoured to act in ways which they and their electorate believed would serve the common interest of everybody in the district.[1] The product of this high ambition became symbolic conflict; the common ideals consisted largely of efficiency and the maintenance of local tradition, expressed symbolically by assault on bureaucracy, during which the parameters were defined from the perspective of business and farm interests.

These processes occurred in a rural district whose people were conscious of a dependent and subordinate relationship with metropolitan Australia. They looked upon their subservience as a contributing factor in impending economic decline. The process of centralisation had removed large amounts of local autonomy, and government policies which had fostered growth and prosperity had been reversed. Cowra people, however, looked to, and may be increasingly dependent on, government support.

Local government was the most important potential medium for obtaining that support. This was one of the factors, which made it *the* arena of local politics. It was important to local people, not just for its role in service provision, but for its potential role as a mediator with other levels of government. Cowra Shire Council showed signs of elitism in its membership, and the reputation survey fueled that interpretation, but at the same time it had not been exclusivist as some earlier studies would suggest that it might have been. Elitist leadership by business and farm people rests easily with the traditional image of local government as a

Conclusion: the machinery of power

managerial institution, as a 'people's corporation'. Individualistic analysis, however, misses the source of elitism, by failing to consider the relationships between interests identifiable in Cowra, and interests which received viable political expression. Local government in Cowra would appear to have been an arena in which a range of interests might pluralistically have been expressed and issues raised for debate.

Difficulty was encountered by those who tried to raise issues over allocation of Council resources, or 'make the wheel squeak'. During the 1950s and 1960s such issues were raised, but Council administration practices had been refined. In 1986, people still perceived provision of services differentially across social areas, with those in the poorer areas perceiving the lower standards. The bureaucratic apparatus, promising efficient and fair administration, was ready to smother issues which might have been raised by people in these areas, as was seen in the West Cowra matters and Taragala's air pollution. Councillors applied their ideologies to determine what was legitimate for their discussion, and those ideologies placed great importance on efficiency of management. While this was easily accommodated by the 'people's corporation' image, it also inhibited pluralism. Moreover, while councillors strove for efficiency they set the agenda in such a way that the interests of resident groups were obscured, and conflict arose between councillors and officers.

What can restrain potential issues can elevate others into political crises. When the power of bureaucracy was seen as a threat by farmers and business people, it became an issue. Issues were raised when conflicts between the interests of the bureaucracy and a general local interest were perceived, as they were most enthusiastically by farmers in the LEP issue. Non-farm, non-business people were very quiet, unless their interests could be expressed as part of a general ratepayer interest, as they were in the Tourist and Development Corporation matters. In the 'people's corporation' image, ratepayer interests were the only legitimate ones, and farming and business interests could easily be equated with a ratepayer interest that was congruent with the interest of the entire locality. Councillors readily made this connection for farm and business people, but did not do so for railway people.

Local interests could be placed in opposition to what was seen as a deviant and malevolent local bureaucracy. This was most obvious in the LEP issue but was also evident in development regulation matters. In the LEP issue, farmers were so strong as to be able to destroy the 'people's corporation' image, casting aside the public participation process that had been designed to limit bureaucratic control, and creating their own. The farmers' 'coup' had popular, though not universally active support, and was seen as defence of a general local interest. Its greatest impact was the deepened division of the Council into two camps: those who supported and those who attacked the officers. This division was also apparent when building regulation problems arose. This time the business interest was put forward, and respected, as a general local interest. The power of business and farm people to create issues is best illustrated by the contrast they presented with railway employees, who were able reasonably to claim a general local interest, and had their concerns voiced in the *Guardian*, but did not see their issue raised. At least, that is, until it was seen as a threat to farmers.

Desire for efficiency was also observed, expressed as ratepayer defence with a dash of localism. It kept human services off the agenda. A human services role would have enabled the Council to better serve the interests of women and Aborigines in particular, but human services had touched rather than penetrated the local political agenda. Those in whose interests provision of human services lay were caught in a double bind. This further protected property interests by appeal to the ratepayer interest which would inevitably be threatened by the increase in local expenditure that human services entail. Human services as a non-issue resembled other matters, such as West Cowra's water, Taragala's air pollution and the decline of the railway, where issues were voiced but not effectively placed on the local political agenda. The Aboriginal non-issue was even further off the agenda due to its history of dissociation with local affairs.

Ideals which stimulated issues were specialised. Ratepayer defence created issues, specifically the controversy about water rates, and the Tourist and Development Corporation matters with a little help from symbolism as status action. Along with the undercurrent of town and country conflict, ratepayer defence could create issues which, when fuelled with localism, could precipitate conflict of pluralistic appearance. I argued, however, that all issues, as against non-issues, became conflict between councillors and officers. Such conflict was the content of local politics, so that while local politics was not enacted by some small cohesive group in the elitist mould, the polity was subservient to a narrow range of interests. There was no incentive to form such a cohesive elite. The political actors saw themselves as defenders of a general interest.

Explanation of this constraint on the polity is enabled by the concept of resources. Possession and deployment of resources were the means by which representatives of the narrow range of interests maintained constraint. Successful deployment of resources required access to the political arena. The most direct path to it ran through councillors and senior officers. Although there was no Bradstow-style agenda-setting clique, both councillors and officers may have been remote because they tended to be white males who were either professionals or self-employed. They did not, however, all fit these categories, and indeed people from all status levels had their needs expressed in Council. The most successful instance of issue-raising took place at the first public meeting about the LEP, not in Council. Lack of representation cannot account for constraints on issues; representation on the Council was not a crucial resource. Under the ideal

Conclusion: the machinery of power

of political neutrality, moreover, representation did not occur; it was defined out of local politics.

The crucial resources were those which legitimated expressed interests as local rather than sectional. Those who could present their wishes as an expression of a general local interest had a prospect of being heard and having an issue raised. Their prospects, however, ranged from very weak in the case of railway workers, through marginal in the case of ratepayers, to significant for business people, and very strong for farmers. The possibility of issue creation was determined by the climate of rural ideology which delineated potential resources. While it denied them to some it reinforced them for others. Rural ideology ratified only those particular expressions of the universal ideals of local government (ratepayer defence, political neutrality and localism) which were compatible with it.

As representation was of secondary importance the political significance of the democratic process was small. Council elections were a ritual which reinforced the ideal of political neutrality, a ritual which denied the reality of democracy it is usually held to represent. Election campaigns were little more than outpourings of apolitical localist sentiment which, in the scarcity of policies and platforms, gave electors little other than efficiency to have a say about, except on the occasional opportunity to express respect for people of high prestige or esteem.

A number of people felt a need to step beyond the democratic apparatus and pursued their interests outside it. Some achieved their aims. Some were discouraged or unable to proceed. Some can be seen to have had an objective interest in acting but did not do so, while wishing to preserve a politically neutral or administratively efficient 'people's corporation'. The first group was enabled by resources; the second encountered opponents' deployment of resources; and the third did not enter the race.

Power was consistently exerted in its second mode. That is, some people benefited while others' interests stayed off the agenda. Power relations stepped beyond the second mode into the third when people failed to recognise their objective interests, while adhering to ideologies which supported the interests of those who were able to extract benefit from the political arena, and those who were able to extract benefit did so, as they maintained popular hegemonic interpretations of local interests. Some politics, especially those surrounding conflict between councillors and officers, were legitimate, and their legitimacy was a product of popular acceptance of the idea of the need for defence against marauding bureaucrats. The third mode appeared in the issues that were raised in those politics: the legitimate issues tended to be those pursued by and for farmers and business people. In this way the values and beliefs that were widely shared became political resources of the powerful. Discouragement of 'sectional' action by the political neutrality ideal, and the double bind for those in whose interests human services lay, illustrated the sharing of values and consequent effects on political activity. As the non-issue of the decline of the railway showed, the power relationship could be seen to extend beyond that which was enabled by the sharing of values. The powerful had such a monopoly of legitimacy that they were able to deny the same shared beliefs as ideological resources for others, when those others were not seen to embody the ideals of rural ideology.

The action which created and reinforced the power relationship need not have been associated with a conscious intention to do so, because these ideologies were widely shared. Just as the powerless believed that their interests were being defended, so the powerful believed that they were defending mutual interests. It is difficult to take an individualistic approach which would interpret such sharing as imposition of values by the powerful onto the powerless and perhaps risk allocating blame to individuals. Rural ideology is a product of a long history of rural settlement, in particular the property relations following nineteenth century land reform, and the on-going relationship between city and country. Localism in particular has a real referent; country districts do have an interest to pursue.

If the bases of Cowra's power structure cannot so usefully be traced to individuals in Cowra Shire, how then can it be explained? The concept of resources provides the key to such an explanation, but not all of it. Possession of resources is a necessary precursor to the exercise of power. But it is not enough merely to have them: resources must also be deployed. Farming and business groups chose to deploy theirs. Resources were deployed when what were perceived to be the interests of business, farming or ratepayers appeared to be threatened. Under the popular technocratic model of bureaucracy, it was the bureaucracy which did the threatening.

The bureaucratic interest was the most often, almost the only, structurally offensive interest perceived. Perceptions of this interest had real referents. It is a mistake to assume all ideology to be self-deception. Cowra people faced a bureaucracy which posed real threats in the form of increased rates and punishment for malefactors, just as the railway workers confronted a city-based bureaucracy which, while determining their career prospects, could not be expected to cater to their interests at the expense of others. Cowra people also faced double binds, notably situations arising from membership of groups with incompatible interests in which ratepayers who would have benefited from new or improved services found themselves.

Farming and business groups did not, however, set up the conditions in which deployment of resources became possible. The most important of such conditions were the property relations of rural society, and the nature of local government as a servant of property interests. These historical circumstances, within which rural ideology had diffused, established both the interest alignments and the resources used to place and maintain those interests in a power relationship. While there is no theoretical or

Conclusion: the machinery of power

empirical necessity for the choice to deploy to be made, the circumstances in which deployment was enabled, and choices guided toward such deployment, existed in the rural ideological climate.

Aspects of these findings are compatible with those of earlier studies, suggesting ways in which Cowra may not be unique. McIntyre and McIntyre (1944), in so far as they found an ideology to maintain an elite in rural Victoria, identified ideology more akin to fatalism than the system of beliefs observed in Cowra. The finding of Oeser and Emery (1957) that politics were defined out of the local arena by a conservative and powerful group rings true in Cowra, but Oeser and Emery, without the theoretical sophistication available to later work, gave their powerful actors a tone of intentionality which could not fairly be applied to Cowra.

Poiner's (1990) observation that an associated ideology of localism was available to property interests is equally applicable to Cowra for the way it obscured interests which, if perceived and acted upon, might have precipitated political conflict. Oxley (1978) is the furthest removed from this study both empirically and theoretically. Yet it is possible to see ideological structures operating in his 'two towns' which had parallels among the resources of the powerful in Cowra. Oxley focused on the denial of structure by an egalitarianism which thereby helped to maintain a status structure. Localism in Cowra denied structural opposition of interests and thereby helped to maintain power relations. Processes similar to those analysed by Oxley operated in Cowra to maintain the status quo. In Cowra, the associated ideologies can be seen as political resources.

The findings of this study are in the broad sense of elitism compatible with those of Wild (1974a), but his individualistic approach left him short of analysis of structural processes. The relationship between this study and Wild (1974a) might be summarised by the finding that an elitist power structure can also occur in a rural service town of normal appearance; that is, one without an aloof gentry attenuating the social ladder. Moreover, such a structure can occur without the conscious agenda-setting processes which appeared to characterise the Bradstow political system. Wild (1974a) shares the shortcomings of the other studies which relied on the largely individualistic techniques exercised in the elitist-pluralist debate.

There appeared to be little prospect of Cowra's power structure changing. There were signs of resistance, as in the West Cowra water supply, Taragala air pollution, human services and Tourist and Development Corporation matters, but these did not alter the structure, and the last-mentioned in particular merely reinforced the status structure and defended the essentially conservative interests of ratepayers. Those who sought a human services role for the Council were caught in a double bind, and those, like the railway workers, who logically had access to resources, may have been prevented from deploying them.

The structure appears immutable under the weight of conservative and localist ideology. Given that Cowra, along with many other small and medium-size country towns, faces the prospect of at best very slow growth while larger towns and cities prosper, the ideology of localism may grow in meaning. Along with it, the ideological resources of the people who are already powerful will also grow. The property relations around which rural ideology has grown, may not, however, be so apparently permanent, with the looming possibility of a decline in family farming. One might expect, however, that like family farming, rural ideology will prove to be durable.

It could be concluded that the value of the study of local power lies in the revelation of processes and associated structures which are largely ideological. Those processes may or may not operate at a societal level. The concepts used to reveal them are ostensibly applicable at any level, but application at the local level has made warnings about any return toward individualism. Structural analysis of Cowra's local politics does not encourage focus of attention on individual action, other than that which reproduces the structures of domination, when those structures are found to be so formidable. Attempts to escape from determinism should be wary of going too far too soon. Resistance has been evident, but it offered a feeble reminder of the views of post-structuralists, such as Foucault (1983), as it highlighted the absence of action threatening to the ideological structures which have pervaded and maintained power. Women sought assistance with human service projects, but had not challenged the beliefs upon which avoidance of human services is now based. The people of West Cowra and Taragala sought a better deal from the Council, but did not challenge the system of allocation. The only group to disorganise legitimacy (Therborn, 1980) was the farmers.

While there is an inherent simplification involved in this analysis, it is set in a situation in which some complications, which might be found elsewhere, are absent. The locale of power processes was a place of individual interaction in which institutions and organisations, other than the 'people's corporation', were few. Local organisations which might have mediated between individual and structure were not prominent as institutional actors divorced from individuals and their interests. Even the farmers' and business organisations were not large in the final analysis, as illustrated by the lack of prominence, despite its participation, of the LGPA in the LEP issue. Obviously, the Tourist and Development Corporation and the Neighbourhood Centre matters would not have arisen without the existence of those organisations, but it is possible to reasonably infer an interest for and another counter to each, and accept that the individuals involved were driven by those interests.

The tradition of community power studies has been left behind other genres of sociology which have explored structural analysis and now search beyond to escape determinism. This study has necessarily been set prior to a 'post-structuralist' approach, but it is not totally constrained by

Conclusion: the machinery of power

determinism. When compared to Vidich and Bensman (1968), it can be seen to contain elements of voluntarism and resistance in its emphasis on acknowledgement of and action upon local interests at the level of the relationship between country and city. It steps past elitism and its specification of static power structures in favour of a dynamic analysis of relationships in which individuals are enabled and constrained by structures of their own making but not of their own intention.

Note

1 When the locally powerful are themselves politically divided, they can be studied without the problems of access which Bell (1978: 33) anticipated. Division within Cowra's 'elite' was so endemic that, were its members ever tempted to do anything that they might subsequently want to hide, the vigour of their political opponents would be strong discouragement. Corruption is rendered unlikely when ties between politicians and bureaucrats are weak. (I am indebted to Dr Eva Etzioni-Halevy for this point.) In any case, the stakes in Cowra's property market are low compared to the enticements to illicit dealing in metropolitan and other local government areas where development is rapid.

Epilogue

I left Cowra in November, 1986 with an enormous debt to all those people who had taken me at face value without much understanding of what I was doing, despite my attempts at explanation. Those who told me about their side of issues (and non-issues) could have held little hope that I could further their cause. Their motives were not selfish, certainly not as selfish as mine would have been if I had intended to take information and give nothing in return. In the case of an overt exchange process, that of the 'Community Needs Survey' (Gray, 1987a), I provided a report in exchange for the extensive support I was given, but that may not have fulfilled the hopes of all my supporters. At times I felt that some people helped me because they thought I might be an ear in the national capital, and while there may be some truth in my interpretation, it would be unjust as a generalisation. I believe that people saw me as a student who was ignorant of life in the bush and, being willing to listen, was worth talking to.

Throughout fieldwork and during the contact I have continued since, I felt from time to time that if Cowra people had the means of sociological understanding, they would be better able to direct their action towards the systems of rule rather than the personalities which just happen to be involved in it. I came to believe that my understanding could be just as valuable to them as their understanding of themselves was to me. I started to hope, naively perhaps, that the sparks of resistance depicted in the study might start fires which would be fuelled by those who, while unwittingly maintaining systems of dominance, were not so intent on doing so that they would fail to see the structures that they had unintentionally created, and start to dismantle the apparatus that maintained them. My debt to Cowra people could be repaid by the dissemination of my research findings, for that intellectual means is all I had to offer as an ear in the national capital. As I have made many friendships in Cowra, it is important at a personal level that I make what could be the most valuable contribution to those friendships: the results of three years work which they in part made possible.

For all these reasons, and the simple pragmatic possibility that Cowra

Epilogue

people close to local politics might correct errors in my reporting, I offered a copy of an advanced draft to the Shire President, Clerk and Engineer. These three were well placed to both understand the thesis and initiate action in response to it, which as Barnes (1970: 237) offered a reminder, is a possible outcome of research which must be borne in mind. They had given me substantial help through the project.

This choice was not, however, an easy one. My dilemma was more complex than the one mentioned by Barnes (1977: 10), which confronts the student of local politics who would find research findings approved by one side of politics while being disapproved by the other. For in Cowra there were no political 'sides', and dissemination of draft material to every identifiable interest group which did or did not have its interests expressed in the local political arena was logistically impossible. The 'people's corporation' was the organisation whose operation was most clearly implicated, so its leadership in terms of both a councillor and officers seemed to be the obvious people to vet the work.

I met Neville Armstrong and Jim Finnimore in Neville's office, after both had read the draft. (Unfortunately Cyril Treasure could not attend.) The meeting was most gratifying, because both Neville and Jim had understood the work and acknowledged value in its approach. It was also gratifying that they had detected only four very minor errors, correction of which has had no effect on the arguments. Their interpretations contrasted with my structural approach: they had observed the actions of individuals and used those observations to construct explanations. While appreciating the difference between our interpretations they were keen to emphasise the limited range of choice of action imposed on local government councillors and officers in discharging their responsibilities, and the effect that this has on local politics. They recognised the structural constraints imposed on themselves and their colleagues.

I had offered in my structural approach a level of understanding that, while it may have been apparent, was certainly obscured in the day to day business of dealing with individuals. We discussed the value of a structural approach to such issues as human services and development matters, as well as Council allocation policy. Neville acknowledged that the policy apparatus presented a formidable structure, having moved the political system away from the squeaky wheel model leaving deserving wheels difficult to 'squeak', but our conversation about possible means of redressing this imbalance reminded me of how difficult it is at a practical level to make a public allocation system work equitably. To the extent that some people in positions of responsibility have gained insight into their locality which they might not otherwise have had, and that those people may try to redress some of the imbalances of power resources that the work has identified, I feel that I can claim some satisfaction, and can believe that I have returned something to the community.

It would of course be vastly arrogant to claim that my insights have or could prompt an attack on the power structure. Such action may only come from those who have led resistance. For some the struggles continue. The Neighbourhood Centre continues its insecure existence into 1991. The few remaining railway employees continue to see their career prospects and working conditions deteriorate. Along with all country people whose livelihood is dependent on the family farming system, Cowra people are confronted with government proposals for deregulation which would take away support for small farmers while making opportunities for those farms which are already large and efficient.

People who have to decide whether to support or reject Neighbourhood Centres, railway transportation and the small farm system would, like the senior officers of Cowra Shire Council, benefit from acquaintance with the structural element in local politics. Interpretation of the local social process at a structural level is essential for research to fulfill any promise of liberation. The old individualistic focus of Australian community power studies may only further the popularity of conspiracy theories, encouraging witch-hunting rather than action to alter the structures of power.

Acknowledgements

I owe my first debt to the people of Cowra, including those whose civic work is illuminated in this book, and many more who are not so visible, for the welcome they offered and the help they gave me. I have valued their insight and their friendship. They made my stay in their district happy, productive and above all, informative.

Many people offered guidance and advice through the course of the project. Stephen Mugford gave me the right proportions of guidance, encouragement and freedom I needed to explore the community research process while I was under his supervision as a doctoral student. Harry Oxley supported me from my earliest plans for the project, offering encouraging comments from fieldwork through to draft chapters.

I am indebted to many other people who generously agreed to read and comment on draft chapters. Barry Hindess and Jack Barbalet provided penetrating advice on the theory components. John Merritt and Bill Gammage encouraged my historical analysis. Chris Paris offered comments which helped me through much of the political analysis. Eva Etzioni-Halevy made some insightful points after her reading of draft material on elitism and local politics. I must also thank Martin Mowbray for his guidance at the early stage of project formulation and my anonymous examiners and manuscript referees at the later stages.

I am indebted to Frank Lewins for his support and advice, especially for the opportunities which were opened by my teaching with him at the Australian National University, and also for being, like many others, a supportive colleague. My stay in the Sociology Department, the Faculties at ANU was particularly happy and fruitful, for which I must thank all my colleagues. I owe particular thanks to Helen Felton for help with the administrative tasks without which research does not happen. My fellow students, Manjula Waniganayake, Alastair Greig, Masao Nobe, Evelyn Hogan, Claire Runciman, Christine Helliwell and Diana Reed persevered through innumerable discussions and arguments over points of theory and analysis; they did this as well as offering the empathy which only fellow students can have. I have more recently benefited from the views of colleagues, Geoffrey Lawrence, Craig Matheson and Perry Share, at

Charles Sturt University – Riverina, who are blessed with sociological, as well as first-hand, understanding of rural life.

I am also grateful to Stephen Mugford, Larry Saha, and the late Eric Broughton at the ANU, and those in the Commonwealth bureaucracy, who supported my application for, and provided me with the Commonwealth Postgraduate Research Award which enabled the project upon which this book is based.

Appendix: Cowra Shire councillors and senior officers, 1985-6

Shire CLERK Neville ARMSTRONG, a career local government officer, had worked for rural local government since completing high school. He came to Cowra to take up the position of Town Clerk in 1968.

Stephen BELL was a high school teacher, and the only councillor to have tertiary education qualifications.

Barbara BENNETT was elected to the Municipal Council in 1971, and served until her retirement in 1987, including five years as Mayor, and three years as Deputy President of Cowra Shire. Barbara had farming and business interests. Her family history goes back to the earliest settlers.

Shire ENGINEER Jim FINNIMORE was, like the Shire Clerk, a career local government officer. He came to Cowra to take up his position with the Municipal Council, in 1971, from a larger town council.

Bruce GOLSBY was a farmer who, with his wife and family, also ran a business in town. He was first elected to the Municipal Council in 1977. His grandfather had been a Mayor in the 1920s.

Don KIBBLER was well known as a councillor, but perhaps better known as President of the Tourist and Development Corporation. He was also a member of Rotary. Don grew up in Cowra with his three brothers who were also in local business. His parents, having migrated from England before World War II, were known for their building firm.

Jack MALLON, a farmer, lived in the village of Woodstock.

HEALTH SURVEYOR Robert MYLES was the only one of the three senior officers who had grown up in Cowra.

Col NEWTON was a long serving alderman and councillor, a motor mechanic and Labor Party member who was first elected to the Municipal Council in 1953.

George NOBLE was a farmer, first elected to Waugoola Shire in 1965. He and Cyril Treasure were, in 1986, the only former Waugoola Councillors on Cowra Shire.

Ab OLIVER was the epitome of a prominent and respected citizen. His impressive record of work in community organisations gained him an MBE in 1974. He was first elected to Cowra Municipal Council in 1954, and served continuously, except for two three-year periods when he did not nominate for personal reasons, until his retirement in 1987. He was Mayor for seven years and Deputy Mayor for eight, and was the first President of Cowra Shire, serving from 1981 to 1985. Ab was raised on a farm, with his eight brothers and one sister. His brother, Ray, was President of Waugoola Shire between 1960 and 1964, having been first elected to that Council in 1950. Their father had served on Waugoola in its early years. Ray was endorsed by the Liberal Party as their candidate for the State electorate of Young in 1955; Ab was endorsed by the then Country (now National) Party for the Federal seat of Hume in 1974. Neither of them won a seat, nor has any other Cowra local politician since World War II.

Neville PENGILLY was a local business proprietor who had served as President of the Chamber of Commerce.

Shire PRESIDENT Cyril TREASURE was first elected to Waugoola Shire in 1950, and held the Shire Presidency from 1964 until its demise in 1980. He was elected President of Cowra Shire in 1985. Cyril had an impressive record of service to local organisations, and in his presidential capacities, was very visible.

Harold UPSTON had a service station and motor dealer business in Cowra. He had been active in the Chamber of Commerce and, being in his early forties, was the youngest councillor.

Tim WEST, a retired farmer, was well known as a prominent member of the Labor Party and as a participant in local organisations. He was endorsed as Labor candidate for the State seat in 1974 and 1981.

Bibliography

Adler, P.A., Adler, P. and Rochford, E.B. (1986) 'The Politics of Participation in Field Research', *Urban Life*, 14 (4): 363–376.
Advisory Council for Inter-Government Relations (1984) *Responsibilities and Resources of Australian Local Government*, Report 7, Australian Government Publishing Service, Canberra.
Aitkin, D. (1972) *The Country Party in New South Wales: a Study of Organization and Survival*, Australian National University Press, Canberra.
Alexander, A. (1982) *Local Government in Britain Since Reorganisation*, George Allen and Unwin, London.
Alford, R.R. (1969) *Bureaucracy and Participation: Political Cultures in Four Wisconsin Cities*, Rand McNally, Chicago.
Anton, T.J. (1963) 'Power, Pluralism and Local Politics', *Administrative Science Quarterly*, 7: 425–457.
Armstrong, N. (1988) 'Local Government', pp. 213–234 in Marriott, J. (ed.) *Cowra on the Lachlan*, Cowra Shire Council, Cowra.
Atkins, R. (1979) *Albany to Zeehan: A New Look at Local Governments*, Law Book Co., Sydney.
Auchmuty, J.J. (1985) '1810–30', pp. 45–81 in Crowley, F.K. (ed.) *A New History of Australia*, Heinemann, Melbourne.
Austin, D. (1982) 'A Framework for Australian Studies: Some Reflections on Community, Class and Culture', *Mankind*, 13 (3): 218–236.
—(1984) *Australian Sociologies*, George Allen and Unwin, Sydney.
Austin, P. (1986) 'Social Problems Ignored Leeton Woman Claims', *The Land*, 27 February: 6.
Austin, P. and Marshall, A. (1985) 'Farm Pressures Bring Wider Role for Women', *The Land*, 19 September: 10.
Australian Bureau of Statistics (1977–1986) *Agricultural Land Use and Selected Inputs*, Publication 7411.1, Canberra.
Australian Electoral Commission (1987) *Election Statistics, 1987, New South Wales*, Vol. 3, Australian Government Publishing Service, Canberra.
Bachrach, P. and Baratz, M. (1970) *Power and Poverty*, Oxford University Press, New York.
Bailey, F.G. (1971) 'Gifts and Poisons', pp. 1–25 in Bailey, F.G. *Gifts and Poisons: The Politics of Reputations*, Basil Blackwell, Oxford.
—(1983) *The Tactical Uses of Passion: an Essay on Power, Reason and Reality*, Cornell University Press, Ithaca.
Barbalet, J.M. (1985) 'Power and Resistance', *British Journal of Sociology*, 36 (4): 531–548.
—(1986) 'Limitations of Class Theory and the Disappearance of Status: the Problem of the New Middle Class, *Sociology*, 20 (4): 557–575.

—(1987) 'Power, Structural Resources and Agency', *Current Perspectives in Social Theory*, 8: 1–24.
Barnes, J.A. (1970) 'Some Ethical Problems in Modern Fieldwork', pp. 235–251 in Filstead, W.J. (ed.) *Qualitative Methodology*, Markham Press, Chicago.
—(1977) *The Ethics of Inquiry in Social Sciences: Three Lectures*, Oxford University Press, Dehli.
—(1979) *Who Should Know What?* Penguin, Harmondsworth.
Barrett, S. and Fudge, C. (eds.) (1981) *Policy and Action*, Methuen, London.
Beaulieu, L.J. and Ryan, V.D. (1984) 'Hierarchical Influence Structures in Rural Communities', *Rural Sociology*, 49 (1): 106–116.
Bell, C. (1969) 'A Note on Participant Observation', *Sociology*, 3: 417–418.
—(1978) 'Studying the Locally Powerful', pp. 14–40 in Bell, C. and Encel, S., *Inside the Whale: Ten Personal Accounts of Social Research*, Pergamon Press, Sydney.
Bell, C. and Encel, S. (1978) *Inside the Whale: Ten Personal Accounts of Social Research*, Pergamon Press, Sydney.
Bell, C. and Newby, H. (1971) *Community Studies*, George Allen and Unwin, London.
—(1976a) 'Husbands and Wives: the Dynamics of the Deferential Dialectic', pp. 152–168 in Barker, D.C. and Allen, S. *Dependence and Exploitation in Work and Marriage*, Longman, London.
—(1976b) 'Community, Communion, Class and Community Action', pp. 189–207 in Herbert, D. and Johnson, R. (eds.) *Social Areas in Cities*, Vol. II, Wiley, London.
—(1977) *Doing Sociological Research*, George Allen and Unwin, London.
Bell, C., Newby, H., Saunders, P. and Rose, D. (1976) 'Community Power in Rural Areas', unpublished paper delivered at 47th ANZAAS Congress, Hobart.
Bell, C. and Roberts, H. (1984) *Social Researching: Politics, Problems, Practice*, Routledge, London.
Benton, T. (1981) 'Objective Interests and the Sociology of Power', *Sociology*, 15: 161–148.
Betts, K. (1986) 'The Conditions of Action, Power and the Problem of Interests', *Sociological Review*, 34 (1): 39–64.
Birch, A.H. (1959) *Small Town Politics*, Oxford University Press, London.
Blowers, A. (1977) 'Checks and Balances – The Politics of Minority Government', *Public Adminstration*, 55 (3): 305–16.
—(1983) 'Master of Fate or Victim of Circumstance? The Exercise of Corporate Power in Environmental Policy-Making', *Policy and Politics*, 11 (4): 393–415.
Bokemeier, J. L. and Tait, J. L. (1980) 'Women as Power Actors: a Comparative Study of Rural Communities', *Rural Sociology*, 45 (2): 238–55.
Bolton, G. (1978) 'How We Got Here', pp. 1–20 in van Dugteren, T. (ed.) *Rural Australia: the Other Nation*, Hodder and Stoughton, Sydney.
Bourdieu, P. (1979) 'Symbolic Power', *Critique of Anthropology*, 13–14 (4): 77–85.
Bowman, M. (n.d.) *The Suburban Political Process in Box Hill Melbourne*, Melbourne Politics Monograph, Melbourne.
—(1983) 'Local Government in Australia', pp. 165–184 in Bowman, M. and Hampton, W. *Local Democracies: A Study in Comparative Local Government*, Longman Cheshire, Melbourne.
Bradley, T. and Lowe, P. (1984) 'Introduction: Locality, Rurality and Social Theory', pp. 1–23 in Bradley, T. and Lowe, P. (eds.) *Locality and Rurality: Economy and Society in Rural Regions,* Geo Books, Norwich.
Brook, E. and Finn, D. (1978) 'Working-Class Images of Society and Community Studies', pp. 125–143 in University of Birmingham, Centre for Contemporary Cultural Studies, *On Ideology*, Hutchinson, London.
Bryson, L. and Mowbray, M. (1981) 'Community: the Spray-On Solution', *Australian Journal of Social Issues*, 16 (4): 255–267.
Bryson, L. and Thompson, F. (1972) *An Australian Newtown*, Kibble Books, Malmsbury.

Bryson, L. and Wearing, B. (1985) 'Australian Community Studies – A Feminist Critique', *Australian and New Zealand Journal of Sociology*, 21 (3): 349–366.

Buller, H. and Hoggart, K. (1986) 'Nondecision-Making and Community Power – Residential Development Control in Rural Areas', *Progress in Planning*, 25: 135–203.

Burdess, N. (1981) 'Women in New South Wales Local Government', *Australian Journal of Public Administration*, 40 (4): 355–358.

——(1984) 'Public Involvement in New South Wales Local Government', *Australian Journal of Public Administration*, 43 (3): 296–300.

Burgess, R.G. (1984) *In the Field: An Introduction to Field Research*, George Allen and Unwin, London.

Buxton, G.L. (1985) '1870–90', pp. 165–215 in Crowley, F.K. (ed.) *A New History of Australia*, Heinemann, Melbourne.

Buxton, R. (1973) *Local Government*, Penguin, Harmondsworth.

Camasso, M.J. and Moore. D.E. (1985) 'Rurality and the Residualist Social Welfare Response', *Rural Sociology*, 50 (3): 397–408.

Campbell, F. and Kriegler, R. (1981) 'Illusion and Disillusion in an Industrial Town', pp. 71–96 in Bowman M. (ed.) *Beyond the City: Case Studies in Community Structure and Development*, Longman Cheshire, Melbourne.

Carr-Gregg, C. (1978) *Japanese Prisoners of War in Revolt*, University of Queensland Press, St Lucia.

Chandler, W. (1985) 'When Local Should Mean Neighbourhood . . . Reforms for Local Government', *Australian Society*, 4 (12): 31–2.

Chapman, R.J.K. and Wood, M. (1984) *Australian Local Government: The Federal Dimension*, George Allen and Unwin, Sydney.

Chatterton, L. (1984) 'The Labor Party and the Paradox of Rural Opinion', *Labor Forum*, 6 (2): 16–20.

Clark, C.M.H. (1978) *A History of Australia*, vol. iv, 'The Earth Abideth for Ever', Melbourne University Press, Melbourne.

Cockburn, C. (1977) *The Local State*, Pluto Press, London.

Coffield, F. and Borrill, C. (1983) 'Entree and Exit', *Sociological Review*, 31 (3): 520–545.

Cohen, A.P. (1975) *The Management of Myths*, Manchester University Press, Manchester.

——(1982a) 'Belonging: the Experience of Culture', pp. 1–17 in Cohen, A.P. (ed.) *Belonging: Identity and Social Organisation in British Rural Cultures*, Manchester University Press, Manchester.

——(1982b) 'Blockade: a Case Study of Local Consciousness in an Extra Local Event', pp. 292–321 in Cohen, A.P., (ed.) *Belonging: Identity and Social Organisation in British Rural Cultures*, Manchester University Press, Manchester.

——(1985) *The Symbolic Construction of Community*, Ellis Horwood/Tavistock, London.

——(1986) 'Of symbols and boundaries, or does Ertie's greatcoat hold the key?' pp. 1–19 in Cohen, A.P. (ed.) *Symbolising Boundaries: Identity and Diversity in British Culture*, Manchester University Press, Manchester.

Colebatch, H.K. and Degeling, P.J. (1986) *Understanding Local Government*, Canberra College of Advanced Education, Canberra.

Connell, R.W. (1977) *Ruling Class, Ruling Culture*, Cambridge University Press, Cambridge.

Connell, R.W. and Irving, T.H. (1985) 'The Ruling Class', pp. 347–359 in Woodward, D. et al. (eds.) *Government, Power and Politics in Australia*, 3rd edn., Longman Cheshire, Melbourne.

Cornish, S. (1985) 'Powerlessness in Peripheral Regions: the Case of the Non-Militant Miner', pp. 43–64 in Rees, G., Bujra, J., Littlewood, P., Newby, H., and Rees, T.L., *Political Action and Social Identity: Class, Locality and Ideology*, Macmillan, London.

Corrigan, P. (1979) 'The Local State: The Struggle for Democracy', *Marxism Today*, 23 (7): 203–9.

Cowlishaw, G. (1988) *Black, White or Brindle: Race in Rural Australia*, Cambridge University Press, Cambridge.
Craig, R. (1983) 'Maintaining the Peripheral Workforce–the Role of Ideology in Family Farming in Australia', unpublished paper presented at the Annual Conference of the British Sociological Association, Cardiff.
Craig, R. and Phillips, K. (1983) 'Agrarian Ideology in Australia and the United States', *Rural Sociology*, 48 (3): 409–420.
Craze, B. (1977) 'The Wiradjuri Tribe Aborigines on the Lachlan – and Their Contact with Explorers and Settlers', *Armidale and District Historical Society Journal and Proceedings*, 20: 11–23.
—(1979) *Cowra's Event of the Year–A History of a Country Show*, Cowra Pastoral, Agricultural and Horticultural Association, Cowra.
—(n.d.) Unpublished notes prepared for Cowra and District Historical Society.
Crenson, M.A. (1971) *The Un-Politics of Air Pollution: A Study of Non-Decisionmaking in the Cities*, The Johns Hopkins Press, Baltimore.
Crutchett, S. (1985) 'Division of Duties the Key to Success of Temora Farm Venture', *The Land*, 12 November: 4.
—(1987) 'Heavy with Promise but Light with Facts', *The Land*, 22 January: 7.
Davidoff, L., L'Esperance, J. and Newby, H. (1976) 'Landscape with Figures: Home and Community in English Society', pp. 139–175 in Mitchell, J. and Oakley, A. (eds.) *The Rights and Wrongs of Women*, Penguin, Harmondsworth.
Davies, J. (1972) *The Evangelistic Bureaucrat*, Tavistock, London.
Dearlove, J. (1973) *The Politics of Policy in Local Government: The Making and Maintenance of Public Policy in the Royal Borough of Kensington and Chelsea*, Cambridge University Press, Cambridge.
Debnam, G. (1975) 'Nondecisions and Power', *American Political Science Review*, 69 (3): 889–904.
Dempsey, K. (1974) 'Lay Power and Ministerial Careers', pp. 427–440 in Edgar, D. (ed.) *Social Change in Australia*, Cheshire, Melbourne.
—(1983) *Conflict and Decline: Ministers and Laymen in an Australian Country Town*, Methuen, Sydney.
—(1986a) 'Gender Relations; the Study of the Practice of Social Closure by Men Against Women', unpublished paper presented to the Annual Conference of the Sociological Association of Australia and New Zealand, University of New England, Armidale.
—(1986b) 'The Impact of Sponsorship on Field Research', unpublished paper presented to the Annual Conference of the Sociological Association of Australia and New Zealand, Armidale.
—(1987) 'Economic Inequality between Men and Women in an Australian Rural Community', *Australian and New Zealand Journal of Sociology*, 23 (3): 358–374.
—(1990) *Smalltown: A Study of Social Inequality, Cohesion and Belonging*, Oxford University Press, Melbourne.
Dick, A. (1986a) 'Clash Over Planning Controls of Farmland', *The Land*, 24 July: 6.
—(1986b) 'SRA Senses Time Right to Close Down Branch Lines', *The Land*, 24 July: 17.
—(1987) 'Government Won't Railroad Us on Option 3', *The Land*, 3 September: 7.
Domhoff, G.W. (1986) 'The Growth Machine and the Power Elite: A Challenge to Pluralists and Marxists Alike', pp. 53–76 in Waste R.J. (ed.) *Community Power: Directions for Future Research*, Sage, Beverly Hills.
Duncan, S. S. and Goodwin, M. (1982) 'The Local State: Functionalism, Autonomy and class relations in Cockburn and Saunders', *Political Geography Quarterly*, 1 (1): 77–96.
Dunleavy, P. (1976) 'An Issue Centred Approach to the Study of Power', *Political Studies*, 24: 423–34.
—(1980) *Urban Political Analysis*, Macmillan, London.

Bibliography

Dye, T.R. (1986) 'Community Power and Public Policy', pp. 29–51 in Waste, R.J. (ed.) *Community Power: Directions for Future Research*, Sage, Beverly Hills.
Edelman, M. (1960) 'Symbols and Political Quiescence', *American Political Science Review*, 54 (3): 695–704.
—(1967) *The Symbolic Uses of Politics*, University of Illinois Press, Urbana.
—(1971) *Politics as Symbolic Action: Mass Arousal and Quiescence*, Markham, Chicago.
Elias, N. (1974) 'Foreword – Towards a Theory of Communities', pp. ix-xli in Bell, C. and Newby, H. (eds.) *The Sociology of Community*, Cass, London.
Elliffe, P. (1987) 'Human Services Stand Reaffirmed', *Local Government Bulletin*, 42 (4): 13–15.
—(1988) 'State and Local Interests on the South Coast', *Local Government Bulletin*, 43 (3/4): 17–18.
Elliott, B. and McCrone, D. (1982) *The City: Patterns of Domination and Conflict*, Macmillan, London.
Etzioni-Halevy, E. (1985) *Bureaucracy and Democracy*, Routledge and Kegan Paul, London.
Fagence, M. (1979) *The Political Nature of Community Decision Making: An Examination of Some Concepts and Theories from Social and Political Science of Relevance to the Conduct of Community Decision-Making and Town Planning*, Planning Research Papers No. 1, Department of Regional and Town Planning, University of Queensland.
Falkemark, G. (1982) *Power, Theory and Value*, Liber Gleerup, Lund.
Fasenfest, D. (1986) 'Community Politics and Urban Redevelopment, Poletown, Detroit and General Motors', *Urban Affairs Quarterly*, 22 (1): 101–23.
Folster, W. (1939) various articles in *Cowra Guardian*.
Forward, R. (1969) 'Issue Analysis in Community Power Studies', *Australian Journal of Politics and History*, 15 (3): 26–44.
Foucault, M. (1983) 'The Subject and Power', pp. 208–220 in Dreyfus, H. and Rabinow, P. (eds.) *Michel Foucault, Beyond Structuralism and Hermeneutics*, Chicago University Press, Chicago.
Frey, F. (1971) 'Comment: On Issues and Nonissues in the Study of Power', *American Political Science Review*, 65 (4): 1081–1101.
Gammage, B. (1986) *Narrandera Shire*, Narrandera Shire Council, Narrandera.
—(1987) 'Who Gained from Land Selection in NSW?', unpublished paper presented to Australian Historical Association Conference, Armidale.
Gaventa, J. (1980) *Power and Powerlessness*, University of Illinois Press, Urbana.
Geer, B. (1964) 'First Days in the Field', pp. 322–344 in Hammond, P. (ed.) *Sociologists at Work*, Basic Books, New York.
Gerth, H.H. and Mills, C.W. (1977) *From Max Weber: Essays in Sociology*, Routledge and Kegan Paul, London.
Giddens, A. (1979) *Central Problems in Social Theory*, Macmillan, London.
Giles, M. W. and Dantico, M. K. (1982) 'Political Participation and Neighborhood Social Context Revisited', *American Journal of Political Science*, 26 (1): 144–50.
Goldsmith, M. and Saunders, P. (1976) *Participation Through Public Meetings: the Case in Cheshire*, Linked Research Project into Public Participation in Structure Planning, Interim Research Paper 9, U.K. Department of the Environment.
Goodman, R. (1972) *After the Planners*, Penguin, Harmondsworth.
Gordon and Gotch, (various dates 1870–1905) *The Australian Handbook*.
Gramson, W.A. (1985) 'Goffman's Legacy to Political Sociology', *Theory and Society*, 14 (5): 605–622.
Granovetter, M.S. (1972) 'The Strength of Weak Ties', *American Journal of Sociology*, 78 (6): 1360–1380.
Gray, I. (1987a) *The Demand for Community Care*, Report to the Cowra and District Home

and Community Care Committee (unpublished), Australian National University, Canberra.
—(1987b) 'A Case for Rural Locality Studies', unpublished paper presented to the Annual Conference of the Sociological Association of Australia and New Zealand, Sydney.
—(1988a) *The Demand for Community Care Among the Aboriginal Population of Cowra*, Report to the Cowra and District Home and Community Care Committee (unpublished), Australian National University, Canberra.
—(1988b) *Family Farming and Social Values*, Report to the Cowra Branch of the New South Wales Farmers' Association (unpublished), Australian National University, Canberra.
Gray, P. (1980) 'Exchange and Access in Field Work', *Urban Life*, 9 (3): 309–331.
Green, D.G. (1981) *Power and Party in an English City*, George Allen and Unwin, London.
Gusfield, J.R. (1963) *Symbolic Crusade*, University of Illinois Press, Urbana.
Gyford, J. (1976) *Local Politics in Britain*, Croom Helm, London.
Hall, R., Thorns, D. and Willmott, E.E. (1984) 'Community, Class and Kinship – Bases for Collective Action Within Localities', *Environment and Planning D: Society and Space*, 2 (2): 201–215.
Halligan, J. and Paris, C. (1984) 'The Politics of Local Government', pp. 58–72 in Halligan, J. and Paris, C. (eds.) *Australian Urban Politics*, Longman Cheshire, Melbourne.
Hampton, W. (1970) *Democracy and Community: a Study of Politics in Sheffield*, Oxford University Press, London.
Heclo, H. (1969) 'The Councillor's Job', *Public Adminstration*, 47: 185–202.
Hill, A. (1985) *The Bunburyists*, Penguin, Melbourne.
Hindess, B. (1976) 'On Three Dimensional Power', *Political Studies*, 24 (3): 329–333.
—(1982) 'Power, Interests and the Outcome of Struggles', *Sociology*, 16 (4): 498–511.
—(1986a) 'Actors and Social Relations', pp. 113–126 in Wardell, M.L.and Turner, S.P. (eds.) *Sociological Theory in Transition*, George Allen and Unwin, Winchester, Mass.
—(1986b) 'Interests in Political Analysis', *Sociological Review Monograph*, 32: 112–131.
Horowitz, R. (1986) 'Remaining an Outsider: Membership as a Threat to Research Rapport', *Urban Life*, 14 (4): 409–430.
Horvath, R. and Tait, D. (1986) 'Socio-Spatial Inequality in Sydney', pp. 191–207 in McLoughlin, J. B. and Huxley, M. (eds.) *Urban Planning in Australia: Critical Readings*, Longman Cheshire, Melbourne.
Irving, T.H. (1985) '1850–70', pp. 124–164 in Crowley, F.K. (ed.) *A New History of Australia*, Heinemann, Melbourne.
Jackson, Teece, Chesterman, Willis and Partners (1982) *Cowra Environmental Study*, prepared for Cowra Shire Council.
James, K. (1979) 'The Home: a Private or Public Place? Class, Status and the Actions of Women', *Australian and New Zealand Journal of Sociology*, 15 (1): 36–42.
—(1981) 'Public or Private: Participation by Women in a Country Town', pp. 97–113 in Bowman, M. (ed.) *Beyond the City*, Longman Cheshire, Melbourne.
—(1982) 'Women on Australian Farms: A Conceptual Scheme', *Australian and New Zealand Journal of Sociology*, 18: 302–319.
Johnson, R. (1979) 'Participation in Local Government', pp. 230–57 in Lucy, R. (ed.) *The Pieces of Politics*, 2nd edn., Macmillan, Melbourne.
Jones, G. and Stewart, J. (1985) *The Case for Local Government*, George Allen and Unwin, London.
Jones, M.A. (1977) *Organisational and Social Planning in Australian Local Government*, Heinemann, Richmond.
—(1981) *Local Government and the People: Challenges for the 1980s*, Hargreen, Melbourne.

Bibliography

Jones, T. (1987) 'Towns Fight to Save Public Service Jobs', *The Land*, 13 August: 6.
Kellogg Rural Adjustment Unit (1977) *Local Government, Community Groups and Social Welfare*, KRAU Miscellaneous Publication No. 4, University of New England, Armidale.
Kennedy, B.E. (1981) 'How Distance Shaped a Community: Broken Hill's First Ten Years', pp. 114–128 in Bowman, M. (ed.) *Beyond the City: Case Studies in Community Structure and Development*, Longman Cheshire, Melbourne.
Kilmartin, L. and Thorns, D. (1978) *Cities Unlimited: the Sociology of Urban Development in Australia and New Zealand*, George Allen and Unwin, Sydney.
Kilmartin, L., Thorns, D. and Burke, T. (1985) *Social Theory and the Australian City*, George Allen and Unwin, Sydney.
Knights, D. and Willmott, H. (1982) 'Power, Values and Relations: A Comment on Benton', *Sociology*, 16 (4): 578–585.
—(1985) 'Power and Identity in Theory and Practice', *Sociological Review*, 33 (1): 22–46.
Laffin, M. and Young, K. (1985) 'The Changing Roles and Responsibilities of Local Authority Chief Officers', *Public Administration*, 63 (Spring): 1–59.
The Land (1986) 'Plan to Revive Ratepayer Body', 14 August: 5.
—(1987a) 'Strong Push for Option 3', 18 June: 3.
—(1987b) 'Option 3 Rejected', 25 June: 20.
Law Book Company (1985) 'A Review of New Country Councils Constituted Since 1976', *Shire and Municipal Record*, 77 (11): 452–456.
Lawrence, G. (1986) 'Family Farming and Corporate Capitalism: the Uneasy Alliance', *Regional Journal of Social Issues*, 18: 1–17.
—(1987) *Capitalism and the Countryside*, Pluto Press, Sydney.
Layder, D. (1985) 'Power, Structure and Agency', *Journal for the Theory of Social Behaviour*, 15 (2): 131–149.
Little, J. (1986) 'Feminist Perspectives in Rural Geography: an Introduction', *Journal of Rural Studies*, 2 (1) 1–8.
Littlejohn, J. (1963) *Westrigg: The Sociology of a Cheviot Parish*, Routledge and Kegan Paul, London.
Livestock and Grain Producers' Association (n.d.) 'Now's the Time to Show your Hand', leaflet distributed in *The Land* of 10 April, 1986.
Local Government and Shires Association of New South Wales (1987) 'Shires have rough road ahead: report on annual Shires Conference', *Local Government Bulletin*, 42(6): 5–12.
Lockwood, D. (1975) 'Sources of Variation in Working Class Images of Society', pp. 16–31 in Bulmer, M. (ed.) *Working Class Images of Society*, Routledge and Kegan Paul, London.
Lomas, L. (1987) 'The Myth of the Yeoman and the Origins of the Country Party in Victoria', unpublished paper presented to Australian Historical Association Conference, Armidale.
Loveday, P. (1972) 'Citizen Participation and Urban Planning' pp. 129–154 in Parker, R.S. and Troy, P.M. (eds.) *The Politics of Urban Planning*, Australian National University Press, Canberra.
Lukes, S. (1974) *Power: A Radical View*, Macmillan, London.
—(1977) 'Power and Structure', pp. 3–29 in Lukes, S., *Essays in Social Theory*, Macmillan, London.
—(1986) *Power*, Basil Blackwell, Oxford.
Lyon, L. and Bonjean, C.M. (1981) 'Community Power and Policy Outputs: the Routines of Local Politics', *Urban Affairs Quarterly*, 17 (1): 3–21.
Lyons, W.E. and Lowery, D. (1986) 'The Organisation of Political Space and Citizen Responses to Dissatisfaction in Urban Communities', *Journal of Politics*, 48 (2): 321–46.
MacColl, M. (1944) *Economic Survey of Cowra*, Sydney University (held in the Mitchell Library, State Library of New South Wales, Sydney).

McIntyre, A.J. and McIntyre, J.J. (1944) *Country Towns of Victoria*, Melbourne University Press, Melbourne.
McKenzie, B. (1986) 'The Word Rural Areas Fear Most', *Inside Australia*, 2 (2): 30–31.
McNab, R. (1970) 'Community Leadership in a Country Town', unpublished BA(hons) thesis, University of Queensland, Brisbane.
McPhedran, I. (1987) 'A "New Dynamism" vs "Dry Economics" ', *The Land*, 16 July: 10.
Madgwick, P., Griffiths, N. and Walker, V. (1973) *The Politics of Rural Wales*, Hutchinson, London.
Magnusson, W. (1985) 'The Local State in Canada – Theoretical Perspectives', *Canadian Public Administration*, 28 (4): 575–599.
— (1986) 'Bourgeois Theories of Local Government', *Political Studies*, 34 (1): 1–18.
Mant, J. (1982) 'A Tale of Three Acts', *Australian Planner*, 20 (1): 74–76.
Marshall, N. (1985) 'Rural Interest Groups', pp. 23–34 in Costar, B. and Woodward, D. (eds.) *Country to National: Australian Rural Politics and Beyond*, George Allen and Unwin, Sydney.
Martin, W.H. (1922) *History of Cowra 1839–1922*, booklet printed by Cowra Guardian (held in the Mitchell Library, State Library of New South Wales, Sydney).
— (1938) 'Lachlan Valley Capital Has Made Remarkable Strides', extracts from Martin (1922) and notes by R.J. Flood, pp. 9–10 of *Cowra Guardian* 18 February, 1938.
Masson, S. (1986) 'Women's Work: Australia Still Isn't Paying Its Debt to Rural Women', *Inside Australia*, 2 (2): 12–14, 19–20.
Melotte, B. (1983) 'Revising Ends by Focusing on Means: Participation at Kwinana', *Australian Planner*, 21 (4): 85–87.
Merelman, R.M. (1968) 'On the Neo-Elitist Critique of Community Power', *American Political Science Review*, 62: 451–60.
Merritt, R.J. (1983) *The Cake Man*, Currency Press, Sydney.
Middleton, H. (1987) 'Aborigines', pp. 344–379 in Encel, S. and Berry, M. (eds.) *Selected Readings in Australian Society: An Anthology*, Longman Cheshire, Melbourne.
Mladenka, K.R. (1980) 'The Urban Bureaucracy and the Chicago Political Machine: Who Gets What and the Limits to Political Control', *American Political Science Review*, 74 (4): 991–8.
Molotch, H. (1976) 'The City as a Growth Machine', *American Journal of Sociology*, 82 (2): 309–30.
Montague, M. (1981) 'Community Structure and Mobility in a Queensland Country Town', pp. 166–187 in Bowman, M. (ed.) *Beyond the City: Case Studies in Community Structure and Development*, Longman Cheshire, Melbourne.
Mowbray, M. (1984) 'Fiscal Welfare and Local Government: Distributive and Ideological Effects of the Rating System', pp. 73–87 in Halligan, J. and Paris, C. (eds.) *Australian Urban Politics*, Longman Cheshire, Melbourne.
— (1985) 'The Medicinal Properties of Localism', pp. 41–58 in Thorpe, R. and Petruchenia, J. (eds.) *Community Work or Social Change?* Routledge and Kegan Paul, London.
— (1986) 'The Red Shire of Kearsley, 1944–1947: Communists in Local Government', *Labour History*, 51: 83–94.
— (1987) 'Community in Austerity', *Australian Society*, July: 41–42.
Mugford, S. (1979) 'Triad Analysis in Organisational Settings: a Theoretical Discussion and an Empirical Example', pp. 253–269 in Dunkerley, D. and Salaman, G. (eds.), *The International Yearbook of Organization Studies 1979*, Routledge and Kegan Paul, London.
Musgrave, W., Conner, N., Gregory, G., Sinden, J. and Wright, V. (1983) *Local Government Amalgamations in Rural New South Wales*, Australian Rural Adjustment Unit, University of New England, Armidale.
— (1985) *Local Government Amalgamations in Rural New South Wales: An Economic and Social Analysis*, Rural Development Centre, University of New England, Armidale.

Bibliography

Nalson, J.S. and Craig, R.A. (1987) 'Rural Australia', pp. 311–343 in Encel, S. and Berry, M. (eds.) *Selected Readings in Australian Society*, Longman Cheshire, Melbourne.

Newby, H. (1975) 'The Deferential Dialectic', *Comparative Studies in Society and History*, 17 (2): 139–164.

—(1977) *The Deferential Worker: A Study of Farm Workers in East Anglia*, Allen Lane, London.

—(1982) 'Rural Sociology in these Times', *American Sociologist*, 17 (2): 60–70.

—(1983) 'Sociology of Agriculture: Toward a New Rural Sociology', *Annual Review of Sociology*, 9: 67–81.

Newby, H., Bell, C., Rose, D. and Saunders, P. (1978) *Property, Paternalism and Power*, Hutchinson, London.

Newby, H. and Buttel, F. (1980) 'Toward a Critical Rural Sociology', pp. 1–35 in Buttel, F. and Newby, H. (eds.) *The Rural Sociology of the Advanced Societies*, Croom Helm, London.

New South Wales Department of Environment and Planning (1981) *The Environmental Planning and Assessment Act, 1979: A Guide for Local Government*, 2nd edn. Sydney.

Newton, K. (1975) 'Community Politics and Decision-Making: The American Experience and its Lessons', in Young, K. (ed.) *Essays on the Study of Urban Politics*, Macmillan, London.

—(1976) *Second City Politics*, Oxford University Press, London.

—(1979) 'The Language and the Grammar of Political Power: A Comment on Polsby', *Political Studies*, 27 (4): 542–7.

Nott, A.J. (1982) *Environmental Planning and Development Law (NSW)*, Penman Press, Sydney.

Nott, M.J. (1983) *Cowra Shire Agricultural Land Suitability Study*, Agricultural Land Bulletin 2, Department of Agriculture New South Wales.

Oeser, O.A. and Emery, F.E. (1957) *Social Structure and Personality in a Rural Community*, Routledge and Kegan Paul, London.

Office of Local Government (1987) *Community Development, Human Services and Local Government*, Report of a Task Force of the Joint Officers' Committee, Local Government Ministers' Conference, 1986, Australian Government Publishing Service, Canberrra.

Omodei, R.A. (1982) 'Beyond the Neo-Weberian Concept of Status', *Australian and New Zealand Journal of Sociology*, 18 (2): 196–214.

Oxley, H.G. (1978) *Mateship in Local Organisation*, 2nd edn., University of Queensland Press, Brisbane.

Pahl, R.E. (1975) *Whose City?* Penguin, Harmondsworth.

Painter, M. J. (1973) 'A Comparative Analysis of the Decision Making Process in Six Local Government Councils in Sydney', unpublished PhD thesis, Australian National University, Canberra.

—(1974) 'Parochialism and Localism in Local Council Elections in Suburban Sydney', *Public Administration*, (Sydney) 33 (4): 346–359.

—(1975) 'Parochialism, Particularism and Maladministration in Local Government', pp. 124–135 in Spann, R. and Curnow, G. (eds.) *Public Policy and Administration in Australia: A Reader*, John Wiley, Sydney.

Pandey, U.S. (1972) 'Power in Barretta: Influence and Decision-Making in an Australian Country Town', unpublished PhD thesis, University of New England, Armidale.

Parenti, M. (1970) 'Power and Pluralism: A View from the Bottom', *Journal of Politics*, 32: 501–30.

Parker, R.S. (1978) *The Government of New South Wales*, University of Queensland Press, Brisbane.

Parkin, A. (1979) 'Cities without Politics', *Politics*, 14 (2): 291–294.

—(1985) 'Power: A Synopsis of the Arguments', pp. 297–307 in Woodward, D. et al. (eds.), *Government, Politics and Power in Australia*, 3rd edn., Longman Cheshire, Melbourne.

Pearson, D., (1980) *Johnsonville*, George Allen and Unwin, Auckland.
Peace, A. (1985) 'Small Town Politics and Crises of Legitimation', *Journal of Australian Studies*, 16: 84-96.
Peat, Marwick, Mitchell Services (1986) *Cowra Economic Development Opportunities*, draft preliminary report.
Peterson, P. (1981) *City Limits*, University of Chicago Press, Chicago.
Petrikas, D. (1986) 'Angry Farmers Call for '87 Rates Freeze', *The Land*, 10 July: 16.
Pettigrew, A. (1972) 'Information Control as a Power Resource', *Sociology*, 6: 187-204.
Poiner, G. (1979) 'Country Wives', *Australian and New Zealand Journal of Sociology*, 15 (2): 56-64.
— (1990) *The Good Old Rule: Gender and Other Power Relationships in a Rural Community*, Sydney University Press, Sydney.
Polsby, N.W. (1979) 'Empirical Investigation of the Mobilization of Bias in Community Power Research', *Political Studies*, 27 (4): 527-41.
— (1980) *Community Power and Political Theory*, 2nd edn., Yale University Press, New Haven.
Powell, J.D. (1985) 'Assault on a Precious Commodity – the Local Struggle to Protect Groundwater', *Policy Studies Journal*, 14 (1): 62-69.
Power, J. (1984) 'Regionalising Programs as Agents of Localist Politics', *Regional Journal of Social Issues*, 15: 11-14.
Power, J. Wettenhall, R. and Halligan, J. (1981) *Local Government Systems of Australia*, Advisory Council for Inter-Government Relations, Information Paper No. 7, Australian Government Publishing Service, Canberra.
Purdie, D.M. (1976) *Local Government in Australia*, Law Book Company, Sydney.
Raucher, R. (1983) 'Participation in a Coastal Shire', *Australian Planner*, 21 (3): 66-68.
Read, P. (1983) 'A History of the Wiradjuri People of New South Wales 1883-1969', unpublished PhD thesis, Australian National University, Canberra.
— (1984) *Down There with Me on the Cowra Mission*, Pergamon, Sydney.
— (1988) *A Hundred Years War*, Australian National University Press, Canberra.
Rees, G. (1985) 'Introduction', pp. 1-15 in Rees, G., Bujra, J., Littlewood, P., Newby, H., and Rees, T.L. (eds.), *Political Action and Social Identity: Class, Locality and Ideology*, Macmillan, London.
Reimer, B. (1986) 'Women as Farm Labor', *Rural Sociology*, 51 (2): 143-155.
Reppel, B. (1986) 'North Coast Subdivision Row Could be 'Test Case'', *The Land*, 23 January: 4.
Rew, N. (1978) Preface to Oxley, H.G. *Mateship in Local Organisation*, 2nd edn., University of Queensland Press, Brisbane.
Rich, R. (1982) 'The Political Economy of Urban Service Provision', pp. 1-16 in Rich, R. (ed.) *The Politics of Urban Services*, Lexington Books, Lexington.
Richards, A. (1981) 'Foreword', pp. xi-xxvi in Strathern, M. *Kinship at the Core*, Cambridge University Press, Cambridge.
Richards, P.G. (1975) *The Reformed Local Government System*, 2nd edn., George Allen and Unwin, London.
Robin, S. (1986) 'Centre Versus the Periphery in State and Local Government Relations', unpublished paper presented to the Annual Conference of the Sociological Association of Australia and New Zealand, Armidale.
Robbins, J.R. (1975) 'Local Government and Community in South Australia', unpublished PhD thesis, University of Adelaide.
— (1978) 'Localism and Local Government in South Australia', *Politics*, 13: 81-91.
Roe, M. (1985) '1830-1850', pp. 82-123 in Crowley, F.K. (ed.) *A New History of Australia*, Heinemann, Melbourne.
Rose, D., Saunders, P., Newby, H. and Bell, C. (1976) 'Ideologies of Property: A Case Study', *Sociological Review*, 24 (4): 699-730.

Rose, G. (1988) 'Locality, politics, and culture: Poplar in the 1920's', *Environment and Planning D: Society and Space*, 6 (2): 151–168
Rowley, C., (1971) *Outcasts in White Australia: Aboriginal Policy and Practice*, Vol. 2, Australian National University Press, Canberra.
Rural Development Centre (1985) 'The New Rush for the Land', *Inside Australia*, 1 (3): 14.
Ryall, J.C. (1928) Recollections published in various issues of *Cowra Free Press*, Cowra.
Ryan, L. (1986) *Lines to the Lachlan*, Macquarie Publications, Dubbo.
Sandercock, L. (1978) 'Citizen Participation: the New Conservatism', pp. 117–132 in Troy, P.N. (ed.) *Federal Power in Australian Cities*, Hale and Iremonger, Sydney.
Sanders, W. (1984) 'Aboriginal Town Camping, Institutional Practices and Local Politics', pp. 141–148 in Halligan, J. and Paris, C. (eds.) *Australian Urban Politics*, Longman Cheshire, Melbourne.
Sands (1878–9 and 1881–2) *Sands Official Post Office and Country Directory of New South Wales*, John Sands, Sydney.
Sands (1884–5 and 1889–90) *Sands Country Directory and Gazetteer of New South Wales*, John Sands, Sydney.
Sargent, S. (1985) *The Foodmakers*, Penguin, Melbourne.
Saunders, P. (1979) *Urban Politics: A Sociological Interpretation*, Hutchinson, London.
—(1981) 'Community Power, Urban Managerialism and the 'Local State'', pp. 27–49 in Harloe, M. (ed.), *New Perspectives in Urban Change and Conflict*, Heinemann, London.
—(1983) 'On the Shoulders of Which Giant? The Case For Weberian Political Analysis', pp. 41–63 in Williams, P. (ed.), *Social Process and the City*, George Allen and Unwin, Sydney.
—(1985) 'Space, the City and Urban Sociology', pp. 67–89 in Gregory, D. and Urry, J. (eds.) *Social Relations and Spatial Structures*, Macmillan, London.
Saunders, P., Newby, H., Bell, C. and Rose, D. (1978) 'Rural Community and Rural Community Power', pp. 55–85 in Newby, H. (ed.), *International Perspectives in Rural Sociology*, John Wiley, Chichester.
Schattschneider, E.E. (1960) *The Semi-Sovereign People: A Realist's View of Democracy in America*, Holt, Rinehart and Winston, New York.
Schatzman, L. and Strauss, A.L. (1973) *Field Research: Strategies for a Natural Sociology*, Prentice Hall, Englewood Cliffs.
Schmalenbach, H. (1961) 'The Sociological Category of Communion', in Parsons, T. (ed.) *Theories of Society*, Vol. 1, Free Press, New York.
Secretariat to the Joint Officers' Committee of the Local Government Ministers' Conference (1980) *The Rural Local Government Study: an Analysis of the Functions and Finances of Rural Authorities*, Australian Government Publishing Service, Canberra.
Self, P. (1987) 'In Pursuit of Local Life', *Town and Country Planning*, 56 (7/8): 210–212.
Share, P. (1985) *Closer Settlement Policy in Australia and Rural Ideology: A Preliminary Investigation*, unpublished paper presented to the annual conference of the Sociological Association of Australia and New Zealand, Brisbane.
—(1987) 'The Liminality of Farmers – Class and Gender Relations in Agricultural Populations', *Regional Journal of Social Issues*, 21: 19–40.
Sharp, E.B. (1984) 'Citizen Demand Making in the Urban Context', *American Journal of Political Science*, 28 (4): 654–70.
Sharpe, L. (1979) *Decentralist Trends in Western Democracy*, Sage, London.
Shearer, D. (1984) 'Citizen Participation in Local Government – the Case of Santa-Monica, California', *International Journal of Urban and Regional Research*, 8 (4): 573–586.
Simms, M. (1984) 'The Politics of Women in Cities: a Critical Survey', pp. 129–140 in Halligan, J. and Paris, C. (eds.) *Australian Urban Politics*, Longman Cheshire, Melbourne.
Sinclair, A. (1987) *Getting the Numbers: Women in Local Government*, Hargreen, Melbourne.

Smith, C.W. (1983) 'A Case Study of Structuration: The Pure Bred Beef Business', *Journal for Theory of Social Behaviour*, 13: 3–28.
Soovere, K.J. (1967) 'Community Power in Mount Isa', unpublished BA (hons) thesis, University of Queensland, Brisbane.
Stacey, M. (1969) 'The Myth of Community Studies', *British Journal of Sociology*, 20 (2): 134–147.
Stanyer, J. (1976) *Understanding Local Government*, Collins, Glasgow.
Stephenson, J.B. and Greer, L.S. (1981) 'Ethnographers in their Own Cultures: Two Appalachian Cases', *Human Organization*, 40 (2): 123–130.
Steel, W.A. (1932) 'Early Settlement and Settlers of Cowra, 1815–36', *Cowra Guardian*, 26 February, 1932.
Stoker, G. and Wilson, D. (1986) 'Intra-Organisational Politics in Local Authorities – Towards a New Approach', *Public Administration*, 64 (3): 285–302.
Stone, C.N. (1980) 'Systematic Power in Community Decision Making: A Restatement of Stratification Theory', *American Political Science Review*, 74 (4): 978–90.
Strathern, M. (1981) *Kinship at the Core*, Cambridge University Press, Cambridge.
— (1982) 'The Village as an Idea: Constructs of Village-ness in Elmdon, Essex', pp. 247–277 in Cohen A.P. (ed.) *Belonging: Identity and Social Organisation in British Rural Cultures*, Manchester University Press, Manchester.
— (1984a) 'Localism Displaced: A "Vanishing Village" in Rural England', *Ethnos*, 49 (1–2): 43–61.
— (1984b) 'The Social Meaning of Localism', pp. 181–197 in Bradley, T. and Lowe, P. (eds.) *Locality and Rurality: Economy and Society in Rural Regions*, Geo Books, Norwich.
Stuckey, R.D. (1975) *Bluett's Local Government Handbook*, The Law Book Company, Sydney.
Therborn, G. (1980) *The Ideology of Power and the Power of Ideology*, New Left Books, London.
Toon, J. (1984) 'A Review of the Environmental Planning and Assessment Act, 1979', *Australian Quarterly*, 56 (2): 183–191.
Urry, J. (1981) 'Localities, Regions and Social Class', *International Journal of Urban and Regional Research*, 5 (3): 455–473.
Vandeloo, E. N. (1983) 'Local Government and Community Organization: Local Politics and Social Change in Victoria', unpublished PhD thesis, University of Melbourne.
Vaughan, A. (1984) *Signalman's Morning, Signalman's Twilight*, Pan, London.
Vedlitz, A. and Dyer, J.A. (1984) 'Bureaucratic Response to Citizen Contacts: Neighborhood Demands and Administrative Reaction in Dallas', *Journal of Politics*, 46 (4): 1207–16.
Verrall, D., Ward, I., and Hay, P. (1985) 'Community, Country, Party: Roots of Rural Conservatism', pp. 8–22 in Costar, B. and Woodward, D. *Country to National: Australian Rural Politics and Beyond*, George Allen and Unwin, Sydney.
Vidich, A.J. and Bensman, J. (1968) *Small Town in Mass Society*, Princeton University Press, Princeton.
Viteritti, J.P. (1982) 'Bureaucratic Environments, Efficiency and Equity in Urban Service-Delivery Systems', pp. 53–68 in Rich R. (ed.) *The Politics of Urban Services*, Lexington Books, Lexington..
Warner, W.L. (1949) *Democracy in Jonesville: A Study of Quality and Inequality*, Harper and Brothers, New York.
Waste, R.J. (ed.) (1986) *Community Power: Directions for Future Research*, Sage, Beverly Hills.
Waterson, D.B. (1968) *Squatter, Selector and Storekeeper*, Sydney University Press, Sydney.
Watmore, P. and Roberson, A. (n.d.) *Pioneers Family Roots Cowra*, Cowra Family History Group.
Whitworth, R.P. (compiler) (1866) *Bailliere's New South Wales Gazetteer and Road Guide*, Bailliere, Sydney.

Widdows, R. (1974) 'Country vs City: A Study of Attitudes to Country and City Living in a Small Country Town', *Australian Journal of Social Issues*, 9 (3): 196–208.
Wild, R.A. (1974a) *Bradstow*, Angus and Robertson, Sydney.
—(1974b) 'Social Status and Political Power', pp. 309–328 in Edgar, D. (ed.) *Social Change in Australia*, Cheshire, Melbourne.
—(1978) 'The Background to Bradstow: Reflections and Reactions', pp. 182–215 in Bell, C. and Encel, S. *Inside the Whale: Ten Personal Accounts of Social Research*, Pergamon, Sydney.
—(1981) *Australian Community Studies and Beyond*, George Allen and Unwin, Sydney.
—(1983) *Heathcote*, George Allen and Unwin, Sydney.
—(1984) *For Community Studies*, unpublished paper presented at the 54th ANZAAS Congress, Canberra.
—(1985) 'Australian Community Studies – A Feminist Critique – Response', *Australian and New Zealand Journal of Sociology*, 21 (3): 367–370.
Wilkinson, K.P. (1986) 'In Search of the Community in the Changing Countryside', *Rural Sociology*, 51 (1): 1–17.
Williams, H. (1986) *The History of Cowra Pre-Schools*, Cowra and District Historical Society.
Williams, R. (1975) *The Country and the City*, Paladin, St Albans.
—(1983) *Towards 2000*, Chatto and Windus, London.
Willmott, W.E. (1985) 'Hearts and Boundaries: Community at Tinui', *New Zealand Geographer*, 41 (1): 15–20.
Wills, J. (1985) *Local Government and Community Services: Fitzroy – a Study in Social Planning*, Hard Pressed Publications, Clifton Hill, Melbourne.
Wiltshire, K. (1985) 'The Significance of the States' pp. 121–130 in Woodward, D. et al. (eds.) *Government, Politics and Power in Australia*, Longman Cheshire, Melbourne.
Wolfinger, R. (1971) 'Nondecisions and the Study of Local Politics', *American Political Science Review*, 65 (4): 1063–80.
Woodward, D., Parkin, A. and Summers, J. (1985) (eds.) *Government, Politics and Power in Australia*, 3rd edn., Longman Cheshire, Melbourne.
Yates, D. (1978) *The Ungovernable City*, MIT Press, Cambridge, Mass.
Young, I.M. (1986) 'The Ideal of Community and the Politics of Difference', *Social Theory and Practice*, 12 (1): 1–26.
Young, K. (1979) 'Values in the Policy Process', pp. 30–41 in Pollitt, C., Negor, J., Lewis, L. and Patten, J. (eds.) *Public Policy in Theory and Practice*, Hodder and Stoughton, London.

Index

Aboriginal people, 26, 70, 120–1, 123–5; Erambie settlement, 3, 69, 121–3; interests, 120, 124, 139; non-issues and, 120–5, 126; status, 32;
acquiescence, 18, 22; theory, 15, see also inevitability, sense of
actors, see agency
agency, 11, 12, 16–17, 149, 186–7, 189
agenda: of Cowra Shire, 78, 83, 84, 86, 117, 120, 124, 138, 139, 149, 184; of local government, 86
agenda setting, 183; in Australian studies, 17, 22, 50–1, 62; theory, 10, 12, 64
agribusiness, 39
agriculture, 112; in Cowra Shire, 2, 24, 28, 33
aldermen, 80, 81
amalgamation (of Cowra Municipality and Waugoola Shire), 24, 83, 85, 87n7, 142–3
apathy, 13, 15
Apex Club, 4
apolitical local government, belief in, 153, 156, 181n2; in Australian studies, 18, 22, 23, 156–7; in Cowra Shire, 144, 157-161
arena: concept of, 15–16, 22, 60, 62; of Cowra Shire, 43, 44, 47

Bachrach, P., 10, 12
Bailey, F., 55, 149
Baratz, M., see Bachrach, P.
Barretta (NSW), 21, 51–2, 172
Bell, C., 14, 23, 129, 141, 144, 161, 168, 189, see also Newby H.
belonging, 18, 166, 170,
boundaries, 163, 166, 170, geographical, 68
Bradstow (NSW), 19, 50, 62, 129, 184
bridges, 27, 77
Brindleton (NSW), 44, 122, 124–5, 134, 166
budget (Cowra Shire), see estimates

bureaucracy, 64, 74, 107, 108, 123, 127–8, 148n1, 155, 179–80, 183; bureaucrats, 57, 63, 99–100, 101, 131, 136, 147, 148n2, 153, 155, see also officers; in local government, 44; organisation interests, 59, 62, 111, 127, 128, 132, 135–6, 183, 186, see also management
business, 56, 59, 156, 174; in Australian studies, 21, 22, 51, 140; Cowra, 26, 27, 28, 29, 35, 36–7, 40, 41, 114, 141, 182; people in Australian local government, 49; people in Cowra local government, 52, 57, 88; interests, 21, 22, 30, 91, 93, 95, 103, 108, 126, 127, 144, 149, see also commerce, interests

caravan park, 61n
census, 1, 27, 32, 33, 34, 35, 36, 40, see also population
centralisation, 36–41, 45, 48, see also dependence, city
Chamber of Commerce, 38, 47–8, 54, 101, 114, 160
children, 31; child care, 46, 115–17
churches, 29, 140
city, 34, 36, 88, 100, 153, 169–70, 172, 186; interests, 30, 168, see also dependence, centralisation, Sydney
civic centre, 33, 65, 72
class, 88, 144, 157, 158, 161; in Australian studies, 1, 18; history, 31, 33; interests,18, 66; and local government, 43–4, 48, 64, see also interests
closer settlement, 30, 32, 36, 39, 41, see also free selection
closure, 18, 113, 114
clubs, see voluntary organisations
coalitions, 137–8, 139
Cohen, A. 163, 164, 168, 170, 181n8
commerce, 27, 28, 32–3, 34, 37, see also business, Chamber of Commerce
committees (Cowra Municipal), 79, 80

Index

committees (Cowra Shire), 3, 132; Finance, 72; Policy and Resources, 72, 74; Works, 72, 75, 92
Commonwealth Government, 4, 41, 44, 45, 46, 47, 79, 115, 126
communion, 20, 161, 162–3
community, 12, 32, 92, 96, 152, 163, 170; concept, 1, 6, 8n1, 20, 161; Cowra, 64, 168
community studies, 1–2, 8n1; power studies, 6, 9, 16, 23, 43, 188
competition, 21
complacency, 21
Concerned Citizens Committee, 101
conflict, 10, 102, 104, 107, 130–1, 134, 157, 182
consensus, 86; in Australian studies, 20, 21, 22, 50
conservatism; in local government, 45, 48; in Cowra, 67, 87n3, 160,
consultants, 77, 78
Council, see Municipal Council, Shire Council
Council Chambers, see Civic Centre
councillors (Cowra Shire), 83, 89, 137–8, 195–6; beliefs of, 86, 108, 149; and elitism, 52–3, 54, 56; interests of, 74, 85, 89, 101; number of, 84; perceptions of, 75, 76, 102, 119–20, 123, 134–6, 183; places of living, 74; rhetoric, 110, 150–1; values of, 76, 82, 86, 147–8, 149; work of, 73–4, 76, 77, 78, 86, 133–4, 135, 148, see also Shire President
councillors (Waugoola Shire), 72, 85
councillor-officer relations, 73–4, 77–8, 86, 93, 96, 102, 104, 107, 127–139, 143, 156, 184, 189n
countrymindedness, 152–3, 157, 168–70
Cowlishaw, G., 44, 49, 52, 122, 124, 134, 139
Cowra Guardian, see newspapers
Crenson, M., 14, 16, 87n5
crisis, economic, 2

decision making, 74; in Australian studies, 51;
democracy, 127; in Australian studies, 50; ideals of, 44; local, 43, 57, 60, 128–9
Dempsey, K., 18, 22, 58, 112, 140, 157, 161, 166, 167, 168, 173
dependence: Cowra's 33–4, 37, 37–8, 182; rural area's 40; town's 141; women's, 112, see also city, centralisation
development: in Australian studies, 51; policy, 63, see also Tourist and Development Corporation
double bind, 172, 184, 186
drainage, 75, see also water
drought, 84

Dunleavy, P., 16, 151, 153

economy, Cowra's, 1, 24; history, 27, 28, 30, 32, 33, 38, 82; and local government, 45, 46, see also business, commerce, development, industry
efficiency, 71, 73, 74, 76, 77, 78, 85, 128, 145, 154, 155–6, 183, 184
egalitarianism, 57, 147; in Australian studies, 50
elections, 157, 181n4; Cowra Shire, 46, 52–3, 84, 120, 126, 159, 160, 173, 174, 181n9, 185; mayoral, 67; Municipal, 46, 47, 51–2, 67–8, 174; Waugoola Shire, 51–2, 67
electors: in Australian studies, 50; Cowra, 53, 147, 153, 158, 160; local government, 44
electricity, 37, 38, 48, 65
elitism: in Australian studies,17, 19, 20–1, 22, 49–52; concept, 9, 53, 189; Cowra Shire, 52–60, 114, 139, 173, 182–3; in local government, 49, 127, 128–132
elitist-pluralist debate, 9, 19, 21–2, 51
Emery, F., see Oeser, O.
employees, 32, 38, 40–1, 82, 88; interests of, 108
employers, 32, 33, 41, 88, 106, 112
employment, 81, 82, 112
equity, 63, 64, 77, 145, 191
esteem, 50, 57, 173, 175
estimates: Cowra Shire, 84; Cowra Municipal, 89

facilities (Cowra Shire), 70–1, see also civic centre, saleyards, town services
families, 30, 40, 57, 112, 167–8, 174, 177
family farms, 112, 152
farmers, 56, 84, 85, 140–3, 157, 182; beliefs, 141, 152, 155; history, 28, 32, 39; interest group, 88, 99, 103, 107, 160; interests of, 30, 96, 100, 103, 104, 108, 126, 127, 149, 152; in local government, 49, 50, 88; organisations, 32, 40, 47, 54, 71; values, 152, 153, see also closer settlement, Farmers' Association, free selection, graziers
Farmers' Association, 4, 40, 47, 54, 71, 84
Federal Government, see Commonwealth Government
Foucault, M., 15, 188
free selection, 28, 29, 30, 31, see also closer settlement
future, 187–8

Gammage, B., 28–9
Gaventa, J., 14, 16

gender: ideology, 111, 112, 126, 152; relations, 18, 112, see also women
geographical location, 24, 25
Golf Club, 93
gossip, 55
government, see Commonwealth Government, State Government, local government
graziers, 31, 49, 50, 139, see also farmers
grouping, 158–60, see also coalitions
Guardian, see newspapers

Health Surveyor: Cowra Shire, 61n, 75, 79, 92, 136, 195; Cowra Municipal, 80
Heathcote (Vic), 19, 51
hegemony, 11, 185
Hindess, B., 14, 23n1
Historical Society, 4, 164
hobby farms, 34, 85, 98
Home and Community Care (HACC), 4, 5
Hospital, Cowra, 37
housing, 68, 81
human services, 110–11, 115–20, 124–6, 184

identity, 164, 166, 167, 169, 170, 178–9
ideological resources: in Australian studies, 17, 18, 20, 22, 23, 62; in Cowra, 108, 125, 149, 155, 160, 171, 177, 180, 185, 186; in local government, 63; theory, 13;
ideology, 2, 21, 22–3; in Australian studies, 18–9, 21, 50; beliefs, 12, 13, 54, 126; in Cowra, 72, 120, 123; in Cowra Shire Council, 76, 85, 113, 120; in local government, 60, 85–6, 151; in power theory,10–11, 12, see also apolitical local government, localism, ratepayer principle, resources, rural ideology, values
incomes, 40, 69
individualism (analytical) 11, 12, 21, 22, 113, 183, 186, 188, 191, 192
industry: attitude to, 81, 93; history, 32, 33, 34, 36, 37, 38, 39, 40, 41, 106; pollution, 79, 82, 101; subsidy to, 93, 145
inevitability, sense of, 22, 56, see also acquiescence, apathy
'influentials', 8n5, 50, 51, 53–6
information, 134
interests, 86, 138, 149, 161, 182; in Australian studies, 17, 20, 21, 22, 50, 51; non-business, 107, 183; non-farm, 88, 96, 107, 183; non-local, 37, 162; perceptions of, 59–60, 85, 161–3, 168, 170, 178, 185; spatial, 72–3, 76, 79, 83, 85, 160; theory, 9, 13–4, 17, 19, 62, see also business, class, employees, farmers, local interests, women

issues, 63, 74; allocation, 71, 74–9, 83–6, 183; in Australian studies, 19–20, 51; councillor-officer relations, 135–39; Cowra local, 55–6, 102, 107, 126, 127, 145, 147, 151, 158; development, 88, 93, 95–96; rates, 145; theory, 16, 62

Japanese Garden, 38, 89–91, 135, 146

Kandos (NSW), 19
kinship, 166–8
Knights, D., 15, 23n3

Labor Party, Australian, 30, 31–2, 36, 41, 67, 122, 156, 157–8, 160, 172; in local government, 48, 49, 157
Lachlan River, 24, 26, 27, 77
leadership, 60, 64, 93, 113, 146
legislation, 44
legitimacy, 96, 149, 156, 161, 176–7, 185, 186; council officers', 57, 62, 136; theory, 13, 55
Liberal Party, 31, 45, 48
Livestock and Grain Producers Association, see Farmers' Association
lobbying, 78
local advocacy, 42, 44, 45, 47, 48
local government, 50, 60, 63, 74, 110, 134, 182; Australian, 43, 44–45, 47, 49; British, 43; in Australian studies, 17, 22, 44, 49–53; Cowra history, 24, 29, 32, 45, 61, 121; ideology in, 151, 153; rural, 111
locale, 16, 46, 55
localism, 153, 161–72, 179, 180, 186; in Australian studies, 18, 19, 21, 22, 23, 50; definition, 161; use of, 92, 120, 141–2; village, 67, see also rhetoric
local interests, 44, 97, 107, 108, 134, 151, 163, 171–2, 180, 183, 184, 189; Cowra's, 30, 38, 178; perception of, 83, 108, 135, 151, 170, 165–6;
'local locals', 167–8, 170, 173–4, 175
locality, 1, 8n1, 22
Lukes, S., 9–11, 16, 23n1, 139

McIntyre, A. and J., 17, 21, 22, 49, 53, 64, 187
Mallee Town, 17, 49, 64
management, 44, 49, 60, 74, 86; of Cowra Shire, 59, 75, 86, 156
Marulan (NSW), 18
mayor, 29, 52, 65, 67, 83, 86–7n, 89, 114, 156–7
meetings: Cowra Municipal, 86; Cowra Shire, 3, 55, 75, 76, 78, 132–3, 160; public, 76, 81, 89, 100–1
methods of research, 2–5; data, 8n2–5; entree, 3; ethics, 5; gatekeepers, 5;

Index

interviews, 5, 8n5; objectivity, 8n2; records, 5; sponsorship, 5; surveys, 4, 52, 59, 70, 74, 76, 86, 190, see also needs surveys; *verstehen*, 14
migrant camp, 35, 36
mobilisation of bias, 10–11, 13
Municipal Council, Cowra: decisions, 115, 122; and economic development, 88–9; history, 24, 29, 38, 83; relations with Waugoola Shire, 142–3

National [Country] Party, 45, 48, 60n, 82, 158
needs surveys, 8n3, 71
Neighbourhood Centre, 3, 46, 117–18, 164–5, 192
neighbourliness, 164, 167
neo-elitism, 10
networks, 55, 60n2, 131, 166–7, 181n6, 181n7, see also gossip
Newby, H., 14, 23, 141, 146, 151, 162, see also Bell, C.
newspapers: Brindleton's, 44; *Cowra Free Press*, 30; *Cowra Guardian*, 3, 8n5, 30, 38; *Cowra Independent*, 30; *Lachlan Leader*, 30
non-decision making, 110, 125; in Australian studies, 20; theory, 10, 16, 62
non-issues, 127, 132, 135, 147, 184; allocation, 74, 79–83, 86, 147; human services, 118, 125–6, 147; theory, 16, 63

occupations, 27, 28, 69; of councillors, 52
Oeser, O., 17–18, 22, 49, 64, 140, 157, 187
officers (Cowra Shire), 5, 54, 57, 61n, 73, 75, 86, 134–6, 154–5, 195, see also Health Surveyor, Shire Clerk, Shire Engineer
outcomes, 15, 22; in Cowra, 78–9, 88
Oxley, H., 17, 19, 20, 21, 22, 49–50, 57, 128, 144, 146, 173, 174, 187

Pandey, U., 21, 22, 51–2, 128, 156, 157, 172
participant observation, 21
participation, 48–9, 55, 64, 67, 97, 107, 128
party politics, 158, 159, 160
'people's corporation', 60, 62, 63, 67, 74, 96, 104, 107, 110, 128, 132, 183
planning, 3, 59, 61n, 95–104, 136
pluralism: concept, 9, 10, 13, 43, 44, 62; in Australian studies, 17, 19: Cowra, 60, 64, 67, 68, 74, 86, 88, 96, 160; local government, 49–50, 60, 127, 129; Waugoola Shire, 67
Poiner, G., 18, 22, 112, 151, 187

policy, 63, 64, 85, 148; in Cowra Shire, 48, 60n, 71–6, 86, 95, 160
pollution, 87n6; air, 14, 79–83, 86, 125
population, 1, 24, 27, 32, 33, 34, 35, 36, 64, 71, 112, see also census
power: in Australian studies, 18, 19, 20, 23, 50–1; concepts, 1, 9–17, 43, see also pluralism, elitism, neo-elitism, conflict, mobilisation of bias
prestige, 57, 172, 175
prisoners of war, 34, 38
professionals, 52, 175
progress associations, 64–8, 71, 75, 86n1
property, 163, 174, 175; in Australian studies, 18, 23; in Cowra's history, 30, 31, 32, 39; interests, 62, 68, 110, 125, 126, 129, 144, 163, 186; rights, 101, 108
property services, 48, 62, 63
propinquity, 163–166
public meetings, see meetings

railway, 4, 24, 104–7, 125, 178–9; history, 2–3, 29–30, 32, 33, 108–9, 178–9, 192
ratepayer principle, 108, 120, 144, 153, 154, 155, 161
ratepayers, 89, 90, 95, 119, 125, 154; interests, 91, 108, 126, 143, 147–8, 151; non-business, 88; Ratepayers Association, 47, 71, 77, 144–5; rural, 84
rates, 44, 84, 85, 88, 110; Cowra's collection of, 61n, 69, 77, 86n3, 119, 125, 141, 142, 144, 156; Cowra's water, 47, 77, 145
Read, P., 121–2, 124
recreation, 61n, 71, 86–7n
regulations, 61, 75, 93, 104, 153–4; building, 48, 92, 93–5, 130–1
representation, 22, 60, 84, 85, 113, 143, 173, 185
reputations, 53–59
resistance, 188, 190; in Australian studies, 20, 22, 50, 51; concept,15; Cowra's 38
resources, 62, 88, 127, 148, 162, 168, 171, 180–1; in Australian studies, 20, 22–3, 62; concept, 12–13, 184, 186; Cowra's, 24; economic, 24; personal, 49; status, 93; technical, 78; time, 82, see also ideological resources
rhetoric, 28, 149–50; community (local), 92, see also localism; local government, 45; use of, 150–1
ridings, 68, 73, 84, see also wards
roads, 32, 45, 61n, 72, 74, 105, see also streets
Rotary Club, 175
rubbish, 45
rules, 12, 'of access', 62–3, 74, 75, 79; of local government, 49, 78

rural ideology, 18–9, 21, 22, 28–9, 30, 31, 111–12, 151–3, 163, 179
rural interests, 83, 85
rural-urban continuum, 1
rural-urban relations, see town and country relations
rural sociology, 2
Ryall, J., 29, 30, 42n

saleyards, 83
Saunders, P., 10–11, 14, 43, 44, 52, 53, 62, 125, 129
self-employed residents, 41
sewerage, 45, 61n, 70, 86n2
Shire Clerk, 133; Cowra, 56, 58–9, 61n, 84, 85, 195; Waugoola, 83
Shire Council, Cowra, 41, 44, 61n, 88; history, 24, 52–3, 83; importance, 46, 54, 116; perceptions of, 53, 56, 154, 156; size, 45
Shire Council, Heathcote, 20
Shire Council, Waugoola: history, 24, 32, 37, 38, 39, 67, 68, 83; relations with Cowra Municipal, 142–3
Shire Engineer (Cowra Shire), 61n, 77, 78, 98, 195
Shire President: Cowra, 56, 74, 84, 196; Waugoola, 83, 84
shops, 27, 28, 36–8, 93–4
Smalltown (Vic), 18, 166
social areas, 68–71
social stratification, 18, 19, 20, 21, 22, 68
social structure, 6, 11, 12
squatters, 26, 28, 29, 30, 39
'squeaky wheels', 64, 71–3, 83
State Government (NSW): applications to, 81, 82, 84, 90–1, 92, 105, 118; co-operation with, 45; decentralisation, 38, 60n; decisions of, 27, 28, 29–30, 79, 83, 169; devolution, 96, 154; funding, 46; and human services, 115; influence of, 44–5, 63, 97–8, 103, 124, 126, 132, 134; local representatives in, 31–2, 41; regulations, 91, 134
State Government (Vic), 20, 51
status, 3, 64, 108, 146–7, 172–7; in Australian studies, 18, 23, 50, 51; concept, 55, 172–3; Cowra's structure, 56, 174, 176, 178; in Cowra's history, 29, 31, 32; socio-economic, 69–71; of women, 113–14, see also esteem, prestige
Strathern, M., 161, 162, 163, 166, 168
streets, 70, 72, see also roads
subordinate groups, 78
surveys: air pollution, 81, see also methods of research

Sydney, 27, 30, 33, 36, 40, 41, 65, 90, 98, 169, see also city

Taragala, 5
telephone exchange, 37
Therborn, G., 13, 96
Tourist and Development Corporation, 39, 47–8, 54, 88–93, 135–6, 146–7, 177
Town Clerk, 83
town and country relations, 83–5, 139–43
town interests, 85
town services, 33, 37, 65, 76, see also civic centre, facilities, saleyards
townspeople, 67, 84, 140–1, 143
transport, 24, 27, 34

unemployment, 33, 69
unintended consequences, 6, 162, 189
user pays principle, 145

values, 11, 13, 55, 163; of councillors, 62, 76, 82, 86, 147–8, 149
villages, 101; and allocation policy, 67, 75, 76; history, 27, 34; populations, 87n4; socio-economic status, 69, 71, 87n4
voluntary organisations: in Australian studies, 17, 44; in Cowra Shire, 46, 47, 48, 57, 60n, 115, 164, 188, see also Apex Club, Concerned Citizens Committee, Farmers' Association, Golf Club, Historical Society, Home and Community Care, Neighbourhood Centre, progress associations, railway, ratepayers, Rotary Club
voting, 84, 89

wards, 67
water, 37, 45, 48, 65, 70, 75, 76–8, 84, 93
welfare, 4, 47; Aboriginal, 3; devolution of 45
wheat, 28, 29
Wild, R., 19–20, 21, 22, 50–1, 52, 54, 55, 59, 62, 68, 129, 130, 144, 146, 156, 161, 162, 168, 173, 187
Willmott, H., see Knights, D.
women: in Cowra local government, 51, 111, 114–15, 120; farming, 31; interests, 111–13, 114, 115, 125, 139; in local government, 111, 113; in workforce, 41, see also gender
working class, 2, 5, 31
workforce, 32, 33, 36, 41, see also employees, employers
Wyangala Dam, 23, 34, 36, 41

LIBRARY OF